ENGLISH

Curriculum Bank

KEY STAGE ONE
SCOTTISH LEVELS A-B

READING

ANGELA REDFERN

Published by Scholastic Limited,
Villiers House,
Clarendon Avenue,
Leamington Spa,
Warwickshire CV32 5PR
Text © Angela Redfern
© 1995 Scholastic Ltd

AUTHOR
ANGELA REDFERN

EDITOR
NOEL PRITCHARD

ASSISTANT EDITOR
JOEL LANE

SERIES DESIGNER
LYNNE JOESBURY

DESIGNER
TOBY LONG

ILLUSTRATIONS
CLAIRE JAMES

COVER ILLUSTRATION
GAY STURROCK

INFORMATION TECHNOLOGY CONSULTANT
MARTIN BLOWS

SCOTTISH 5-14 LINKS
MARGARET SCOTT AND SUSAN GOW

Designed using Aldus Pagemaker
Printed in Great Britain by Ebenezer Baylis & Son, Worcester

British Library Cataloguing-in-Publication Data
A catalogue record for this book is available from the British
Library.

ISBN 0-590-53365-7

Contents

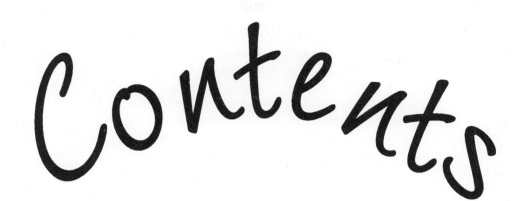

ACKNOWLEDGEMENTS

The publishers gratefully acknowledge permission to reproduce the following copyright material:

© Leo Lionni for 'Frederick' from *Frederick's Tales* (Andersen Press, 1986); © Rosemary Wells for an extract from *The Voyage to the Bunny Planet* (HarperCollins, 1992); © Rosemary Wells for an extract from *Noisy Nora* (HarperCollins 1978); © Susan Nunes for an extract from *Tiddalick the Frog* (Hodder & Stoughton, 1990); © Fiona French for an extract from *Aio the Rainmaker* (OUP, 1975) by permission of Oxford University Press; © Verna Aardema for an extract from *Bringing the Rain to Kapiti Plain* (Macmillan Children's Books, 1986); © Adrian Henri for 'The Dark' from *Rhinestone Rhino* (Methuen, 1989) reproduced by permission of the author c/o Rogers, Coleridge & White Ltd; © the estate of James Reeves for 'I can get through the doorway without any key', reprinted by permission of John Johnson Ltd, London; © Lynley Dodd for an extract from *Hairy Maclary's Rumpus at the Vet* (Mallinson Rendel Publishers); © Kathy Henderson for an extract from *The Babysitter* (André Deutsch, 1988); extracts from *Tyrannosaurus Was a Beast* illustrated by Arnold Lobel, text © 1988 Jack Prelutsky, permission granted by the publisher (Walker Books Ltd, London); © David Lloyd and Clive Scruton for an extract from *Cat and Dog* (Walker Books Ltd, London, 1983).

Every effort has been made to trace copyright holders for the works reproduced in this book, and the publishers apologise for any inadvertent omissions.

Introduction

Scholastic Curriculum Bank is a series for all primary teachers, providing an essential planning tool for devising comprehensive schemes of work as well as an easily accessible and varied bank of practical, classroom-tested activities with photocopiable resources.

Designed to help planning for and implementation of progression, differentiation and assessment, *Scholastic Curriculum Bank* offers a structured range of stimulating activities with clearly-stated learning objectives that reflect the programmes of study, and detailed lesson plans that allow busy teachers to put ideas into practice with the minimum amount of preparation time. The photocopiable sheets that accompany many of the activities provide ways of integrating purposeful application of knowledge and skills, differentiation, assessment and record-keeping.

Opportunities for formative assessment are highlighted within the activities where appropriate, while separate summative assessment activities give guidelines for analysis and subsequent action. Ways of using information technology for different purposes and in different contexts, as a tool for communicating and handling information and as a means of investigating, are integrated into the activities where appropriate, and more explicit guidance is provided at the end of the book.

The series covers all the primary curriculum subjects, with separate books for Key Stages 1 and 2 or Scottish Levels A–B and C–E. It can be used as a flexible resource with any scheme, to fulfil National Curriculum and Scottish 5–14 requirements and to provide children with a variety of different learning experiences that will lead to effective acquisition of skills and knowledge.

SCHOLASTIC CURRICULUM BANK ENGLISH

The *Scholastic Curriculum Bank English* books enable teachers to plan comprehensive and structured coverage of the primary English curriculum, and enable pupils to develop the required skills, knowledge and understanding through activities.

Each book covers one key stage. There are four books for Key Stage 1/Scottish levels A–B and four for Key Stage 2/Scottish levels C–E. These books reflect the English programme of study, so that there are titles on Reading, Writing, Speaking and listening and Spelling and phonics.

Bank of activities
This book provides a bank of activities that can be used in many different ways: to form a framework for a scheme of work; to add breadth and variety to an existing scheme; or to supplement a particular topic. The activities are designed to encourage children to develop as enthusiastic, responsive and knowledgeable readers.

Lesson plans
Detailed lesson plans, under clear headings, are given for each activity and provide material for immediate implementation in the classroom. The structure for each activity is as follows:

Activity title box
The information contained in the box at the beginning of each activity outlines the following key aspects:
▲ *Activity title and learning objective:* For each activity, a clearly stated learning objective is given in bold italics. These

learning objectives break down aspects of the programmes of study into manageable, hierarchical teaching and learning chunks, and their purpose is to aid planning for progression. These objectives can easily be referenced to the National Curriculum and Scottish 5–14 requirements by using the overview grids at the end of this chapter (pages 9 to 12).
▲ *Class organisation/Likely duration:* Icons †† and ⏰ signpost the suggested group sizes for each activity and the approximate amount of time required to complete it.

Previous skills/knowledge needed
Information is given here when it is necessary for the children to have acquired specific knowledge or skills prior to carrying out the activity.

Key background information
The information in this section outlines the areas of study covered by each activity and gives a general background to the particular topic or theme, outlining the basic skills that will be developed and the ways in which the activity will address children's learning.

Preparation
Advice is given for those occasions where it is necessary for the teacher to prime the pupils for the activity or to prepare materials, or to set up a display or activity ahead of time.

Resources needed
All of the materials needed to carry out the activity are listed, so that the pupils or the teacher can gather them together easily before the beginning of the teaching session.

What to do
Easy-to-follow, step-by-step instructions are given for carrying out the activity, including (where appropriate) suggested questions for the teacher to ask the pupils in order to help instigate discussion and stimulate investigation.

Suggestion(s) for extension/support
Ideas are given for ways of providing easy differentiation where activities lend themselves to this purpose. In all cases, suggestions are provided as to ways in which each activity can be modified for less able children or extended for more able children.

Assessment opportunities
Where appropriate, opportunities for ongoing teacher assessment of the children's work during or after a specific activity are highlighted.

Opportunities for IT
Where opportunities for IT present themselves, these are briefly outlined with reference to particularly suitable types of program. The chart on page 159 presents specific areas

Assessment

The system of level descriptions in the National Curriculum presents the teacher with the task of matching the typical performance of individual children with a set of descriptive statements. In this book, each activity presents advice on what the teacher should look out for during the course of the activity. The notes made while observing the children can contribute to a descriptive profile of the child's performance, compiled and refined throughout the school year, which might also be supported by annotated samples of the work that the child produces. The important point is that assessment is integrated into everyday performance.

At the end of each chapter, there are activities which are designed to provide a summative measure of a range of key competencies linked to the type of reading dealt with in that chapter. These activities do not differ in their organisation from the preceding ones, and focus on a number of learning objectives covered in the chapter. Assessment activities are indicated by the ✍ icon.

Photocopiable activity sheets

Many of the activities are accompanied by photocopiable activity sheets. For some activities, there may be more than one version; or an activity sheet may be 'generic', with a facility for the teacher to fill in the appropriate task in order to provide differentiation by task. Other sheets may be more open-ended, to provide differentiation by outcome. The photocopiable activity sheets provide purposeful activities that are ideal for assessment and can be kept as records in pupils' portfolios of work.

Cross-curricular links

This book emphasises that reading and writing skills should not be taught in isolation, but integrated into the work children do in other areas of the curriculum. Information retrieval strategies are not confined to study skills lessons, but can be developed through the perusal of texts on topics of contemporary concern. Where photocopiable pages have been supplied for particular activities, these are intended as demonstration materials, providing opportunities to rehearse procedures which can then be applied to more relevant texts. In many cases, the activities open routes for links between different subject areas – techniques for mathematical representation can be applied to media texts; the musical dimensions of spoken and printed language can be explored; historical change and geographical variation in language usage are examined; and throughout, children are encouraged to respond to all forms of printed material via a range of types of graphic representation.

Cross-curricular links are identified on a simple grid which cross-references the particular areas of study in English to the programmes of study for other subjects in the curriculum, and (where appropriate) provides suggestions for activities. (See page 160.)

of IT covered in the activities, together with more detailed support on how to apply particular types of program. Selected lesson plans serve as models for other activities by providing more comprehensive guidance on the application of IT, and these are indicated by the bold page numbers on the grid and the 🖥 icon at the start of an activity.

Display ideas

Where they are relevant and innovative, display ideas are incorporated into activity plans and illustrated with examples.

Other aspects of the English PoS covered

Inevitably, as all areas of English are interrelated, activities will cover aspects of the programmes of study in other areas of the English curriculum. These links are highlighted under this heading.

Reference to photocopiable sheets

Where activities include photocopiable activity sheets, small reproductions of these are included in the lesson plans together with guidance notes for their use and, where appropriate, suggested answers.

READING

In educational terms, in today's world, literacy counts above all else. It is the foundation for all learning, and the aim of every Early Years teacher is to enable all children to leave the Infant school as fluent independent readers who read with understanding and critical awareness. To this end, teachers should provide a rich language environment that offers children the opportunity for hearing stories read aloud daily, for listening to taped stories and poems, for group reading, choral reading, paired and shared reading, individual reading conferences and bookshares, and writing book reviews. There should also be time for playing with language, savouring the rhymes and rhythms of language, and playing with meanings and patterns in words. In addition, it is important to devote time to using books and other resources for learning across the curriculum, so that children are taught to locate and retrieve information from non-fiction books and make it their own.

Teachers need to keep books in high focus by encouraging parents to become involved with their children's literacy development, by arranging visits to the local library, by running book clubs, by inviting authors and illustrators to visit the school, by organising book week celebrations, and by ensuring that the children's own writing is viewed as valid reading material both for themselves and for others.

The starting-point must be with what the children bring with them to school – that is, the fund of knowledge they have acquired about print from their everyday lives at home with their families. Teachers need to capitalise on children's understanding of print in the environment, and this is where we begin.

Surveys tell us that most families spend some time each day in a shared experience involving the parent and child with a book, often at bedtime. In these safe non-threatening situations, children first learn to enjoy books: they learn about narrative structure, about predicting what will come next, about the cadences and rhythms of language; they learn to join in with favourite bits and with rhyming words; they may even learn to recognise some words and letters, and they learn the words for talking about books such as 'author', 'title', or 'chapter'. Schools must make the most of this and develop it further.

In the second chapter, therefore, we look at opportunities for enhancing children's reading experiences through narrative. This is a crucial section, as it is through literature that children learn to make sense of their world, come to terms with their emotions, learn to see things from someone else's point of view and grapple with social and moral issues.

The third chapter builds on poetry and rhyme, another area that children begin to develop before they come to school. Parents from every branch of society sing to their babies, chant rhymes with them and play action games. Thus children begin to develop an ear for language and a curiosity about language that continues through their street and playground play in ring games, skipping rhymes and clapping songs that are passed from generation to generation. The activities provide teachers with opportunities to celebrate this dynamic language in the classroom and extend it into riddles, puns, similes, alliteration and the world of poetry.

Finally, we turn to another vital element of reading development: reading to learn. To cope in the modern world, children must have at their fingertips the skills to locate, select and digest information across all areas of the curriculum. Here we start the process by teaching children the early steps towards study skills: how to use structural devices for finding their way around a text, how to make choices between sources, and how to focus on the important elements of a passage and reject redundant information.

Teaching children to read is not only the most important job a teacher has, it is also the most exciting and rewarding: there is nothing quite like the thrill of seeing young children take off as readers and become totally absorbed in books.

Learning objective	PoS/AO	Content	Type of activity	Page
Environmental print				
Early concepts about print.	2a, b; 3. *Reading: Awareness of genre, level A. Talking: Talking about texts, level A.*	Taking the children on a walk to observe and discuss print in the locality.	Whole-class discussions, sharing and reflecting on findings of the walk; activities in small groups and pairs.	14
Meaning can be conveyed in a variety of ways.	1b; 2a, b; 3. *Reading: Awareness of genre, level A. Talking: Talking in groups, level A.*	Investigating similarities and differences between T-shirt logos.	Whole class for discussion and review; small groups and pairs for the activities.	16
Interpreting symbols and key words.	1b; 2a, b; 3. *Reading: Reading for information, level B. Talking: Talking in groups, level B.*	Evaluating T-shirt labels.	Whole-class discussions and reporting back; pairs for the activities.	18
Sequencing and text completion using a range of reading strategies; alphabetical order.	1b; 2a, b; 3. *Reading: Reading for information, level B. Talking: Talking in groups, level B.*	Reading and comparing information and instructions on tins of soup.	Whole class for discussion and feedback; small groups and pairs for the activities.	22
Vocabulary extension and scanning techniques.	1b; 2a, b, d; 3. *Reading: Reading for information, levels B, C.*	An investigation of estate agents' adverts.	Whole-class discussions; small groups and pairs for the activities.	28
Language awareness: alliteration, rhyme and rhythm.	1b; 2a, b; 3. *Reading: Awareness of genre, level B. Talking: Talking in groups, level B.*	Comparing and evaluating TV adverts.	Whole-class discussions; small groups and pairs for the activities.	32
Developing knowledge of language and punctuation through studying comics.	1a, c, d; 2a, c; 3. *Reading: Awareness of genre, level B. Talking: Talking about texts, level B.*	Investigating the vocabulary and language styles found in comics.	Whole-class discussions; small groups and pairs for the activities.	36
Demonstrating language awareness and understanding of the style conventions of comics.	1a, c; 2a, b, c; 3. *Reading: Awareness of genre, level B. Writing: Imaginative writing, level B.*	Writing and making a class comic.	Whole class, working in small groups or pairs.	40

Learning objective	PoS/AO	Content	Type of activity	Page
Narrative				
Narrative structure and reader response.	1a, c, d; 2a, b, c; 3. *Reading: Reading to reflect on the writer's ideas and craft, level B.*	Becoming familiar with the work of a well-known children's author.	Whole class for storytime and discussions; pairs for the activities.	42
The role of illustrations in fictional texts.	1a, c, d; 2a, b, c; 3. *Reading: Reading for information, level B. Talking: Talking in groups, level B.*	Evaluating illustrations and investigating artists' techniques.	Whole class for discussion and review; small groups and pairs for the activities.	46
Recalling events in sequence and retelling known stories.	1a, c, d; 2a, b, c; 3. *Talking: Talking about texts, level B. Listening: Listening in order to respond to texts, level B.*	Listening and responding to a range of stories on the theme of babysitters.	Whole class for storytime; small groups and pairs for the activities.	50
Prediction, word recognition, language awareness.	1a, c, d; 2a, b, c; 3. *Reading: Reading to reflect on the writer's ideas and craft, level B. Talking: Talking in groups, level B.*	Coming to terms with personal experiences through fiction.	Whole class for listening to stories and discussions; small groups and pairs for the activities.	54
Inferential comprehension, language awareness.	1a, c, d; 2a, b, c; 3. *Reading: Reading to reflect on the writer's ideas and craft, level B; Awareness of genre, level B. Talking: Talking in groups, level B.*	Comparing a range of books on the theme of holidays.	Whole class responding to stories; small groups for the activities.	58
Increasing listening stamina and visualising in the mind.	1a, c, d; 2a, b, c; 3. *Listening: Listening in order to respond to texts, level B. Talking: Talking about experiences, feelings and opinions, level B.*	Listening to stories, chapter by chapter, and talking in a large group about personal fears.	Whole class for storytime; small groups for the activities.	62
The structure of traditional tales.	1a, c, d; 2a, b, c; 3. *Reading: Awareness of genre, level B. Listening: Listening in groups, level B.*	Investigating similarities and differences in tales from a range of cultures.	Whole class for listening and responding to stories; pairs for the activities.	64

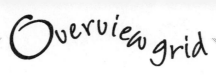

Learning objective	PoS/AO	Content	Type of activity	Page
Language awareness: phonics (blends and digraphs) and alliteration.	1a, c, d; 2a, b, c; 3. *Reading: Reading aloud, level A. Writing: Spelling, level A.*	Preparing a dramatisation of a story for a class assembly.	Whole class for rehearsing; small groups and pairs for the preparatory activities.	68
Demonstrating awareness of the conventions of the folk-tale genre and language skills.	1a, c, d; 2a, c; 3. *Reading: Awareness of genre, level B. Talking: Talking about texts, level B.*	Listening to folk-tales, understanding the conventions and language of this genre.	Whole class, then individual or pair work.	71
Poetry				
Rhythm: keeping the beat.	1c, d; 3. *Music: Using the voice, level A; Using instruments, level A.*	Singing and playing ring games, action songs. Keeping the beat with different body parts.	Whole class in the hall; small groups and pairs for the activities.	74
Recognising rhyme, phonological awareness.	1a, c, d; 2a, b; 3. *Reading: Reading aloud, level A.*	Learning rhymes by heart, reading 'big books'.	Whole class for reciting; pairs for the activities.	77
Recognising rhyme and producing rhyming words. Predicting via rhyming features.	1a, c, d; 2a, b, c; 3. *Talking: Talking about texts, level A; Talking in groups, level A.*	Shared and choral reading; turning a narrative into a drama.	Whole class for responding to stories; small groups and pairs for the activities.	80
Recognising rhyme and rhythm, playing with language.	1a, d; 2a, b, c; 3. *Listening: Listening in groups, level A.*	Chanting playground rhymes, exploring language diversity, making a class collection of rhymes.	Whole class for listening and learning rhymes.	84
Awareness of alliteration, similes, phonological awareness.	1a, c, d; 2a, b; 3. *Listening: Listening in groups, level B.*	Creating alliterative texts, quizzes, poems and riddles; making a class collection of jokes.	Whole class for discussions and review, small groups and pairs for the activities.	87
Recognising the characteristics of a poem; rhyme and rhythm; knowledge about language.	1a, c, d; 2a, b, c; 3. *Reading: Reading for enjoyment, level B. Writing: Imaginative writing, level B.*	Learning poems by heart; reading 'big books'; paired reading; writing their own poems; text completion.	Whole class for discussions and sharing work; small groups and pairs for the activities.	92
Demonstrating awareness of rhyme and rhythmical patterns in language.	1a, d; 2a, b, c; 3. *Writing: Knowledge about language, level B.*	Reconstructing incomplete texts through cloze procedure.	Whole class, working in pairs or small groups.	99

READING

Learning objective	PoS/AO	Content	Type of activity	Page
Information and instructional texts				
Recognising structural guides.	1b; 2a, b, d; 3. *Reading: Reading for information, level B.*	Evaluating a range of non-fiction books.	Whole class for discussions, small groups for the activities.	102
Strategies for retrieving information from texts.	1b; 2a, b, d; 3. *Reading: Reading for information, level B.*	Locating and selecting material, formulating questions, putting new information to use.	Whole-class discussions and review, small groups and pairs for the activities.	104
Developing information retrieval skills; reading and carrying out instructions.	1b; 2a, b, d; 3. *Writing: Functional writing, level B.*	Keeping records of the weather, making a rain gauge, making a brochure about the local area.	Whole class for discussing, sharing work and reporting back; small groups and pairs for the activities.	108
Learning alphabetical order, sound-symbol relationships, upper- and lower-case letters, awareness of audience, linguistic terminology.	1b; 2a, b, d; 3. *Writing: Functional writing, level B.*	Making an alphabet book for the nursery.	Whole class for discussion, small groups and pairs for the activities.	112
Retrieving information from a variety of sources and representing it in a different form.	1b; 2a, b, d; 3. *Writing: Functional writing, level B.*	Investigating similarities and differences between toys of today and toys from the past; making a peg doll; writing a set of instructions.	Whole class for storytime and discussion, small groups for the activities.	114
Demonstrating awareness of the conventions of information books.	1b, c; 2a, c; 3. *Reading: Awareness of genre, level B. Writing: functional writing, level B.*	Using knowledge gained in previous sessions to write and produce a class 'information book'.	Whole class, then individual or pair work.	120

English National Curriculum links relate to the programmes of study for Reading.
Links to the Scottish curriculum are given in italics and relate to the English Language 5–14 guidelines.

Environmental print

We live in a print-rich environment. From birth, children see adults reading notes, letters, cards, newspapers, magazines and official forms. Everything they buy from small corner shops or vast supermarkets is packaged in paper covered in print, and clothes come festooned with logos and labels detailing a wealth of information. Children arrive at school with a wealth of knowledge about print: about the different purposes and audiences for print, about its orientation on the page, about specific letters and figures. They may have been curious about print and been asking adults questions about it for a long time.

It is this prior knowledge which children bring with them to school that we aim to harness and extend in this section. By making children aware that they are already readers, we aim to remove some of the mystique surrounding the reading process that might otherwise hinder their progress.

The activities focus on the children's immediate environment, the streets around their home that the children are familiar with and feel confident about; then move on to food and clothing, the everyday items the children are used to handling; and finally draw on the two main strands of popular children's culture, namely television and comics, where they are indeed 'experts'.

There are opportunities here to learn about the letters of the alphabet, capital and lower-case letters, individual word recognition, punctuation conventions, abbreviations, the use of symbols to convey meaning, strategies for making meaning from print, and the need to come to a text as a critical reader to avoid being manipulated by the writer.

READING

'WE'RE GOING ON A PRINT HUNT'

For the children to:

▲ *understand that messages can be conveyed in a variety of forms;*

▲ *understand that print is used for a range of different purposes;*

▲ *realise that print is all around them and that they successfully 'read' these signs and words daily;*

▲ *realise that letters can be printed in different fonts and cases for a variety of reasons;*

▲ *recognise letters (for example, from their own names) and whole words on sight;*

▲ *show an interest in language use and in languages other than English (if available in the locality).*

†† *Sessions One and Two: whole-class involvement; Session Three: children paired with an adult helper; Session Four: small-group work.*

🕐 *Session One: about 20 minutes; Session Two: about 35 minutes; Session Three: 45–60 minutes; Session Four: 35–45 minutes.*

Key background information

This series of sessions provides the context for children to develop their early concepts about print; to increase their alphabetic knowledge, their language awareness and their writing skills; to make informed choices about format and presentation when recording their experiences; and to enhance their self-image as readers and writers.

The topic involves storytime sessions, outside visits, focused group work, creating displays and 'publishing' children's work.

Preparation

When deciding the final route for your class walk, bear in mind the children's physical stamina, safety factors and the amount of time necessary to complete the walk. Make arrangements for adult helpers to accompany the class on the walk (two children per adult if possible), and agree with them the main points for discussion arising from the intended learning outcomes.

Collect books on street furniture, signs and so on, and put together an initial stimulus display to awaken children's interest and extend their knowledge. Draw a simple, poster-sized street plan of the area around your school.

Resources needed

We're Going On a Bear Hunt by Michael Rosen and Helen Oxenbury (Walker, 1993), paper for making rubbings, notes and sketches, clipboards, pencils of various barrel thicknesses and degrees of hardness/softness, a camera loaded with film.

What to do

Session One: Introducing the topic

Read *We're Going On a Bear Hunt* to the whole class, and encourage the children to join in with the actions and words whenever they can. At the end of the story, encourage them to express their spontaneous reactions to it. Did they like it? Why? Which part was best? Were they frightened?

Reread the story at a more vigorous pace to heighten the fun, and shift the emphasis of your questions at the end by asking if there are any bears to be found near where you live. Other questions might include 'Could we go on a bear hunt?' or if not, 'Could we go on some other sort of hunt?' Discuss all the children's suggestions.

Session Two: Developing the topic

Recap the events in the story. The children will probably insist on hearing it again! Explain that you have had an idea about a very special sort of hunt they can go on: instead of searching for a bear, they are going to be special investigators and search for print in the local area. Ask them if they have any ideas about what they might find. Use the books from the display to stimulate interest and comments, making links with the local area. Do the children remember noticing any letters, words, signs or symbols on their way to school? Perhaps they can remember bus stops, shops, hoardings, street names and so on.

Next, encourage the children to share the responsibility for organising the walk. Work together to decide what preparations will have to be made.

Using your large-scale plan of the nearby streets, talk through the actual route together and mark it with a felt-tipped pen. You will need to discuss the safety factors to be considered during the walk, and decide on any visits to be

made *en route* (for example, permission may be needed from local shopkeepers if you plan to visit their shops). It can be a valuable experience for the children to set up these visits with letters or phone calls in advance. Stress the value of learning how to greet shopkeepers and thank them in their first language, if this is not English. Where do the children think they can find out how to do this?

You will also need to make lists together of the things the children will need to take on the walk, and to work co-operatively to compose a letter to parents telling them about it and asking for helpers.

Session Three: The walk

Hand out the necessary resources to the children and remind them of the road safety rules before you leave the school. Also, remind the children and the adult helpers of the features to look out for during the walk – for example, shop signs, street names, hoardings, banners, street furniture, cinema signs, labels, posters, notices, road signs, bus stops, goods in shop windows, plaques.

En route, make short stops for the children to take rubbings, copy the details of signs, keep tallies and make sketches. Encourage them to observe carefully, to make comparisons and to comment on letters and words – in fact, to note all the features of print as listed in the intended learning outcomes. When children have a common first language other than English, encourage them to use it in discussion.

Session Four: Follow-up

Back in the classroom, the children can work in small groups with an adult helper.

Encourage them to comment spontaneously on the things they saw and discuss the observations they made. Each group can share its findings with the rest of the class; you can list important points on a flip chart or board, classifying the types of signs and scripts, their purpose and the impact they make on the passer-by. Reflect on what has been learned, and discuss which features need further investigation and how to go about it – by interviewing people, by carrying out a library search, by inviting 'expert' speakers to talk to the class, and so on.

Finally, reread *We're Going on a Bear Hunt* – if possible, altering the text to fit the children's experiences on their print hunt.

Suggestion(s) for extension

Children can make a book about the walk, using the photographs taken on the way as well as their own drawings. This can then be published on a word processor – cover design, blurb, title, contents page and layout will have to be negotiated, so that everyone has a role to play.

The children can share the finished product with the whole school in an assembly. They can read the text aloud and give

an account of the walk. The book can then be added to the classroom book collection or the school library. Copies of the book could be delivered to the local people visited during the walk. If English is not their first language, perhaps a version of the book in the appropriate language could be compiled.

Suggestion(s) for support

During the walk, adult helpers may have to point out items of interest to less experienced readers and to explain, rather than ask about, similarities and differences between letters and words.

It is important for inexperienced writers to be involved in the publishing process. Adults can act as scribes or word-processing 'secretaries' to make this possible, or the children can take on the role of illustrators or designers.

The text can be translated and transliterated into the languages of all the children in the class, with the help of adults or older children in the school.

Assessment opportunities

The children's conversation when planning, carrying out and reflecting on the walk, when planning the displays and the publication, and when translating, will highlight their understanding of basic concepts to do with print, their alphabetic knowledge and their language awareness.

Written materials produced for display and for publication will provide evidence of the children's ability to read back what they have written.

Opportunities for IT

In Session Four, children could make a list of the print they have seen using a word processor. They might experiment with different sizes of print or different font styles. This could

READING

be used as a part of a class display showing the range of styles of print that they have found.

Children could make a book using a word processor, with different children being responsible for different sections of the book. The cover could be created using a simple art package and the final design incorporated into the word processor. Children could use a simple desktop publishing package for this work, which would allow a common page layout to be used. This could be in the form of a frame for the print seen, then another frame for information about the print: its purpose, who it is for, the meaning of the words, and so on.

Alternatively, the children could work as a class to create a simple multimedia presentation of their walk, using simple authoring software which enables them to link pages together so that the walk can be reconstructed on the computer screen. It is even possible to include actual pictures taken with a camera and scanned into the software, or to incorporate digitised pictures taken with an ion still camera or a video camera. This work will need considerable teacher support.

Display ideas

Children could create a display explaining how to go about organising a print walk. The display could include the marked-out street plan, a poster about road safety considerations, drafts and final versions of all the letters written and received, the list of resources needed for the walk, and the reasons for visiting certain places *en route*.

After the walk, working in pairs or small groups, the children could make a display of the rubbings, sketches and photographs of interesting items they have discovered in the area. Captions incorporating children's comments recorded on the walk, together with the main points from the discussions back at school, could frame the display.

Other aspects of the English PoS covered

Speaking and listening –1a, b, c; 2a, b.
Writing – 1a, b; 2a, b; 3a.

T-SHIRT BAZAAR

For the children to:
▲ *understand that meaning can be conveyed in a variety of ways;*
▲ *understand that abbreviations can represent words;*
▲ *understand that design features affect the impact of the message;*
▲ *recognise and write upper- and lower-case letters;*
▲ *consider the moral issues involved in advertising and marketing;*
▲ *read known texts clearly, audibly and with expression to a large audience.*
†† *Session One: whole-class and pair work; Session Two: individuals with an adult helper; Session Three: whole-class and small-group work.*
🕐 *Session One: 45 minutes; Session Two: 30 minutes; Session Three: 35–45 minutes.*

Previous skills/knowledge needed
Children should have some experience of basic printing techniques.

Key background information
Starting with the children's own real-life experiences, this series of activities provides a context in which they can develop their skills in letter and word recognition, letter formation and reading a familiar text aloud to an audience.

Storytime sessions can serve as useful introductory sessions, since there is no shortage of children's books about clothing. Work on this topic can also involve practical workshops, focused group work, performing in front of a large audience and 'publishing' a book.

Preparation
Collect a range of different T-shirts, posters and pictures from magazines of T-shirts with logos. Encourage the children to bring in items from home to contribute to an initial display focused on T-shirts.

Resources needed
Tools such as letter stencils, rollers and blocks for printing on to cotton fabric; dyes, writing and drawing materials, a tape recorder. Each child will need an old T-shirt for the printing workshop session.

What to do
Session One: Introduction
Talk about the children's T-shirts and what can be seen on the front of them. Which are their favourite T-shirts and why are these special? When do they like wearing T-shirts and why? When wouldn't they wear them and why? What shops did these T-shirts come from?

READING

Ask the children to work in pairs, looking at the logos on their favourite T-shirts. Encourage them to compare and contrast their T-shirts with those in the assembled collection and to note the different types of logo (personal names, the name of a designer, membership of a club, university names, and so on), slogans (political or concerned with gender or environmental issues, and so on) and whether words or images are most popular.

Then, as a class, move on to discuss the purposes and effectiveness of logos. Do the children think that anything and everything should be allowed on T-shirts? Encourage them to give their reasons for and against. Are they concerned about the actual language used? Have they seen words they think are offensive? Are they concerned about the messages being conveyed and their effect on people?

Suggest to the children that they become designers and create their own logo. Perhaps there is a local group or place they would like to support, such as their school? Perhaps they would prefer to design a T-shirt logo dealing with a wider issue, for example litter, pollution or an endangered species? Brainstorm all the children's ideas and help them to make a final decision about their individual choices.

Session Two: Printing workshop

Before the children begin to design their own logo, recap the features that make the strongest impact on people. Using examples of T-shirts to assist the decision-making process, consider the amount of space available, print size and font, colour choices for background and lettering.

Tell the children to prepare their designs on paper, using stencils for letters (if appropriate), trying out a variety of lettering styles and sizes, and making adjustments if necessary, until they are satisfied with the result. Then, as a whole-class group, evaluate the designs and offer constructive criticism regarding the accuracy of spelling, the careful spacing and the evenness of lettering, effectiveness and aesthetic appeal, so that changes can be made (if necessary) before the printing stage.

Finally, let the children work individually with an adult who can offer them support and technical advice when they are printing their T-shirts.

Session Three: Preparing for the fashion show

The children then need to share out the writing tasks between them. Encourage them to work in pairs or small groups to write descriptions of their T-shirts for a fashion parade, to design and make posters for the school noticeboards, to write invitations to parents and teachers, and to make programmes and tickets for the event.

Children can rehearse reading their commentaries, using a tape recorder to help improve their intonation and expression. They will need at some point to rehearse in the hall where the fashion show will take place, to ensure clarity and audibility. General features of presentation such as

pacing, emphases and body language will also need to be considered.

Finally, the children can present the fashion show to the whole school in assembly.

Suggestion(s) for extension

Some children could make individual zigzag books about their favourite T-shirt and the memories associated with it. These could then be read out to the class and/or recorded on tape to add to the classroom stock for the listening corner.

Suggestion(s) for support

Some children should be paired with a more able partner when designing logos; others may need the support of an adult helper.

Inexperienced writers can take on the tasks that demand less writing stamina, such as making posters, tickets or programmes for the fashion show. Inexperienced readers will need the support of more able readers when rehearsing their commentaries for the fashion show.

Assessment opportunities

When the children talk in groups and whole-class situations as they set about planning their designs, printing their logos,

debating issues, planning for the fashion show and presenting work in assembly, they will demonstrate their skills in questioning, explaining and taking turns, as well as their expressive skills and confidence.

The children's reading of words in isolation on T-shirts, reading aloud to the class or whole school and taping their zigzag books and commentaries, will all highlight their range of reading strategies.

Written work such as the zigzag books, invitation cards and programmes for the fashion show will provide material for monitoring the children's skills in handwriting, layout on the page and spelling. You should also note their attitude to their work – their sense of pride, the care they take and their attention to detail.

Opportunities for IT

In Sessions One and Two, children could use a simple art package to design their own logo for a T-shirt. It is possible to make the printouts on special transfer paper which can then be used to print on to the T-shirt itself. The activity can be used to introduce some of the important features of using an art package, such as drawing and editing lines, changing the thickness and colour of lines, creating, editing, moving, resizing and colouring shapes and adding text in different fonts and colours.

In Session Three, the children could prepare their fashion show script using a word processor, enabling them to draft and redraft their work. They could also design the fashion show tickets in this way. As there is a limited amount of text entry required for the activity, the children can concentrate on the layout commands, such as centring, or the use of different fonts or features, such as underlining, bold or italics.

Other children could write invitations to parents, using a standard letter layout, but personalising the letters by including parents' names. This could lead on to discussion about the benefits of using a word processor, and the children could look at examples of 'junk mail' where personal details are included on each letter sent out.

The children should be taught how to use the tape recorder for editing and replaying their commentaries. This work will give them experience of simple control applications and show the limitations of a tape recorder.

Display ideas

Children could create a shop window display of their printed T-shirts, including pieces of writing giving instructions to help other children make a special T-shirt of their own.

You could also mount a 'work in progress' display, showing the children's written work for the assembly as it evolves from lists of ideas and first drafts to the final product.

Other aspects of the English PoS covered

Speaking and listening – 1a, b, c, d; 2a, b.
Writing – 1a, b, c; 2a, b, d; 3b.

BENEATH THE SURFACE

For the children to:
▲ *understand that symbols represent meaning;*
▲ *know that there are international conventions for instructions on labels and discuss why these are necessary;*
▲ *recognise the symbols used to indicate care of clothes and sizing on clothes labels;*
▲ *recognise words using prior knowledge of clothes-washing routines, of the language of instructions, and of sound-letter relationships;*
▲ *compare the different languages used on labels;*
▲ *make analogies with real-life examples and design their own labels and symbols for clothing;*
▲ *develop their knowledge of alphabetical order.*
†† *Session One: whole class; Session Two: working in pairs, then groups of four; Sessions Three, Four and Five: whole class; Session Six: working in pairs.*
🕐 *Session One: 20 minutes; Session Two: 25 minutes; Session Three: 30 minutes; Session Four: 30 minutes; Session Five: 20 minutes; Session Six: 25 minutes.*

Key background information

This series of activities continues work on T-shirts, and emphasises ways of making meaning by using a range of strategies such as knowledge of real life, word and letter recognition, word-symbol correlation and knowledge of one language to support understanding in another. Children will reflect on obstacles to meaning, the need for consistency, and possible ways of influencing decisions by writing to appropriate people.

Previous skills/knowledge needed
Children will need basic keyboard skills for word-processing.

Preparation
Collect a range of headlines or captions from newspapers and magazines, and adverts and consumer reports relating to the care and quality of clothes or to manufacturers' claims about clothes. Make a collection of books and brochures related to the clothing industry.

Resources needed
Three or four T-shirts for each pair of children, a flip chart or OHP, writing and drawing materials, a computer, one copy per child of photocopiable sheet 122.

What to do
Session One: Introducing the topic
Tell the children that you want them to investigate the labels on T-shirts. Work as a class to collect (on a flip chart or an OHP) all the information the children feel should be included on a label. Ask them if they think this information is usually provided. What can they remember about the labels on T-shirts? (For instance, how many there are, where they are situated, what information they provide, how the information is presented, how easy it is to understand, which languages are used and why.)

Session Two: Hands-on investigations
Recap with the children the points they raised in Session One. Next, arrange the children into pairs and give each pair a selection of three or four T-shirts to see if they can find the information discussed. Suggest that they make a note of the different ways the information is presented, and also note any 'gaps' or any extra information that they find.

Ask two pairs to join together to share their findings and decide on the key points to report back to the whole class.

Session Three: Reporting back on manufacturers' labels
Ask the groups to report in turn and write down all their findings. Discuss whether there was consistency regarding the number of labels found, their location, the amount of information provided on them and the purposes of the different labels.

The children could then list the countries of manufacture in alphabetical order (for example, Canada, China, Greece, India, Ireland, Singapore, Sweden, Taiwan, Turkey, United Kingdom). They could also organise the names of manufacturers in alphabetical order (for example, Laura Ashley, ASK, and so on).

Discuss the different ways of saying the same things on the labels, such as: *made in ...,* *manufactured in ...,* *fait au ...,* *fabriqué au ...,* *tillverkad i ... .*

Discuss the different materials used to make T-shirts and the ways in which these are presented, such as: *50%* *polyester, 50% cotton; 100% cotton; cotton; coton; cotone; algodon; Baumwoll; bomull; katoen.*

Discuss the different sizing systems using letters, words and measurements, for example: *S, M, L, XL; Small, Medium, Free Size, One Size; To Fit Chest 38–40in.*

Discuss why any extra numbers might be included on the label, for example: *CA 18345; RN 13785; 2080/5320 044.*

Comment on any scripts other than Roman – Chinese characters, Arabic, Greek – and why they might be there.

Finally, praise the children for their sharp observational skills and the vast amount of information they have discovered.

Session Four: Taking care of T-shirts
Tell the children that you want them to continue collecting information in their groups. This time, they should collect all the information concerning the care of garments they can find. Throughout this session, make comparisons with the children's experiences of washing clothes – whether by hand, by machine or at the launderette, who does it, how it gets dried, and so on.

First of all, ask them to consider *washing* and to collect all the phrases used on labels in connection with washing,

READING

such as: *wash deep colours separately, wash before wearing, machine wash in cold water, do not soak, do not bleach, machine wash warm, machine or hand wash 40°, hand wash only, do not dry clean.* Do not forget to include phrases in other languages, such as: *lavar separadamente, laver en machine a l'eau tiede, ne pas javeliser.*

Next, consider instructions for *drying* the clothes, such as: *do not tumble dry, tumble dry low, do not dry in the sun, lie flat to dry, pull into shape and dry flat, reshape while damp, drip dry, keep away from fire.* Once again, remember to note phrases in other languages, such as: *ne pas secher dans sechoire rotatif, mantened separado del fuego.*

Lastly, collect the information about *ironing*, for example: *do not iron if decorated, cool iron, warm iron, steam iron.* Note foreign phrases too, such as: *repasser à fer moyen, no planchar al dibujo.*

Reflect with the children on how easy it is to read these instructions, and discuss the cues we can use to help interpret them. Show how what we know about washing clothes in general and the order in which we do things when washing clothes can help us work out the words and meanings. Sometimes the initial letter of a word can help us to identify the word, sometimes the length of the word gives us a clue, and sometimes we know the word as soon as we see it. Go through a few examples of labels with the children to demonstrate these cues in action.

Together, decide on strategies for reading the words in languages other than English. Is there any accompanying English text to help us? Do any of the words look like English words? Are there any symbols next to the words that we could refer to?

Round off the session by considering the reasons for having instructions, and asking whether people actually bother to read them and what factors might put them off. Raise the issue of people with visual impairment.

Ask the children to suggest one thing that might improve the current labelling situation, for example standardisation of the order of information provided and of vocabulary used.

Session Five: Using symbols

Collect all the symbols the children find on the labels and draw them on a board or flip chart. Discuss with the children what they think the symbols mean. Is the meaning for each symbol always obvious, or could there be misunderstandings? Encourage the children to suggest alternative symbols, and include these on the chart.

Arrange the children into pairs and give each pair a copy of photocopiable sheet 122. Tell the children that you want them to decide which of the three labels is the easiest to read and why. Also encourage them to note whether all the necessary information is provided each time, and whether further improvements could be made.

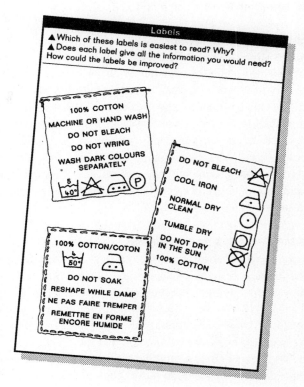

Session Six: Designers' workshop

Encourage children to design their own labelling systems for the T-shirt they printed in 'T-shirt bazaar' on page 16, using information gathered during the class discussions as guidelines. Remind them that they will have to decide on:
▲ whether to use words and/or symbols;
▲ the layout of the label to support easy understanding;
▲ the size and style of lettering to support easy reading;
▲ which languages to use for export abroad.

Suggestion(s) for extension

There are opportunities for individual writing tasks, such as letters of complaint to manufacturers in the light of the findings. Children would need to give consideration to the format and the wording of a formal letter, and the final draft

could be word-processed. They could be encouraged to locate the address of the firm and write it on the envelope themselves.

They could also write descriptions of the different textiles used in the manufacture of T-shirts, commenting on the feel, elasticity, thickness and durability of the material. They could hunt in the library to find out which languages *coton*, *algodon*, *Baumwolle* and *cotone* belong to.

Drawing on children's knowledge of adverts, consumer reports and television consumer programmes, as well as materials collected beforehand, you could hold a debate on the moral concerns regarding honest or false claims by manufacturers; the quality and price of products; or the effect of a famous designer's name on the price.

Suggestion(s) for support

Some children will need adult support for reading the labels and for scribing and organising their notes.

Assessment opportunities

During discussions, note the children's strategies for making meaning from words and symbols on labels and for comparing meanings across different languages.

Children's written work, such as letters to manufacturers, captions for display, lists and notes, will provide evidence of their strategies for translating ideas on to paper and will give you the opportunity to evaluate the quality of the content, the directionality of the writing, the spacing between words, the degree of handwriting control, the spelling strategies and the use of punctuation. The children's manual and aesthetic skills when creating displays should also be noted.

Opportunities for IT

In Session Four, children could use a word processor to write and sequence the instructions for washing one of the garments they have selected. They could work from the information given on the labels. It might be possible to photocopy the label and include this in a final display, or even scan the label to enable a picture to be included with the writing.

Children could collect some of the data from the labels, such as the country of manufacture or the material, and use graphing software to draw graphs to show the most common countries of origin or materials.

A simple graphics package could be used to draw the symbols seen on the labels, and the children could write in their own words what the symbol means. These could be printed out and collected together for display purposes.

In Session Six, the children could use a word processor or graphics package to design their own label. Computer-drawn symbols could be used on their labels. These could be created by the children themselves, or be drawn in advance by the teacher and saved on to disk so that children could include them in their label design.

Display ideas

A summative display could be created showing everything that the children have found out about labelling systems, care of garments and other languages. It could also include their own designs and the letters they have written to manufacturers.

Remember to involve children as much as possible in the preparation and mounting of displays, in making titles and in writing captions.

Other aspects of the English PoS covered

Speaking and listening – 1a, b, c; 2a, b; 3a, b.
Writing – 1a, b, c; 2a, b, d; 3b.

Reference to photocopiable sheet(s)

Photocopiable sheet 122 requires children to evaluate the clarity and adequacy of clothing labels, thus collating information given in verbal and in numerical form.

FOOD FAIR

For the children to:
▲ *sort words into alphabetical order;*
▲ *learn to recognise key words;*
▲ *use a range of cueing strategies to make meaning from print and to resequence and complete texts;*
▲ *develop their knowledge about language by spotting words within words and recognising abbreviations and common English letter patterns;*
▲ *compare words in different languages and understand that there are different alphabetic scripts;*
▲ *know that design features affect the accessibility of text to readers.*

†† *Session One: whole class; Session Two: small groups with an adult helper; Session Three: whole class; Session Four: whole class, then small groups; Session Five: whole class; Session Six: small groups; Sessions Seven and Eight: working in pairs.*

🕐 *Session One: 20 minutes; Session Two: 30 minutes; Session Three: 20 minutes; Session Four: 45 minutes; Session Five: 30 minutes; Session Six: 30 minutes; Session Seven: 25 minutes; Session Eight: 25–35 minutes.*

⚠ *Bear in mind food allergies and dietary restrictions if the children taste any of the soups.*

Key background information

This activity provides a familiar context in which children can use a range of reading strategies to reorder and complete texts and to create their own texts. It also provides the opportunity to reinforce alphabetic knowledge and letter-writing skills, and to extend the children's descriptive language. Links can be made with topics on shops and shopping, food, health, growing things, seasons, the world of business and industry, and the local environment.

Preparation

A stimulus display can generate interest and can be used as the basis for much of the later work. Children can contribute items to the display if appropriate. The display might include: a wide range of different types of soup (reassure contributors that the tins will be returned unopened once the project is over); recipes, magazines and cookery books from around the world, including examples in languages other than English (if possible) and in scripts other than Roman; a range of children's fiction related to the theme of food and eating (especially soup); aprons and towels decorated with logos; and kitchen utensils from around the world. The home corner could also be set up as a shop, supermarket or café.

Practise writing the words *bortsch* and *shchi* in Cyrillic script and *avgholemono* in Greek, and check the facts about the derivation of unusual soup names. (See illustration on right.)

Resources needed

Tins of soup (empty tins with jagged edges are not safe for use in the classroom), one copy of photocopiable pages 123 (or 124) and 125 for each child, utensils and ingredients for the cookery session, scissors and adhesive ready for Session Six, a tape recorder, a version of the traditional story 'Stone Soup' *(Scholastic Collections: Tales, Myths and Legends* contains one adaptation; some versions are called 'Nail Soup'), a flip chart or OHP, writing and drawing materials.

What to do
Session One: Introducing the topic

Start by reading the story 'Stone Soup' to the class, either in the traditional version or in one of the more modern versions. Encourage the children's spontaneous response to the story, then guide the discussion towards which soups the children like. Ask why their favourite soup is special to them. Is it home-made, and if so, by whom? Which utensils are needed to make it – for example, grater, chopper, sieve, blender, food processor? If it is bought, does it come in a tin, a packet or a carton? Where was it bought – corner shop, supermarket? When do they eat it – what time of year, what

αὐγολέμονο	*avgholemono*
борщ	*bortsch*
Щи	*shchi*

time of day? How do they eat it – hot or cold; as a whole meal, as a starter or at the end of the meal (as in China)?

To close the session, reread the story and encourage the children to join in.

Session Two: Development

After recapping the children's favourite soups, scribe on to a flip chart or OHP the names of as many types of soup as you and the children can think of. Encourage the children to draw on the initial stimulus display if they run out of ideas.

Together, regroup the names into alphabetical order – for example: Asparagus, Beef broth, Broccoli, Brown Windsor, Butter bean and parsnip, Carrot and butter bean, Carrot and coriander, Carrot and orange, Celery, Chicken, Leek and potato, Leek and mutton broth, Lentil, Lettuce, Minestrone, Mushroom, Onion, Pea and ham, Pumpkin, Spicy parsnip, Tomato, Turnip, Vegetable, Watercress.

Discuss the names on the list. Which names did the children know already? Which ones are new to them? Which soups do they like and which do they dislike? Draw the children's attention to interesting linguistic features such as letters that also occur in the children's names, matching initial letters or capitals and lower-case letters, common features such as double letters (ee/bb/rr/ss/tt), words within words (a, pa, us, rot, row, own, in, so, mat, snip, range).

Session Three: Names

Together with the children, look at the names of all the soups on the class list and note how many tell you what is in them – Carrot, Pea, and so on. Next, consider the other sorts of names, such as Brown Windsor and Minestrone. Have a recipe book to hand and find other examples – Mulligatawny, Bird's nest soup, Goulash, Gazpacho, Cock-a-leekie, Cawl mamgu, Cullen skink, Highlander's broth. Ask the children

to guess what might be in them and how they might have got these names. You could also encourage them to think of some humorous reasons. Give the children one minute only to brainstorm their ideas with the person sitting next to them, giving reasons for their choices.

Discuss the children's answers and comment on their ideas; then provide the correct information and tell the children where you found it, commenting on any interesting linguistic features (such as the Welsh word for soup, *cawl*, and its link with the Latin *colis/caulis*, meaning the stem of hollow cabbage-like vegetables).

Session Four: Labels

Show the children a tin of soup and look at all the information on the label. Discuss with them what information they would ideally like to find there and why. Write down all the questions the children might include:

▲ How much does it cost and how much does it contain?

▲ What's actually in the soup? (The list of ingredients could be very important for people with food allergies.)

▲ How should we cook it?

▲ How wholesome is it? Might there be possible risks to health?

▲ Do tins last forever? If not, shouldn't there be a date by which we should eat the contents to avoid any risk of food poisoning?

▲ Where could we write to complain if we were not satisfied? Would we get our money back?

▲ Have the manufacturers taken environmental factors into account in their packaging?

▲ Divide the class into groups. Then, armed with their list of questions and one tin of soup per group, the children can leap into their special investigators' shoes and work (with the help of an adult where necessary) on a specific focus.

Before they start, run through the points to bear in mind and note these on a board for the children to refer to as and when necessary – for example:

▲ Is all the information provided that they need? If not, what is missing?

▲ Is the information given in words and/or symbols?

▲ Are the symbols easy to read? Are the words well chosen?

▲ What clues help us to read the print? Are there any key words we need to know?

▲ Are headings signalled in large print?

▲ Is the print big enough to read easily?

▲ Is there a common format on the tins which helps us to find what we are looking for?

Now appoint specific tasks to each group.

Group One

Suggest to the children that they should list all the words found under the heading 'ingredients' on a large sheet of paper, for example: water, preservative, colour, starch, modified starch, modified maize starch, wheat flour, herbs, spices, garlic powder, flavourings, sugar, salt, mustard, pepper, stabiliser, emulsifier, thickener, monosodium glutamate, milk protein, white wine, skimmed milk powder, cream, tomato purée.

Discuss the meanings of 'ingredient' words with the children when necessary and talk about which of these ingredients were unexpected, which they think are acceptable, which they are worried about and why. The group could arrange their list in alphabetical order, ready to report back to the whole class later.

Group Two

Tell this group that their task is to list on a large sheet of paper all the words found under 'Nutrition(al) Information'. For example: Composition: per 100g/per can/per serving; *Energy*: 492kJ/118kcal; *Protein*: 3.699g; *Carbohydrate*: 14.499g, *of which sugars*: 1.699g; *Fat*: 5.099g, *of which saturates*: 1.699g; *Fibre*: 0.899g; *Sodium*: 0.899g. Note variants such as dietary fibre.

Discuss unfamiliar terminology and the use of continuous text or charts. Which is the most useful way of presenting this sort of information? List the conclusions for class discussion.

Group Three

Explain to this group that they are to list on a large sheet of paper all the words appearing under 'Preparation Guidelines' on the food labels. Point out variants such as 'Cooking Instructions' and 'Serving Instructions'.

Note introductory phrases such as 'All appliances vary, the following are guidelines only. Adjust times according to your particular oven.' Talk about why manufacturers might put this on the tin. Warn children to watch out for conventional as well as microwave oven instructions. Discuss why tinned soup manufacturers say DO NOT BOIL and often put this in capital letters.

Group Four

Set this group the task of listing all the general information about the product – such as the name, for example: 'Soups of Britain', 'The traditional range', 'The vegetarian range'; the brand name, for example: Tesco, Campbell's, Baxter's, Heinz, Sainsbury, Waitrose; the advertising blurb, for example: 'Britain's leading independent soup maker', 'For further information about our other fine food ranges, please write to...', 'A source of fibre', 'A low fat food, tasty and wholesome'; the weight or the amount ('This can contains two servings'); the price, the bar-code, the 'best before' date, and so on.

Talk about abbreviations such as JUL 98/APR 98; BBE NOV 97; MAR 98, and what they might stand for. The children could record these along with their meanings.

Group Five

Tell this group to list on a large sheet of paper all the information given in the form of symbols. Figure 1 below shows some examples.

Discuss how easy the symbols are to read. Could they stand on their own without words? Again, the children could record their findings for the benefit of others or for reference at a later date.

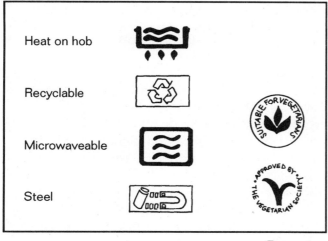

Heat on hob	
Recyclable	
Microwaveable	SUITABLE FOR VEGETARIANS
Steel	APPROVED BY THE VEGETARIAN SOCIETY

Figure 1

Group Six

Tell this group to list all the information about 'consumer rights' given on can labels on a large sheet of paper. For example: 'If you are not satisfied with any of our products please return it to the store where it was purchased, where we will be pleased to replace it, or send it with the packaging to the Consumer Relations Manager at the following address stating where and when it was purchased. This offer does not affect your statutory rights.' Or 'If this soup fails to satisfy, please write to our Customers Services Manager for a full refund. Your statutory rights are not affected.' Discuss whether every tin gives such information and, if given, how easy it is to read. Talk about the language used, and how and why this might be changed. For instance, why use *purchase* instead of *buy*?

Discuss how difficult it might be to carry out these instructions. What might be an easier and simpler way of making your concerns known? What are the pitfalls of this type of complaints system? Who might lose out?

Session Five: Reporting back

Each group in turn can report back to the class on what they found, reading back from their recording where appropriate. Aim for child-led rather than teacher-directed discussions as the children grow more used to working in this way. Go over

the concerns the children have and discuss what can be done about them. Encourage the class to compose a joint letter to one of the firms concerned, perhaps; or to the local newspaper, the local MP or the Consumer Council. Make sure it gets posted, as it is important that the children receive a reply.

Session Six: Resequencing

Divide the children into pairs and give each pair a copy of photocopiable sheet 123. Explain that the soup manufacturer has muddled up the cooking instructions, and that it is their task to resequence the instructions into the correct order. Before starting, the children should read the instructions out loud. Encourage them to discuss the factors that will help

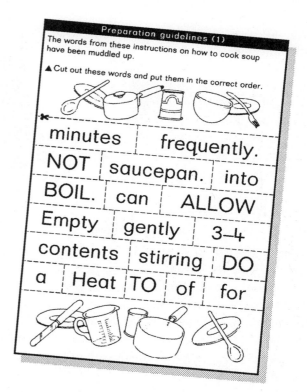

them to decide on a logical sequence – for example: the title, prior knowledge of how soup cooking instructions are usually laid out, words that they recognise, punctuation such as full stops and capital letters. Once they have completed the sequencing task, they can read the final version out to another pair and compare their results, giving reasons for their particular sequence.

when commenting on the taste and the texture of the soups – for example: bland, sour, too watery, too spicy, too salty, too runny, too thick, too floury; and to make comparisons and use similes to sharpen the accuracy of their descriptions and make them more interesting.

The children could write to the manufacturers, describing the test they have carried out and detailing the results.

Suggestion(s) for extension

Drawing on your own and the children's family or holiday experiences as well as recipe books, encourage the children to talk about the interesting soup names they have come across – for example: bortsch, bouillabaisse, clam chowder, avgholemono, soupe bonne femme, bisque de homard, Leghorn fish stew, vichyssoise, soupe à l'onion, consommé. Group them in sets to support the children's thinking – fish soups, vegetable soups, and so on.

Discuss what language the names are in and what the soups might be made of, and compare these with types of British soups from the children's earlier list. Consider why so many French words for food are used in English recipes and restaurants. Consider links with names of places or people – for example, bonne femme, mamgu (granny), Vichy, Leghorn. Note interesting linguistic features such as accents, and combinations of letters that do not occur in English.

Children could list words for soup in as many languages as possible: soup, cawl, potage, consommé, soupe, garbure, sopa, zuppa, suppe, broth, bouillon, velouté. Look for similarities and differences between these words. Make a display of these words alongside verbs connected with eating

Session Seven: *Filling in the blanks*

Divide the children into pairs and give each pair a copy of photocopiable sheet 125. Explain that their task is to complete the names of the soups on the labels, as an error in production has caused all the vowels to be omitted.

Discuss helpful cues with the children first. For example: remind them of the five vowels plus y (and w); point out that knowing some soup names already will be of use; check which common three-letter words are likely to crop up; discuss which vowels are most likely to occur at the ends of English words, and which two vowels often go together in the middles of words.

Encourage the pairs to share their results. The children can make up a similar game with other soup names for their friends to complete.

Session Eight: *The proof of the pudding*

Set up a tasting test for the children to carry out. Remove the names of the soups from four or five tins of soup and lay out the labels in a row.

Carefully heat the soups in turn, according to the manufacturer's cooking instructions, to ensure a fair test; then ask the children to taste a spoonful of soup and to match the soup to the correct label.

Encourage them to use precise, descriptive vocabulary

▲ Preparation guidelines (2)

Each sentence below has been muddled up. Cut up the word strip for each one, and arrange them into the correct order to make complete sentences. Then put the sentences in order to make the instructions for heating a can of soup.

3-4
Heat   frequently.
    for   gently
minutes   stirring
not boil. to Do allow
saucepan.   into
contents of Empty a
can

soup: slurp, suck, slither, chew, swallow, sip, gobble, drink, blow, and so on.

Children could write out a soup recipe of their own to add to the collection in the class recipe book. Bilingual adults or older children could translate the text into other languages and transliterate where necessary. These recipes could be recorded on tape for the benefit of children in the Nursery.

Suggestion(s) for support

Some children will need an adult's help when working on the photocopiable sheets. The task on photocopiable sheet 124 is a simpler alternative to that on photocopiable sheet 123. Extra emphasis could be given to matching upper- and lower-case letters. The children could then reinforce recognition of DO and DO NOT by devising a list of rules that would help to keep the classroom a 'permanently happy place'.

Many young children's ideas are far in advance of their scribing skills, so activities that do not demand too much writing stamina are ideal. To reinforce letter-sound correlation, the children could make a dictionary or an alphabet chart of soups, with each child being responsible for one letter of the alphabet. Stress the importance of attention to careful handwriting, letter formation, detailed drawing, attractive borders, and so on.

Using the work of famous artists (for example, Andy Warhol's work based on tins), discuss the customer appeal of labels and encourage the children to design a label for their own favourite soup. Recap all the information needed and the important points that designers have to bear in mind.

Assessment opportunities

The children's comments when noticing words within words and the similarities and differences between words, their recognition of letters from their own names on soup tin labels, their use of specialised vocabulary when cooking, and their sequencing, coherence and relevance when reporting back on their findings will all provide evidence of their language and reading development.

Note their use of a range of reading cues when reading text on tins, and when completing and resequencing texts. Remember to use the children's writing to provide reading opportunities on a regular basis.

Opportunities for IT

In Session Four, children could use an art or graphics package to design their own soup label, taking account of the items already discussed. They could experiment with different colours, and with the size and style of text on the label.

In Session Five, children could compose and redraft their letters of complaint using a word processor. This could be used to introduce letter layout and some of the simpler format commands, such as 'right justify' for the address and 'full justification' to even up the right-hand margin.

For younger children, in Session Six the teacher could set up a concept keyboard linked to a word processor. The overlay for the keyboard could contain the sentences for the instructions in the wrong order. Children could resequence the order by pressing on the relevant word or sentence, which will then appear on the screen.

Older or more able children could use a prepared file with the sentences in the wrong order. They could either use the 'cut' and 'paste' commands of the word processor to delete the sentence and then paste it into the correct place, or use the drag and drop facility on more modern word processors to mark the sentence and then drag it to its new position.

In Session Seven, children could be introduced to a program like *Developing Tray* (available from ILECC) in which they must replace all of the letters in a word or sentence. The aim is to make the replacement in the shortest possible number of goes. The words can be entered without vowels or without consonants, and you can then ask the children to replace them. Children need to look for letter clues such as double letters, common consonant blends, and so on, to inform the selection of letters.

Different files can be prepared for pupils at different levels, giving them more, or less, starting information.

Display ideas

The children's work resulting from these activities can be used to expand the initial stimulus display. Presentation can be improved if the children use a word processor and give their work decorative borders.

A summative display of all that the children have found out from their surveys and investigations, with their constructive and critical comments framing it, would be effective.

A display of the children's 'award-winning' soup tin designs would be a colourful addition to the classroom.

Other aspects of the English PoS covered

Speaking and listening – 1a, b, c; 2a, b; 3b.
Writing – 1a, b, c; 2a, b, c, d; 3a, b.

Reference to photocopiable sheet(s)

Sheet 123 requires children to rearrange words into a set of instructions; sheet 124 is a simpler version. Sheet 125 requires children to fill in the missing vowels or vowel sounds.

SELLIT, QUICKE AND RUNNE

FOR SALE

ESTATE AGENTS' ADVERTISEMENTS

For the children to:
▲ use a range of strategies to make meaning from text;
▲ develop scanning strategies to read for information, ignoring redundant material;
▲ recognise adjectives;
▲ increase their descriptive vocabulary;
▲ match text to photographs;
▲ read between the lines and sharpen their critical awareness as readers;
▲ reflect on the ethical issues involved in advertising.
†† Session One: whole class; Session Two: working in pairs; Session Three: small-group work; Session Four: small-group work with adult support; Session Five: working in pairs.
🕐 Session One: 20 minutes; Session Two: 35 minutes; Session Three: 35 minutes; Session Four: 25 minutes; Session Five: 30 minutes.

Key background information

This series of activities provides a real-life context in which children can use information retrieval skills, further their grammatical knowledge of parts of speech (such as adjectives) and write in a particular style for a particular purpose. Links can be made with projects on homes, climates, the world of work and communication.

Preparation

Collect a range of adverts from estate agents' offices aiming to cover as broad a range of types of houses as possible; local and national newspaper and magazine sections on property advertising, sales and letting; sets of photographs of different types of houses cut out of magazines.

Gather a selection of children's fiction related to homes, moving house, travellers and the homeless. With the children's help, arrange the home corner as an estate agent's shop. Make shop signs, cards for adverts, forms for customers to fill in, cheques, receipts, bank cards, an appointments book and a complaints book.

Resources needed

Writing and drawing materials, one copy per child of photocopiable sheets 126, 127 and 128, recyclable materials, adhesive, paint.

What to do

Session One: Introduction to the topic

Introduce the topic in storytime by reading a story about moving – for example, *Ming Lo Moves the Mountain* by Arnold Lobel (Walker Books, 1991) or *Moving Molly* by

Shirley Hughes (Red Fox, 1991). Invite the children's spontaneous responses to the story and encourage them to make links with their own homes: where they live, who lives with them, the type of house (or flat) they live in, the materials the building is made of, the local amenities in the neighbourhood, what they would feel about moving house, and so on. Make sure that when discussing types of houses, you use the terminology that will be used during the topic (detached, semi-detached, terrace, maisonette, bungalow, chalet, and so on). In this way, the children will be prepared for the vocabulary they will meet in the printed texts.

Session Two: Development

Start this session by talking with the whole class about what would happen if the children had to move house. What would they look for in the adverts for houses to buy or rent? Ask them what facts they would need to know and list these on the board or a flip chart. Suggestions might include:

▲ where the house is situated (*location*);

▲ what *type* of house it is;

▲ what *rooms* it contains;

▲ what's *outside* it;

▲ what extra *amenities* there are;

▲ what special *features* it has.

Explain to the children that you want them to pretend to be house-hunters, scanning newspapers for specific information about houses for sale or rent. Organise the children into pairs or small groups and stipulate that each pair/group will look for different features of the houses, using key words from the class list to focus their attention. Distribute the newspapers among the children and allow them time to underline any relevant information that they find.

The children can report their findings to the class, and you should scribe all the information they contribute on to large sheets of paper under the various criteria headings, so that everyone can read them.

▲ *House type*: detached, semi, terrace, self-contained flat, apartment (ground floor, first floor, second floor, penthouse), maisonette, cottage, studio, townhouse, farmhouse, family residence, converted manor house, bungalow, chalet.

▲ *Location*: riverside, close to town centre, easy access to all local amenities, overlooking woodland, village location, semi-rural position, quiet location, cul-de-sac, university area.

▲ *Number of rooms*: hall, downstairs cloakroom, lounge, dining room, study, utility area, breakfast room, two receptions, bathroom, shower room, separate WC, three double bedrooms, master bedroom with balcony and *en-suite* bathroom, loft room.

▲ *Outside*: single/double garage, ample parking, parking nearby, car port, allocated parking; small/medium/large garden, mature garden, enclosed garden, walled rear garden, 100ft rear garden, ¼ acre plot, lawned garden, two ponds and a well, larger than average plot, outdoor swimming pool.

▲ *Amenities*: gas-fired central heating, oil-fired central heating, double glazing, electric radiators, storage heaters, power-assisted garage door, fully-fitted kitchen, refitted kitchen with oven and hob. (Note the use of abbreviations such as GFCH.)

▲ *Features*: brick fireplace, cast-iron fireplace, Victorian fireplace, inglenook fireplace, patio doors, internal beams, open-plan dining room, archway to dining room, security entrance system, split-level apartment, newly-installed kitchen, recently redecorated.

Talk about the terminology used. Explain any unfamiliar words or abbreviations, and comment on the similarities and differences between the words. Check whether the children think they have enough information to choose a house to buy or rent, or whether they have any doubts or any gaps in their knowledge of this area.

Session Three: Critical readers

Discuss what the job of an estate agent entails, and suggest that the children look very carefully at the ways in which estate agents try to persuade people to buy houses. First of all, look together at the photographs of the houses. Are they always in colour and taken from the best angle, and do they stress particular effects? What do the children think might *not* be shown in the photographs?

Then look at the adjectives used. Are they honest or exaggerated? Explain to the children that they are going to hunt for adjectives, working in pairs or groups, using the same adverts as before so that they will be familiar with the text. Ask them to collect all the adjectives they can find, and then to report back to the class later.

Write their collection of adjectives on to a flip chart. Likely words are: spacious, luxury, modern, superb, comfortable, pleasant, excellent, charming, immaculate, picturesque, Victorian, traditional, Georgian-style, extended, purpose-built, old-style, turn of the century, 1920s, exclusive, bay-fronted, and so on. Discuss with the children the reasons why the estate agents might have chosen each of these adjectives: the effect they are trying to conjure up, and the clients they are trying to appeal to. Ask the children if they think this is fair or misleading. Talk about the legal aspects of advertising – estate agents are not supposed to tell outright lies. Work through the list of words and suggest possible alternatives – more accurate – for each adjective.

Session Four: Matching words and pictures

Divide the class into small groups and give each group a copy of photocopiable pages 126 and 127. Explain to the children that they will need to group-read the advertising blurbs on one sheet and then match them to the correct pictures on the other sheet. Can they decide which blurb best describes which house? Encourage ongoing discussion and close attention to detail.

Groups can share their decisions with the class afterwards, explaining their reasons.

Session Five: Adjectives

Divide the children into pairs and tell them to read the estate agent's blurb provided on photocopiable sheet 128. Explain that their task is then to underline any adjectives they feel are likely to be an exaggeration of the truth, making joint decisions about which words to underline after discussion.

They can then discuss humorous alternatives that exaggerate the bad points for a change, and rewrite a humorous version of the blurb pinpointing the awful truth about why people should not buy this house!

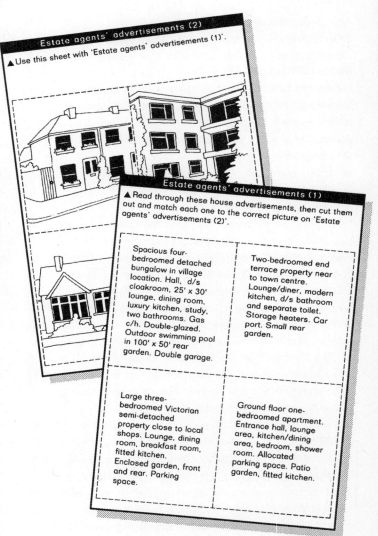

Estate agents' advertisements (2)
▲ Use this sheet with 'Estate agents' advertisements (1)'.

Estate agents' advertisements (1)
▲ Read through these house advertisements, then cut them out and match each one to the correct picture on 'Estate agents' advertisements (2)'.

Spacious four-bedroomed detached bungalow in village location. Hall, d/s cloakroom, 25' x 30' lounge, dining room, luxury kitchen, study, two bathrooms. Gas c/h. Double-glazed. Outdoor swimming pool in 100' x 50' rear garden. Double garage.	Two-bedroomed end terrace property near to town centre. Lounge/diner, modern kitchen, d/s bathroom and separate toilet. Storage heaters. Car port. Small rear garden.
Large three-bedroomed Victorian semi-detached property close to local shops. Lounge, dining room, breakfast room, fitted kitchen. Enclosed garden, front and rear. Parking space.	Ground floor one-bedroomed apartment. Entrance hall, lounge area, kitchen/dining area, bedroom, shower room. Allocated parking space. Patio garden, fitted kitchen.

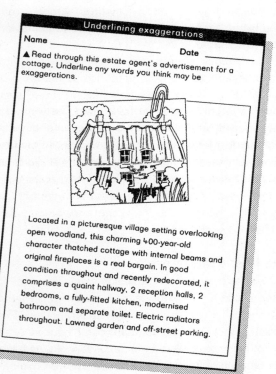

Underlining exaggerations

Name _____ Date _____

▲ Read through this estate agent's advertisement for a cottage. Underline any words you think may be exaggerations.

Located in a picturesque village setting overlooking open woodland, this charming 400-year-old character thatched cottage with internal beams and original fireplaces is a real bargain. In good condition throughout and recently redecorated, it comprises a quaint hallway, 2 reception halls, 2 bedrooms, a fully-fitted kitchen, modernised bathroom and separate toilet. Electric radiators throughout. Lawned garden and off-street parking.

Suggestion(s) for extension

Children could research in the library the less usual types of housing, such as caravans and houseboats. They could also investigate the lives of travellers or the homeless. Another possibility is to research building materials used in different parts of the world and how these are suited to climate and local resources.

Suggestion(s) for support

The activities centred on the photocopiable sheets could be done as purely oral activities, with an adult reading the text and leading the discussion. Alternatively, an adult could act as scribe.

Assessment opportunities

Note the children's reading strategies when they are trying to find information quickly, and their ability to match text to pictures; and their understanding of the need to read between the lines. Listen to their conversation for signs of critical reading skills when they are hunting for adjectives, reasoning and questioning, discussing important concerns about housing and reporting to the class.

Opportunities for IT

In Session Two, the children could use a database containing 'estate agent' information which has been set up in advance by the teacher; or they could create their own database. In either case, they should have opportunities to use the database to answer such questions as: *How many houses are there in the country? Which is the house with the largest number of rooms?* or more complex questions, such as: *How many houses have a double garage and are in the town? Which houses have double glazing and gas central heating?*

If the children are going to set up their own database, they will need to spend some time as a group or class to discuss the headings (field names) of the database. They will also need to decide how to classify information such as the size of the garden, or the location. It is often useful to create a data collection sheet which gives children a limited number of available responses, one of which they must use to describe a feature. Gardens, for instance, might be classified as: none, patio, small, medium, large. This helps with consistency within the database, and makes it much easier to use. It is also a good idea to make sure that children

collect the data in the same order that they will enter it into the computer.

Once the children have collected their data, they might work in pairs or with the support of an older child or an adult to type in their data. If they work in pairs, one child should check the work of the other, both for keying errors and for mistakes in the data itself. Extra spaces or full stops can often cause havoc with later searches!

The database might contain the following fields:

Location	town/country/city, etc
Rooms	6
Bedrooms	4
Type	detached, semi-detached, terrace, etc
Garage	none, 1, 2, etc
Garden	large, small, etc
Features	GCH, DG

Some databases have tokenised fields, which means that children can only select from the offered choices which are set up in advance. This makes entry and later searching much more consistent and reliable.

Once the children start to search, they will need to be introduced to facilities such as simple searches, sorts and printing out their answers (in table or even graph form). Make sure that you allow plenty of time for this activity, which will probably need to be spread over several weeks. It is important that children have time to use the database and do not just enter their information.

The children could write their own descriptions of a house using 'estate agent' language. This could be done using a word processor or simple desktop publishing package. A standard page layout could be created in advance, giving spaces or frames for pictures, main details and a room by room description. Alternatively, this could be reduced to just a single front page, giving the key features of the house, picture and price.

Display ideas

The children could make a frieze of a local street with houses and shops, and write imaginary estate agents' adverts for each property. The children could draw or paint pictures of their own homes and display these alongside descriptions of them that an estate agent might write, together with accounts of their real feelings about their homes. Warning posters of do's and don'ts for house-hunters could also be included.

Other aspects of the English PoS covered

Speaking and listening – 1a, b; 2a, b; 3b.
Writing – 1a, b, c; 2a, b, c, d; 3b.

Reference to photocopiable sheet(s)

Matching the advertisements on sheet 126 with the pictures on sheet 127 requires children to interpret the text. Sheet 128 leads children to examine an advertisement critically.

TELEVISION ADVERTISEMENTS

For the children to:

▲ *listen to, understand, respond to and recall information disseminated by a disembodied voice;*

▲ *read key words from a television screen and make inferences;*

▲ *complete a cloze procedure, match catchphrases to products and illustrations to text by using a range of cueing strategies;*

▲ *develop their awareness of language use and evaluate language features that capture listeners' interest (alliteration, rhyme, rhythm, repetition, style, vocabulary).*

†† *Sessions One and Two: whole class; Session Three: working in pairs; Session Four: whole class, then pair work; Session Five: small groups; Session Six: whole class, then pair work; Session Seven: pair work.*

🕐 *Session One: 20 minutes; Session Two: 30 minutes; Session Three: 25 minutes; Session Four: 25–30 minutes; Session Five: 30 minutes; Session Six: 40–45 minutes; Session Seven: 35 minutes.*

Key background information

This topic provides a highly motivating context in which to build on children's natural curiosity in order to raise their awareness of how language is used to influence and persuade. It also provides opportunities to use prior knowledge, as well as linguistic and orthographic knowledge, to make meaning from print and to supply missing words and letters in incomplete texts. These sessions can link with projects on advertising, food, rhythms and pattern.

Preparation

Record on video a selection of popular adverts from television, and note down the salient facts about text and spoken script that will be used in the teaching sessions. For Session Three, prepare an old, tattered 'original' document from the *Marie Celeste* (based on Figure 1).

Resources needed

Writing materials, musical instruments for sound effects, a tape recorder, a video recorder and television, one copy per child (or pair of children) of photocopiable sheets 129, 130, 131 and 132.

What to do

Session One: Introduction to the topic

Elicit the children's general views about adverts they have seen on the television.

▲ Do they mind the interruptions to programmes?

▲ Are there too many, too few, or just the right number of adverts?

▲ Do they think all channels should be allowed to advertise? Why/why not?

▲ Who do children think the adverts are aimed at – parents, children, old people, single people?

▲ Do the children think that adverts really influence people's buying habits?

▲ Do they think adverts make people greedy? Is it fair on people out of work to keep seeing lots of expensive things advertised on television – especially at Christmas, when their children might get upset?

Write a list of the adverts the children can remember well on a flip chart or a very large sheet of paper that can be seen by the whole class, and leave it on display for the children to read during the week. Together, try to sort the adverts into sets – for example, ones about food, toys, holidays, washing powder, and so on.

Ask the children if they can think of any reasons why some adverts are so easy to remember. Is it the rhyme, the rhythm, the tune, the humour, the visual impact, the snappy catchphrase? Discuss what they believe to be the most important factors – for instance, the music, the voice-over, the special effects.

Discuss whether the speed of presentation hinders understanding. Do they have time to read all the words of the text or to hear all the words of the songs and jingles?

Session Two: Modelling how to evaluate a television advertisement

Many advertisements aimed at children feature traditional stories: for example, adverts for porridge often centre around the story of 'Goldilocks and the Three Bears'. This aspect of advertisements can be used to stimulate children's interest and is worth investigating.

Recap from earlier discussion the features you might look for in an advert, for example: music, sound effects, special effects, humour, reference to familiar things, type of text (print/capitals/cursive), how long text is on screen, language use (vocabulary, playing with words).

Now model the routine for the children to follow when working in pairs or small groups on other adverts. Watch and listen carefully to the adverts on the videotape you have prepared, using the rewind and pause buttons as necessary to capture phrases as they appear, and note down the phrases.

During this process, focus on reading skills. Encourage the children to join in when they can, mirroring the intonation of the speaker. Point to the text as it is shown on the screen. Prompt children's reading with pertinent questions if possible, and read aloud any text shown with or for the children if necessary.

Investigate whether the children noticed the different sorts of script — capitals, fancy glowing letters, and so on. Did these have the desired effect on the watcher? Discuss whether the words were on screen long enough for the children to read them. Were there enough words, or would more be an improvement? What would the children like to add or leave out? Do they like adverts with humorous content, or with memorable characters?

Next, focus on listening skills and discuss the music and sound effects. Were they appropriate? Was there enough? Would the children like to make any additions? How effective was the voice-over text?

Round off the session by suggesting to the children that they bring in some packaging from products advertised on the television to display in the classroom, so that they can read the advertising blurbs on the different packets and compare them.

Session Three: Cloze procedure

Pirates and shipwrecks are common themes in television adverts. Briefly tell the tale of how the *Marie Celeste* sank long ago but divers never found anyone on board, and how this has never been explained. A television advert for breakfast cereals used this mystery story, maintaining that the sailors had abandoned ship to get some Weetabix for their breakfast! Ask the children if they think this is true. Tell them that they now have the chance to find out, because a manuscript was rescued from the *Marie Celeste*. It was found rolled up inside a bottle, badly damaged, and parts of it are now unreadable.

Present the faded, crumpled and torn 'original' you have prepared; but explain that it is much too precious to hand round, so you have made photocopies of it for use in class today. Can the children, as eminent historians, decipher what the pirates were trying to tell us?

Give each of the children a cloze procedure text based on Figure 1. Ask them to work in small groups to supply the words missing from the text, using the rhyme, the rhythm, grammatical cues, meaning cues and prior knowledge of the text. Encourage them to float as many suggestions as possible for the missing words, as extending vocabulary and justifying choices have an important role in the learning process. It is not just a question of finding a right answer!

When complete, the children can read their version to the whole class. Discuss the various suggestions offered and decide on final choices that best fit the style of the advert.

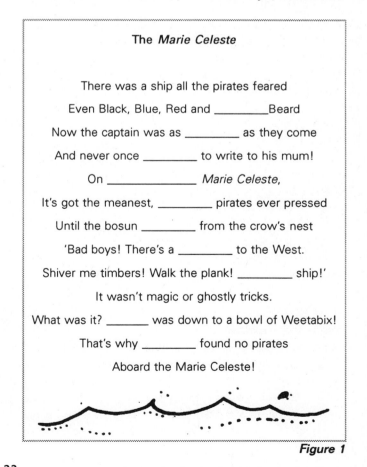

The *Marie Celeste*

There was a ship all the pirates feared

Even Black, Blue, Red and _____Beard

Now the captain was as _____ as they come

And never once _____ to write to his mum!

On _____ Marie Celeste,

It's got the meanest, _____ pirates ever pressed

Until the bosun _____ from the crow's nest

'Bad boys! There's a _____ to the West.

Shiver me timbers! Walk the plank! _____ ship!'

It wasn't magic or ghostly tricks.

What was it? _____ was down to a bowl of Weetabix!

That's why _____ found no pirates

Aboard the Marie Celeste!

Figure 1

READING

Session Four: Chocolate bars

Prime the children for this activity by discussing in advance all the chocolate bars on sale in the shops (Mars, Crunchie, Snickers, Yorkie, and so on) and listing them in alphabetical order on a board or flip chart. Encourage the children to name and describe their favourites and to give reasons for their preferences. Ask them to watch out for television adverts for chocolate bars at home. At the end of the week, take feedback from the class about the advertisements that they watched – the visual images, the words and phrases used to persuade people to buy the products, the background music played. Ask for the children's opinions on how effective the adverts were and how they could be improved.

Distribute copies of photocopiable sheet 129 to the children and ask them to work in pairs or small groups to complete the text to make an advertisement for their favourite chocolate bar. They can choose whether to fill the gaps with single words or with whole phrases for best effect. If they wish, they can add musical accompaniment and sound effects, then prepare a reading for the whole class.

other characters used in adverts, might say before and after eating the chocolate.

Tell the children that they are going to create an advert for one of their own favourite chocolate products based on the story of 'The Three Little Pigs'. Distribute copies of photocopiable sheet 130 to the children and suggest that they work in small groups to complete their advert. They will need to draw on their knowledge of the original story, and of the humorous version discussed in class, to supply appropriate words to fit the characters' actions and thoughts. (Remind the children of the difference between speech and thought bubbles.) Encourage them to discuss alternatives with their partners and to use a humorous tone to suit the genre, with plenty of exclamation marks, question marks and noise effects.

Perhaps they could invent new adverts for their favourite chocolate based on other stories.

Session Six: Slogans and catchphrases

Talk with the children about common linguistic features of adverts such as alliteration, rhymes and wordplay. Share examples of such features that are used in well-known adverts. Which ones do the children like? Which do they find particularly catchy and memorable? Do they think they can write better ones?

Decide on a random product and then create a catchphrase for it together. You can model the creative process by scribing first suggestions, crossing out, adding and changing vocabulary until everyone is satisfied with the result. Then distribute copies of photocopiable sheet 131,

Session Five: Traditional stories

Remind the class of how adverts often use well-known stories to capture children's interest, especially when advertising food that children enjoy. For instance, Cadbury's used the story of 'The Three Little Pigs' to show how the wolf could be transformed from a 'baddie' into a 'goodie' by eating some of their chocolate buttons! Discuss what the big bad wolf, or

and ask the children to work in pairs to invent names for new products and to devise a catchy advertising slogan for each one. Afterwards, the pairs can share their versions with their friends, giving reasons for their choices.

Session Seven: Inventing adverts

Distribute copies of photocopiable sheet 132 to the children. Explain that some of the phrases may be familiar to them already from adverts they have seen, but ask them to consider what a stranger who had never seen any of the adverts might think if he saw these phrases. Tell them to read through the catchphrases carefully, working in pairs, and to decide what they think each catchphrase might be advertising. Discuss what clues might help them to decide. For example, the word 'step' in phrase 5 might suggest shoes, slippers, socks or a shoe shop. Encourage the children to list as many options as possible – for example, possible answers for phrase 1 might include chocolate bars, biscuits, cakes, cereals, and so on. The pair must then invent a product and product name for each catchphrase, and prepare a script for an advert for this product to record on to tape. This will probably take more than one session to complete. When each pair have finished, they can play their tape to the class and invite constructive comment.

Suggestion(s) for extension

In pairs, the children can create an alternative text for one of the adverts you have discussed or viewed on videotape.

In pairs, or individually, the children can write a slogan for a well-known product, to be displayed so that children in other classes can 'guess the product'. Drawings of the product could be attached under a flap to provide the hidden answer.

Ask the children to view and *evaluate* adverts with their families at home. They could compose a letter to take home to the family, telling them about this project.

Children could discuss whether people should be able to advertise anything and everything, regardless of health, harm and danger factors. They could debate the stereotypical images portrayed in adverts and investigate the accuracy of descriptions, the omissions, the half-truths and the legal restrictions. They could use similar criteria to investigate other forms of advertising, such as billboards around town, newspapers, magazines, radio and so on.

Suggestion(s) for support

Throughout paired activities, less experienced children should have the support of an adult helper, an older child or a more experienced reader whenever the text is too long or too complex for them. They might also benefit from the services of a scribe for written activities. At times, a tape recorder would suffice to make a permanent record of the children's work. Differentiated follow-up activities could also be devised as follows:

▲ Painting posters to advertise products.

▲ Making a collection of words featuring spelling patterns encountered in the adverts.

▲ Composing their own song for a product that would appeal to young children in the Nursery. Remind them not to forget the musical accompaniment.

Assessment opportunities

Children's discussions when evaluating adverts, expressing personal opinions, justifying their choices, commenting on language use, making comparisons and explaining reading cues used to complete texts all offer valuable information about their reading progress.

Children's reading skills, accuracy and fluency, as well as their confidence, will be evident when they read their own writing to the class. Also note their attitudes towards writing, their developing secretarial skills and the quality of the content of their written work.

Opportunities for IT

In Session Six, the children could write their slogan using a word processor. They could use the editing facilities to redraft their slogan until they are satisfied with it. As the keyboarding aspect of this task will be quite short, children can then concentrate on the writing and the presentation of the slogan, using different fonts or colours to make it stand out. The completed catchphrases could be printed out and used as a part of the class display.

The children could create an advert using an art or graphics package to draw a picture of their product, add text and use colour to make the picture more eye-catching. They could incorporate the slogan they have already written.

Display ideas

The classroom walls could be used as billboards with children's adverts displayed all around.

Other aspects of the English PoS covered

Speaking and listening – 1a, c, d; 2a, b; 3a, b.
Writing – 1a, b, c; 2a, b, c, d; 3b.

Reference to photocopiable sheet(s)

Photocopiable sheets 129, 130, 131 and 132 require children to relate images to advertising copy in various ways: filling gaps in copy, writing text for a picture story, inventing brand names and slogans, interpreting slogans.

CHILDREN'S COMICS

For children to:
▲ *appreciate the distinctive style of writing in comics, and the similarities with, and differences from, other genres such as storybooks, newspapers and reference books;*
▲ *collect instances of the use of exclamation marks and question marks in comics, and consider the reasons why these feature so highly;*
▲ *understand how punctuation can enhance an action-packed narrative;*
▲ *note invented words and how they relate to everyday words;*
▲ *supply appropriate speech for comic characters.*
†† *Session One: whole class; Session Two: working in pairs; Session Three: whole class; Session Four: whole class, then group work; Session Five: working in pairs.*
⏱ *Session One: 20 minutes; Session Two: 30 minutes; Session Three: 25 minutes; Session Four: 20 minutes; Session Five: 30 minutes.*

Previous skills/knowledge needed

The children should be able to recognise exclamation marks and question marks, and to use scissors.

Key background information

Within the context of writing a class comic book, children will investigate the language conventions used in comics – for example, aspects of punctuation such as exclamation marks and question marks, the distinctive style of writing, expressive verbs and onomatopoeic language. They will also explore orthographic patterns of English. The work done in these sessions lays the groundwork for the activity on page 40. This topic can link with class projects on communications, illustrators, gender stereotyping and the mass media.

Preparation

Collect and display a range of children's comics – both old and new, and in as many languages as possible. Children can make a major contribution to this.

Resources needed

A range of materials for writing, drawing and book-making, a tape recorder, a flip chart or large sheets of paper, one copy of photocopiable sheet 133 for each child.

What to do

Session One: Introduction to the topic

Gather the whole class together and tell the children that they are going to write a comic for the class library. To ensure a top-quality product, they must first do some research to make sure that they know all there is to know about comics!

All the way through the following sessions, make reference to the comic the children will write and point out useful factors to include in their work.

Start off by inviting the children's spontaneous comments about their favourite comics. Who are the best-known characters? What do they like particularly about the humour in these comics? Are there different sections to a comic, and if so, what exactly is available for the reader? Who prefers comics to storybooks and why? What do their parents think about comics?

Then look at an example of a comic and go through the sections with the children, noting strip-cartoon stories, quizzes, adverts, letters, riddles, and so on. Ask them what they noticed about the way the text is laid out on the cartoon pages. Point out that it is mainly dialogue, with speech bubbles everywhere, and with some special vocabulary. What effect do they think this might have on the reader?

Check for common features with comics in other languages – there is an abundance of comics written in Punjabi, for instance.

Session Two: Exclamation marks

Tell the children that they will be working in pairs as detectives, to hunt out all the exclamation marks and question marks in their comics. Give at least one comic to each pair and explain that they will have only a couple of minutes to carry out this task, so they will have to be very attentive. They are to keep a tally of all the !s and ?s that they spot. Set the stopwatch and let the count begin. At the end of the two minutes, discuss the findings of all the pairs.

Now explain to the children that their next search will be a little different, as this time they have to copy out (or cut out, if copying is too laborious) all the phrases where exclamation marks are used. Allow about five or six minutes for the children to do this.

Ask the children to read out their findings to the class while you scribe their offerings on to a flip chart or a very large sheet of paper. Group the results into two sections, such as what people say in the speech (or thought) bubbles and the actions described in text outside these bubbles. The resulting list should be similar to the one given below:

▲ Recognisable words or phrases, such as: No fear! We missed you! Thank you! There it is! Hi! Shucks! Help! Gee! Whoops! No-o-o! Golly! Yes! Bravo!
▲ Made-up words to describe the noises people make, such as: Uh-oh! Aaak! Aarrgh! Yuk! Hic! Glub! Oooer! Eeeekkk! Cor! Yow! Boohoo! Wheee! Uck! Yikes! Phew! Whew! Yeeow! Bah! Arf Arf! Yeah! Gurk! Heh heh heh! Uhhh! Bpthh Blabbabla! Yay! Waaah! Oops! Nah! Oof! Coo! Urrrgh!

▲ Recognisable verbs, such as: Whisk! Whine! Yell! Slurp! Sniff! Bash! Biff! Sob! Thud! Bang! Chomp! Snap! Shove! Pop! Roar! Crack! Slam! Rumble! Scream! Click! Smack! Bump! Splutter! Gurgle! Scratch! Kick! Jab! Scuttle! Wail!
▲ Made-up words that describe the sounds of actions, such as: Pow! Vroom! Brmmm! Sproing! Boink! Skreek! Boom! Bopp! Pong! Wham! Ding Dong! Thwap! Zzunk!

Discuss with the children the effects writers create by using all these exclamation marks. How could a writer get across the same information in a storybook that just one picture and one word (like SLAM!) manage to convey in a comic? Invite a few verbal suggestions.

Finally, children can work individually, choosing a word each to write out in large print and decorate with colourful felt-tipped pens to make a display of comic-style vocabulary in the classroom.

Session Three: Letter strings and meanings

Explain to the children that in this session, they will first of all look carefully at the letter patterns in words; so they need to be at their most observant. Remind them of the convention that English words have no more than two of the same letter together, and ask for examples of words with double letters in them. List these on the board and demonstrate how odd they would look with treble letters. Then look closely at a selection of the made-up words from the class collection and encourage the children to describe how these differ from ordinary words – for example, the repetition of the vowels and/or consonants. What effect do the children think the writer is

Then the children could work in groups to prepare speeches for and against violence in comics, and role-play this as a court case. In subsequent writing sessions, the children could write newspaper reports arguing for or against the use of violent episodes in comics and discussing the effect these might have on children.

Session Five: Text completion

Challenge the children to work in pairs on photocopiable sheet 133, supplying the missing text to fit the pictures. Ask them to 'read' the illustrations and to tell the story together in their own words. They then have to decide what the characters might be saying in the situations shown in the pictures. They should draw on their previous experiences in earlier sessions to select the sort of language likely to be used, and redraft their suggestions accordingly.

Encourage the children to check the number of exclamation and question marks they have used, and to adjust their text to fit their previous findings about the punctuation conventions in comics.

Remind them to check the likely spelling of the made-up words, remembering what they have discussed earlier about doubling and trebling vowels and consonants for graphic interpretation of sound effects.

When the children feel happy with their drafts, they can fill in the speech bubbles on the sheet, checking to see if they need to add any exclamations outside the speech bubbles to describe events or noises.

Finally, the pairs of children can read their completed work to other pairs and compare results.

searching for by putting three As and three Rs in *Aaarrrgh!*

Discuss the feelings that are being described by these made-up exclamatory words from the class list. In the children's opinion, is it always possible to tell what the characters are feeling from the sounds they shout? Which exclamations suggest fright, fear, terror, anger, hurt, distress, misery, shock, surprise, delight?

Now ask the children to work in pairs with their original copied or cut-out pieces of comics from Session Two, sorting the exclamations into sets under different headings that relate to the whole range of human emotions. When they have finished the task, gather together as a class to see if there is a consensus of opinion. The important element is the quality of the ensuing discussion as the children justify their own choices and question other people's.

Session Four: Developing language awareness

Recap with the children what they have learnt so far about the language used in comics; then move on to discuss whether there are any patterns. Who says what? Does it make a difference if they are 'goodies' or 'baddies'? Winners or losers? Bullies or victims? Men or women? Adults or children? People or animals? How would people respond in the real world to the events in the comics? Look at a specific example together.

Ask the children if they think it is the exaggerated language that makes comics funny. Talk about how they respond to the aggressive language used in comics. Do they feel that it sets a bad example? Do they think that it should be banned? If so, why; or if not, why not?

Suggestion(s) for extension

Confident readers and writers might like to compose collective or individual onomatopoeic poems using the verbs collected from comics, such as *chomp* and *sloosh*, and then prepare a choral reading on tape to add to the class resources in the listening corner.

Some children might like to make a quiz game for younger peers based on questions about comic characters, using sets of cards with 'who', 'what', 'why', 'where' and 'when' questions on them to support word recognition and fix the visual image of these common words in the mind.

Suggestion(s) for support

Less experienced readers and writers would benefit from the support of a more confident child when working in pairs, or they could work with an adult helper. To reinforce alphabetical order, letter recognition and letter strings, early readers (working with an adult helper) could make a class dictionary of all the exclamatory words collected from comics.

To reinforce initial sounds, a group of early readers (together with an adult helper) could search the comics for alliterative character names such as Desperate Dan, Corky the Cat and Winker Watson, and could invent some names of their own.

Assessment opportunities

Listen carefully to the children's discussion when they are sharing their work, to assess their knowledge of punctuation marks. Note also the children's ability to scan the comics to find specific items. From their writing, you can monitor their ability to provide appropriate language in speech bubbles to fit the pictures provided.

Opportunities for IT

As an extension to Session One, children could collect data about the most popular comics read in the class and then use graphing software to produce block graphs to represent this. Different groups could select different types of comics to survey, or collect data from different classes in the school.

Children could work in pairs to explore the composition of different types of comics, recording the information for their chosen comic on a simple tally chart and then transferring it on to graphing software. A tally of the number of pages could be kept for such things as: adventure stories; animal stories; jokes; quizzes; sports stories; humorous stories; advertisements; hobbies, and so on.

Children might need to discuss how they are going to categorise different types of features to maintain a consistent approach across all of the comics examined.

Different comics might throw up different types of articles. Children could explore the differences between comics aimed at boys and girls, or younger and older children.

The class could combine their data on to a simple database, which could contain a single record for each comic. This would allow searches and further analysis, from which different kinds of graphs could be made. (For instance, which comics have the most pages of sport, or jokes.)

In Session Two, children can write out their selected word using a word processor. They can then decide how to present their work in the most unusual or striking way using the features available to them. This might include the print size, the font style, the use of colour or even changing the font size within a word.

Software is also available which enables children to print out words along the computer paper strip in a banner or headline form. This would allow comic words to be displayed as a form of frieze, perhaps in word groups depicting different noises.

Display ideas

The children's work resulting from these sessions can be used as a backdrop to the initial stimulus display. Be sure to include words found in comics from other cultures, where appropriate. Large comic picture sequences from which the words have been deleted could also be included, and children could be asked to supply the missing dialogue.

Other aspects of the English PoS covered

Speaking and listening – 1a, b, c, d; 2a, b; 3a, b.
Writing – 1a, b, c; 2a, b, c, d; 3a, b.

Reference to photocopiable sheet(s)

Photocopiable sheet 133, like photocopiable sheet 130, requires children to add text to a picture story; but here, they are writing in the style of a children's comic.

CREATING A CLASS COMIC

For the children to:
▲ **use language appropriate to its purpose;**
▲ **use punctuation effectively;**
▲ **use a range of reading strategies when reading aloud.**
†† *Introductory session: whole class. Subsequent sessions: small group or pair work.*
🕐 *Introductory session: 30 minutes. Subsequent sessions: 30–40 minutes depending on children's stamina.*

Key background information
It is assumed that children will already have taken part in the previous sessions, working with children's comics in order to acquire a knowledge base from which to create a comic of their own. This activity will test the effectiveness of those sessions. It is important to allow children several sessions in order to plan, develop ideas, reflect and redraft.

Preparation
Provide a selection of comics to refer to if necessary.

Resources needed
Writing and drawing materials, bookmaking materials, a computer.

What to do
Recap with the children everything they have learned about comics from the previous sessions, and tell them that it is time to start the class project on writing their own comic. Brainstorm, on to a flip chart or board, ideas about what to include – comic strips, riddles, quizzes, fan mail, adverts, an editorial letter, readers' letters, 'spot the difference', mazes, number puzzles, and so on. Ask the children to choose their favourite sections and to take responsibility for preparing them for publication. Decisions about the cover page and general layout will also have to be taken.

The children will need several writing sessions and should work in pairs or small groups, with adult support as appropriate, to complete their drafts and illustrations. Before the final draft is produced, gather as a whole class to share the work, make final decisions and agree any changes. The children may wish to word-process the final draft of their text.

The planning and drafting sessions, together with the final whole-class session, will provide opportunities for you to ask the children questions about design devices such as when to use symbols and logos, headings, bold print, capital letters, coloured print, multiple exclamation marks, zigzag lines around text, thought and speech bubbles, and how to signal time lapses in the text, in order to assess what they have learned from the previous teaching sessions in this chapter. Analysing the various drafts and the finished product will provide evidence of achievements in the development of spelling strategies, punctuation and handwriting skills, as well as appropriate use of language. Annotated photocopies of the work could be included in children's portfolios.

When the class comic is finished, the children will need to prepare their reading of the section they have composed for presentation in a school assembly.

Observing and listening to the children as they plan their contributions to the comic, as well as listening to them reading it aloud to their peers, will provide the evidence you need to make a summative assessment of individual children's confidence and their self-image as readers, their ability to recognise key words and to use phonic and meaning cues. Note also whether they read audibly, at a reasonable speed, with appropriate emphasis and pauses to mark punctuation breaks.

Suggestion(s) for extension
Experienced writers might well finish their contributions more quickly than other members of the class and could then make posters for the school library to advertise the arrival of the comic. They could also prepare notes to support their presentation of the comic in a school assembly.

Suggestion(s) for support
Less confident readers and writers will benefit from the support of a more experienced partner when working in pairs, or they could work with an adult helper.

Display ideas
A display of work showing different stages in the production of the class comic would be very effective, as it would show how writing develops from first ideas through planning and drafting to the final form. Photographs of the children at work on the various stages could also be included.

Other aspects of the English PoS covered
Speaking and listening – 1a, c; 2a, b; 3a, b.
Writing – 1a, b, c; 2a, b c, d; 3b.

Narrative

A growing involvement in narrative and a deepening response to it are essential qualities for becoming a reader. Thus this section aims to provide suggestions for getting children 'hooked on books' by developing their love of fiction, using storytime as the major opportunity in every school day to highlight children's literature and model reader response.

This process involves getting to know authors and illustrators and recognising their style; learning to love characters in books and wanting to hear or read about them over and over again; making comparisons between events in books and events in real life; noticing similarities and differences between books; showing a greater awareness of the language of books; becoming increasingly knowledgeable about different genres; developing an interest in cultures other than our own; and, perhaps most importantly of all, engaging fully with the emotional impact of books. It goes without saying that children need to feel secure in their environment before they will be ready to take risks and express their feelings openly to a large group. It is particularly important to dispel the myth of the 'tough guy', so that boys and girls accept that it is perfectly natural for everyone to feel afraid and upset at times.

This section also aims to enhance children's image of themselves as readers through successful reading experiences with familiar texts, and to develop reading stamina by taking children on from picture books to books with chapters, requiring them to listen and concentrate for longer periods and to create images in their minds.

INTRODUCING A CHILDREN'S AUTHOR

For the children to:

▲ *understand the concept of an author and celebrate the work of one particular author of children's fiction;*

▲ *become familiar with the characters in books;*

▲ *know how narrative structure operates, and put that knowledge to use in their own writing;*

▲ *recognise and respond to rhythm and rhyme;*

▲ *relate the emotions of everyday family life, as expressed in books, to their own experiences;*

▲ *engage with the moral issues in the world of books and make analogies with the real world.*

†† *Sessions One, Two, Three and Four: whole class; Session Five: working in pairs; Sessions Six, Seven and Eight: whole class; Session Nine: whole class, then paired or individual work.*

🕐 *Session One: 35 minutes; Session Two: 30 minutes; Sessions Three, Four and Five: 20 minutes each; Session Six: 25 minutes; Sessions Seven and Eight: 20 minutes each; Session Nine: 40 minutes.*

Previous skills/knowledge needed

It is not essential, but it would be helpful, for the children to have some experience of listening and responding to stories in a large group and of paired and shared reading.

Key background information

This series of sessions provides a context for children to begin to appreciate why we read books; what we can learn from books; how we can come to terms with aspects of our own lives through discussion about important issues that affect the characters in a book; that there is more than one valid point of view; and that the rights of others have to be acknowledged as well as our own. There are possible links with class projects on Starting School, Friends, Families and Similarities and Differences.

Preparation

Gather together a collection of all Rosemary Wells's books to mount an initial display in the classroom. (Her books are used as exemplars throughout these activities; but of course, the same activities could be adapted for any children's writer.) A weekly session of paired reading with older children in the school could be arranged if necessary. Timetable individual reading conferences and opportunities for shared reading.

Resources needed

A flip chart or some very large sheets of paper, a copy of *Making a Book* by Mandy Suhr (Wayland, 1993) optional, various books by Rosemary Wells including *Noisy Nora, Stanley and Rhoda, Benjamin and Tulip, The Little Lame*

Prince and the *Bunny Planet* collection, writing and drawing materials, cut-up paper for making little books, staples, clay, a tape recorder, one copy per child of photocopiable sheet 134.

What to do

Session One: Introduction to the topic

Discuss with the children where they think books come from. Who has the ideas for them? Who writes them down? Who does the illustrations? Who publishes them, and who prints them? It may be helpful to look at *Making A Book* by Mandy Suhr (Wayland, 1993) together; talk about each stage, and compare the result with children's 'publications' in school.

Point out the books from the display to the children. Explain that they were all written by the same person, Rosemary Wells, and that you will be enjoying these together over the next few weeks during a Rosemary Wells readathon.

Tell the children that you are going to start the readathon by reading one of your favourites to them: *Noisy Nora* (Picture Lions, 1993).

Read the story aloud to the class, paying due attention to the rhythm and rhyme of the text. Encourage the children to join in the refrain as soon as they feel confident. Pause and encourage prediction at the point where silence falls in the story and Nora goes missing. Ask the children where she might be. Do they think the family will miss her? Do they think anyone will find her? Then read on to the end.

Next, discuss what the children liked about the story. Why do they think Nora was so noisy? Encourage them to notice details in the illustrations. See if they spotted all the tricks that Nora used as the story progressed in an attempt to get attention: how she pulled at her mother's dress, threw the chess-pieces about, put the baby's bowl on her head, scattered the marbles everywhere, threw the soap on the floor, dropped the baking tray, jumped into the bucket, upset

the furniture in the hall, climbed up the cot, poked Kate with a pencil.

Discuss with the children what it is like being the middle child in a family. Do they have older sisters or baby brothers who take up a lot of their parents' time? What do they feel about that? What can they do about it?

It is important to explain to the children that adults do get hassled at times, as the children may need reassurance that Nora's parents do care for her and that lack of time does not mean lack of love.

Reread the story and stop for the children to complete *'Nora had to wait!'* each time it occurs. Encourage them to supply some of the text: *First she banged the ......, then she slammed the ....,* etc.

Invite them to chant the rhythmical refrain with you:
'Quiet! said her father, Hush! said her mum.
Nora! said her sister, Why are you so dumb?'
and to join in with a sad *'No Nora...'* at each repetition, while shaking their heads. It is important for children to rehear favourite stories; and at subsequent readings during the week, the children will soon be joining in the entire reading with you. Encourage them to read the book for themselves as well, in small groups, in pairs and/or individually.

You could record the whole class reading the story with you on tape, and add this to the classroom reading resources for the listening corner.

Over the week, read other books on the same theme by different authors – such as *Not Now, Bernard* by David McKee, *The Shrinking of Treehorn* by Florence Parry Heide and *Gorilla* by Anthony Browne – and make comparisons between them.

Session Two: Text completion and choral reading

Explain to the children that you want them to think about the story of Noisy Nora and to recall the events from the story. Give them copies of photocopiable sheet 134 and ask them to work in pairs to fill in the missing words in the text. When they have completed the text together, ask one child in each pair to read the questions and the other to read the answers, one verse at a time, to make a question and answer poem. Discuss with the children the features that helped them to supply the missing words: prior knowledge of this story and the rhythmical pattern of the phrases. Encourage the class to clap out the rhythm as they chant the poem. The children can rehearse as a class and then record a choral reading of the poem on tape, with half of the children reading the questions and half the answers.

Session Three: Continuing the readathon

Introduce the next of Rosemary Wells' books, *Stanley and Rhoda* (Picture Lions, 1993) to the children. Show them that it is not one long story, but a collection of short stories. Point out how you can use the contents page and the page numbers to find the story you want to read. Read the first story in the collection aloud to the children: 'Bunny Berries'.

When you have finished reading the story, listen and respond to the children's spontaneous comments. Then ask them if they would like to have a little sister like Rhoda. If so, why? If not, why not? Discuss how well Stanley and Rhoda get on.

Ask the children who actually did most of the tidying up in the story. Find out what they think about Stanley's behaviour, and about what he did at the very end of the story. See if the

Introducing a children's author

Name _____

Date _____

▲ Answer these questions and fill in the missing words.

Who had dinner early?
Who played with Kate?
Who needed burping?
So who had to wait?

_____ had dinner early,
_____ played with Kate,
_____ needed burping,
So _____ had to wait.

Refrain: Quiet! said her father, Hush! said her mum.
Nora! said her sister, Why are you so dumb?

Who was very filthy?
Who cooked with Kate?
Who needed drying off?
So who had to wait?

_____ was very filthy,
_____ cooked with Kate,
_____ needed drying off,
So _____ had to wait.

Refrain: Quiet! said her father, Hush! said her mum.
Nora! said her sister, Why are you so dumb?

Who was getting sleepy?
Who read with Kate?
Who needed seeing to?
So who had to wait?

_____ was getting sleepy,
_____ read with Kate,
_____ needed seeing to,
So _____ had to wait.

children feel he should or should not have done that. Ask them why they think he did it.

Encourage the children to share personal incidents from their relationships with siblings: occasions when they were helpful, or perhaps not so helpful. Comment on the phrase 'Shake a leg!' – what does it mean exactly, and why? It could become the class phrase of the week to get things done quickly.

Session Four: Getting further acquainted with Stanley and Rhoda
Children enjoy meeting favourite characters again and again, so reacquaint the class with Stanley and Rhoda.

This time you could read 'Don't Touch It, Don't Look At It'. After the children's initial response to the story, find out if any of them have ever been stung by a bee. If so, ask them to tell the class what it felt like. Do they think Rhoda was making a fuss about nothing?

Encourage the children to recall Stanley's suggestions in sequence and to note how they get worse! Why did that do the trick?

Discuss with the children why they think Stanley never gets cross with Rhoda. Invite them to say what they would have done in this situation. Why?

Session Five: More of Stanley and Rhoda
Introduce 'Henry', the last story in the book about Stanley and Rhoda, then read it to the class.

Find out why the children think Rhoda was so hostile to Henry at first, and why she changed her mind. Who do they think saved the situation? Do they feel that Stanley's tactics worked well with Rhoda? What might have happened if he had tried to force her to do things?

Encourage the children to talk about the lessons they might learn from this story for times when they are in an awkward mood. How do they think they can help each other to stay calm?

Reread the story and encourage the children to join in with the exclamatory comments: 'No', 'Never', 'More', 'Yes'.

Session Six: Emotional growth through stories
Explain to the children that now you have finished reading the short stories about Stanley and Rhoda, it is time to meet someone new.

Read Benjamin and Tulip (Kestrel, 1977) to the class, and guide the discussion to include the important issues that it raises for young children when they are starting school: making relationships on the first day; worries about nobody liking you, not fitting in, not knowing what to do.

Discuss with the children the positive things they can do to help people starting at their school.

As a co-operative writing activity, scribe on to a flip chart or a very large sheet of paper all the suggestions that the children come up with, and display them on the wall for everyone to see.

Session Seven: Introducing box collections of little books
Little books often become treasured items for young children, and having them all together enclosed in a special box adds to their appeal. The children love handling them, putting them in the box and taking them out.

Introduce the box collection of the Voyage to the Bunny Planet books (Collins, 1992). Read The First Tomato from the set to whet the children's appetite. Chant together the short Bunny Planet rhyme:
'Far beyond the moon and stars,
Twenty light years south from Mars,
Spins the gentle Bunny Planet
And the Bunny Queen is Janet.'

Talk to the children about the rhyming words stars/Mars and Planet/Janet. Encourage the class to sway to the left and right with the rhythm as they chant the refrain.

Encourage the children to sympathise with Claire, and to compare her situation with their own experiences of things going wrong and feeling fed up. Discuss together how the Bunny Planet helped matters. Find out from the children what they do when things go wrong. What options do they have instead of a Bunny Planet?

In the next writing session, children will almost certainly want to make their own little books about times when they would like to go to the Bunny Planet. In subsequent storytimes, read and respond to the other Bunny Planet stories: Moss Pillows and The Island Light.

Does she work every day? With a pen, pencil, typewriter or computer? How long does it take her to write a book? What is she working on now? Does she have a favourite character from her own books? Has she been to the Bunny Planet?

Ask the children whether it would be a good idea to tell her something about themselves. Discuss what she might like to know. Should they send a photo of the class? Should they write some stories to send to her as a gift?

The children can then work individually or in pairs, according to their preference, drafting their letters (and stories if they wish to include these). Remind the children about the format of a letter and how to address the envelope, with capital letters for the postcode.

With a bit of luck, they might eventually get a reply from the United States!

Suggestion(s) for extension

Some children may like to write a love/hate poem about their brother or sister, with the first verse describing why they like their sibling and the second verse describing occasions when they don't!

Children could make bookmarks with Wells' characters on, or design book covers for a new edition of a Rosemary Wells book. They could write reviews of the books they have read. They could make clay models of Wells' animal characters, with museum-type captions.

Children could make up quiz questions about the various characters or events in the books for friends to answer: 'Who did/said...'; 'What happened to...'; 'Why did...'

More experienced readers could read the works of Beatrix Potter, and compare and contrast the two authors.

Suggestion(s) for support

Some children may need the help of a more experienced reader from your class, or an older child in the school, when working with the photocopiable sheet. Emergent writers will benefit from having an adult helper when writing their letters to the author.

Assessment opportunities

Children's talk when responding to books, making comparisons, expressing their feelings and asking questions will provide evidence of their growing critical awareness. Note also their confidence in choosing books to read, their knowledge of authors, their interest in specific characters in

Session Eight: Attitudes to difference

Read *The Little Lame Prince* (Picture Lions, 1993) to the children. Listen and respond to the children's initial reactions to the story; then ask if it strikes a chord with any traditional tales they have heard. Discuss with the children what they would do with a magic cape, a magic carpet or a magic lamp. Then talk about the moral of the story – 'If your head is wise and your heart is kind...'

Children may wish to talk about their own experiences of feeling left out, being picked on, being called names or being bullied, which could lead to a discussion of equal opportunities. Some children may wish to follow up this discussion with drawings, paintings or writing about their experiences.

Session Nine: Writing to the author

Suggest to the children that because they have enjoyed Rosemary Wells' books so much and think they are really special, they should write to her to let her know how much they like them.

Discuss with the children what to put in the letter. For instance, are there more things they would like to know about the author? If so, talk through all the questions they might want to ask her about herself. They will almost inevitably come up with: How old is she? Is she married? Has she any children? What was she like as a little girl? Has she always wanted to be a writer? You will need to discuss with the children the issue of privacy and whether or not they should ask personal questions.

They could ask questions about her work: Who does she base her characters on? Does she start by thinking about the words or the illustrations? Does she ever get stuck?

books, and their attitude towards themselves as readers. Note specific cueing strategies when working with the photocopiable sheet.

Opportunities for IT

Teachers with access to computers that have a CD-ROM facility might like to introduce children to the growing number of books which are available on CD-ROM. These books are presented to children on the computer screen with pictures and the text. The text is often read by a well-known actor. Children can listen to the story and follow the text at the same time. They can also click on the text using a mouse, to listen to the whole sentence or specific words and move backwards and forwards through the story. The graphics often have animated sequences or sound effects, which the children also enjoy.

In Session Seven, children could use a word processor or simple desktop publishing package to produce their own mini-books. The teacher could set up a standard page layout in advance so that the children can write their story, leaving spaces for illustrations to be drawn by hand later. Some children may want to create their own pictures using an art package and include them in the story itself. Children could also use an art package to create a cover for their mini-story.

In Session Nine, children could write their letters to an author using a word processor to draft and redraft their work. They can also be introduced to a standard letter format and the use of formatting commands like 'right justify' for the address and 'full justification' to even up the righthand margin. Children should be taught how to position text on the screen using these commands rather than the space bar.

Children could write simple book reviews using a word processor or simple desktop publishing package. If a DTP package is used, a simple format could be set up in advance with frames for different parts of the review to help children structure their writing. The reviews could be printed out and included in a class review file for others to read.

Display ideas

The entire works of Rosemary Wells as classroom 'author of the month', with information about her from magazines and journals, would make an effective initial stimulus display.

Children's book covers could be displayed, as well as their paintings of Wells' characters, their book reviews and their clay models of figures from the stories.

Children could create a large map of the Bunny Planet, with directions for getting there written above it. Descriptive pieces of writing about the planet could encircle the map.

Children's 'published' zigzag books about Stanley, Rhoda, Benjamin and Tulip could be displayed alongside the class reading resources.

Other aspects of the English PoS covered

Speaking and listening – 1a, c; 2a, b; 3b.
Writing – 1a, b, c; 2a, b, c, d, e; 3a.

Reference to photocopiable sheet(s)

Photocopiable sheet 134 is a simple question and answer poem; the children have to fill in the missing names (from memory).

INTRODUCING A CHILDREN'S ILLUSTRATOR

For the children to:
▲ *understand the role of a book illustrator;*
▲ *know the crucial part that illustrations can play in presenting a narrative;*
▲ *recognise artistic conventions, such as how to represent the passage of time and how to convey that people are dreaming, thinking or speaking;*
▲ *interpret the clues that artists provide for readers – on the cover, in endpapers and title pages, through changes in the size of frames or the position of a character within a frame;*
▲ *recognise a particular illustrator's distinctive style;*
▲ *reinforce word recognition and develop vocabulary;*
▲ *create a story by sequencing pictures and writing appropriate dialogue for the characters.*

†† *Sessions One, Two and Three: whole class; Session Four: whole class, then small groups; Session Five: whole class, then paired work.*

⏲ *Sessions One, Two and Three: 25 minutes each; Session Four: 35–45 minutes; Session Five: 40 minutes.*

Previous skills/knowledge needed

It would be helpful, but it is not essential, for the children to have had some experience of activities that demand close observation and attention to detail.

Key background information

In the context of one illustrator's work (Gerald Rose), the activity provides children with an opportunity to 'look with intent' at the visual details on the page and to discuss the effects in order to enrich their enjoyment of books, deepen

their level of involvement and increase their range of techniques to use in their own creation of texts.

Preparation

Collect together, as an initial stimulus display, a collection of work by Gerald Rose (including *The Tiger Skin Rug*, *Ah Said Stork*, *The Bird Garden*, *Scruff* and *Grumps*) plus any posters or magazine articles about him.

Resources needed

A range of writing, drawing, painting and book-making materials and tools, one copy per child of photocopiable sheet 135, small pieces of card, felt-tipped pens.

What to do

Session One: Introduction to the topic

Introduce the session by asking the children to reflect on the books shared recently in class, and to say how important they believe the illustrations in a book to be. Make links with what the children found out about the role of an author in the 'Introducing a children's author' activity.

Ask the children if they already know the names of any illustrators. Perhaps they know and recognise the work of Quentin Blake, Tony Ross or Michael Foreman. Discuss what sort of illustrations the children like best.

Then present a new illustrator to the class: Gerald Rose, who, like Rosemary Wells, is an author *and* an illustrator. Point out the collection of his books on offer in the initial display and read one of them, *The Tiger Skin Rug* (Picture Puffin, 1986), to the class.

Afterwards, encourage the children to respond in their own personal way to the events in the story. Then ask if anyone had guessed the tiger's intentions. Find out if the children felt sorry for him when he was beaten like a rug and dragged across the garden, or when he was scrubbed, hung out to dry and then bumped back up the stairs. Did they predict what the tiger would do to stop the robbers?

Next, move the emphasis of the discussion to the illustrations:

▲ Ask the children what clues they can spot before a text begins. Look again at the cover, the half-title and the title page.

▲ Browse through the pages once more, paying particular attention to the illustrations. How do they enhance the telling of the tale? Draw the children's attention to the opening jungle setting, teeming with life and noise, a threat to the tiger's peace of mind. Then note the change of mood outside the Sultan's palace in the stillness of the moonlight, offering the promise of calm and contentment.

▲ Tell the children to note the different expressions on the tiger's and the people's faces. Ask if they can tell when the tiger is delighted, in pain, feeling fierce, or being gentle like a pet cat.

Once the children know *The Tiger Skin Rug* well, suggest to them that they bring the book to life and act out the story for the whole school in an assembly. Make sure that all the children are involved in some way: either acting the roles of the various animals, the Rajah's family or the robbers, or being Indian musicians who will set the scene and accompany the actions with appropriate percussion. Once the roles are decided upon, there is plenty to do: music has to be composed, clothes organised, the script agreed on, bilingual reading arranged if possible, and invitations sent to parents to come and watch the performance on the day.

After the event, photos, together with children's drawings and writing, can be published in a class book.

Session Two: Using picture clues

Very inexperienced readers can be empowered by reading, along with a teacher, a book that offers very clear cues to meaning through the illustrations. *Ah Said Stork* (Picture Mac, 1986) is a perfect example of such a book.

Read the book to the children, talking about the events as the pages unfold; encourage the children to predict, by

scanning the pages for cues, how the animals will try to smash the egg.

On a second reading, encourage the children to feel confident about joining in with you in reading much of the book. You may have to ask relevant questions to prompt them, such as 'What did the hippo do?' – then, pointing to the illustration, read out 'Hippo rolled on it' as you point to the words.

Use the same technique as you go through the whole queue of animals: Lion bit it, Chimp hit it, Elephant stamped on it, Rhino sat on it, Snake squeezed it, Zebra kicked it. Accept alternative suggestions as long as they don't change the meaning.

Tell the children how clever they are to read nearly a whole book so well. Next, look closely at the illustrations together. Note the markings that make the elephant's skin look just right, leathery and wrinkled; the monkey all furry; the snake smooth and beautifully patterned; the crocodiles knobbly and tough.

Leave the book out for paired or small-group reading during the week, to reinforce the children's feelings of being successful readers.

Later, the children might like to tape a class reading of the story. Different sections of the class could read out how the different animals tried to smash the egg, and you could read out the longer bits of text at the end. This could then be added to the class resources in the listening corner.

Session Three: Getting to know Gerald Rose's work

Introduce another Gerald Rose classic, *The Bird Garden* (Magnet, 1988). Invite the children to look at the front cover, endpapers and title pages for any interesting clues as to what the book is about, then read it to the class. Make sure the children notice how the scene is set, with the arches drawing our gaze out to the garden of a Mogul palace; the colours, patterns, beaks and legs of the myriad different birds; the mynah bird like a triumphant statue on the half-title page, an image that will appear again inside; the patterned page borders that signal the Islamic culture of the Sultan.

Ask who spotted the tiger (a reference for the reader to another favourite Gerald Rose character!)

Comment on special effects like the swirling feathers that give the impression of the birds fighting and the upside-down text for the cockatoo.

Next, turn the children's attention to the storyline. Discuss the birds' treatment of a newcomer and how the children feel about that.

Discuss with the children the issue of the mynah bird getting her own back in the end. Who feels she had every right to do that? Who feels that she should have been more generous and forgiving?

Ask the children to reflect on their own attitude towards newcomers in school. Encourage the children to compare the situation with the Benjamin and Tulip story from the Rosemary Wells activity.

Session Four: Recall and word recognition

Introduce the book *Scruff* (Magnet Books, 1986) to the children. Once again, model for the class the cues that readers pick up before they start reading the text. Discuss what the cover tells us about the character of Scruff; look carefully at the expression on his face, the flower in his mouth, his fur sticking out all over the place. Show how the muddy paw-marks on the endpapers reinforce this view, as does the half-title page where Scruff is scratching as if he's got fleas. As you read the book to the class, ask the children to comment on other indications of a humorous approach, such as the comic-style exclamations (*woof, sniff, arrrchoo, grr*);

the smelly sock escaping from the frame; the juxtaposition of the dog's view and the people's views of the obnoxious smells.

Then recall in sequence what gets blamed for the smells: a compost heap, a bonfire, paint, perfume, ripe bananas, fish, cheese, petrol fumes, dustbins, mucky shoes, old boots, Scruff.

Hand out small pieces of card and felt-tipped pens to the children. Ask them to work in groups to create games based on this story for other classes to play. They can print the words for the items causing each of the smells on to card, and draw pictures (in the style of Gerald Rose) to go with these on separate pieces of card. The cards can then be used to play a matching Lotto or Pelmanism game to reinforce word recognition. Encourage the children to add more ideas of their own for other smells besides those in the book.

Session Five: Resequencing pictures and creating text
Read the story of *Grumps* (Bodley Head, 1991) to the class. Listen and respond to children's individual reactions to the story. Ask the children if they picked up clues from the cover and predicted the storyline and the eventual outcome before you read them the story.

Compare this with other books the children know about youngsters pestering their relatives, or with other books about grandparents (such as *All in One Piece*, *Peace at Last*, *Grandpa* or *Supergran*). Talk about the usual image of grandparents in books. Does this fit the children's own grandparents? Give out copies of photocopiable sheet 135 and tell the children to work in pairs, looking carefully at and discussing the pictures on the sheet. They should then cut

out and resequence them to make a logical story. Finally, they should provide appropriate dialogue in the speech bubbles to fit the pictures.

When they have finished, the children can read out what they have written to the class and compare each other's ideas.

Suggestion(s) for extension
Confident writers might like to find out more about Gerald Rose's life by writing to his current publisher (Picture Puffin) for information. They might like to include paintings or drawings in the style of Gerald Rose as a gesture of appreciation to be sent on to the author. They could follow up the story of *The Bird Garden* and make a non-fiction book about the birds in the story, with careful drawings and accurate descriptions to accompany the text.

Confident readers might like to read the rest of Gerald Rose's books independently: *Rabbit Pie* (Faber, 1980), *The Bag of Wind* (Julia MacRae, 1993), *Trouble in the Ark* (Bodley Head, 1985), *Polly's Jungle* (Picture Puffin, 1994) and others.

Suggestion(s) for support
Some children will need the support of an adult or of a more experienced partner when working on the photocopiable sheet; or alternatively, they could carry out the activity orally.

Early readers may like to make cardboard stick puppets of the animals in *Ah Said Stork*, to act out the story as they read it.

To extend children's vocabulary, an adult could work with a small group to investigate the verbs used in *The Bird Garden* which tell us what the birds did: sing, dance, quarrel, jump, pull, peck, chatter, chortle, flutter, scream, etc. Discuss with the children what the words mean, and ask them to think of possible alternatives. Remind the children to think carefully about their choice of vocabulary when writing their own stories, so as to make them as interesting as possible for their readers.

Assessment opportunities

Note the children's confidence and willingness to experiment and take risks when responding to stories, discussing illustrations and searching for clues. Note the children's reading strategies when they are completing the speech bubbles and when they read their work to the class.

Opportunities for IT

In Session One, children could use a word processor to write the invitations to a class performance of *The Tiger Skin Rug*. If their invitation is written in the form of a ticket, children can discuss the information that is needed (place, time, title, RSVP). The text entry part of this activity can be quite short so that children can concentrate on the layout of their ticket, using 'centre' commands, different fonts and sizes of text. The ticket could be personalised by adding parents' names as well. The children could work in pairs and use simple editing commands to change the names on the ticket.

The same task could be undertaken on a simple art package, so that the children could add a picture to illustrate the ticket. Alternatively, the children could create a poster to advertise the performance.

Display ideas

There are several opportunities here for making large friezes based on the stories of Gerald Rose – for example, *The Tiger Skin Rug* or *Ah Said Stork*.

An artists' workshop display of all the birds in the Sultan's garden (mynahs, cockatoos, birds of paradise, peacocks, toucans, parrots, parakeets, flamingos, storks, humming birds, hoopoes), with a careful choice of materials and techniques, would make a colourful contribution to the visual environment of the classroom. You could also create an art gallery with the children's own choice of paintings in the style of Gerald Rose.

Other aspects of the English PoS covered

Speaking and listening – 1a, b, d; 2a, b; 3b.
Writing – 1a, b, c; 2a, b, c, d, e; 3b.

Reference to photocopiable sheet(s)

Photocopiable sheet 135 is a picture story; the children have to arrange the pictures into an appropriate sequence (there may be more than one solution) and invent text for the speech bubbles.

BABYSITTERS

For the children to:
▲ *recall events from a familiar book;*
▲ *retell familiar stories in their own words;*
▲ *respond to stories by expressing their feelings about their own experiences;*
▲ *reconstruct a known text in the right sequence using meaning cues;*
▲ *match pictures and captions;*
▲ *create stories using experiences from real life and from fiction;*
▲ *recognise sound patterns and rhymes.*

†† *Session One: whole class; Session Two: working in pairs or small groups; Session Three: whole class, then pair work; Sessions Four, Five and Six: whole class.*

⊕ *Session One: 20 minutes; Sessions Two and Three: 30 minutes each; Session Four: 35–45 minutes; Sessions Five and Six: 20 minutes each.*

Previous skills/knowledge needed

It will be useful for this activity if children are already in the habit of listening and responding to stories in a large group every day.

Key background information

Recalling real-life experiences that listening to stories brings to mind, provides an opportunity for children to talk about their worries and fears, as well as about their most pleasurable experiences. These activities could be linked to

classroom projects on Change, Growth, Babies, Families and Ourselves.

Preparation
Collect a variety of books on the theme of babysitting for a display in the classroom. Make several copies of the different parts of the text from *Mr and Mrs Pig's Evening Out* by Mary Rayner (Piccolo, 1976).

Write out the words from Garth Pig's song books: *Garth Pig's Wall Song* and *Garth Pig's Rain Song* (Pan Macmillan, 1994) on an OHP or flipchart.

Resources needed
Writing and book-making materials, a tape recorder, one copy per child of photocopiable sheets 136 and 137, musical instruments, a word processor.

What to do
Session One: Introduction to the topic
Read the story *The Babysitter* by Kathy Handerson (André Deutsch, 1988) to the class, making sure that the children enjoy the humorous aspects of the story. Respond to the children's spontaneous reactions to the story, and invite discussion of their own past experiences with babysitters.

Encourage the children to recount the events of the story in the correct sequence. Then discuss with them what they might have done in a similar situation, and whether the children in the story should have behaved in the way that they did. Next, ask the children to view the situation from the babysitter's point of view. What do they think she would have been thinking?

Session Two: Cloze procedure
Explain to the children that they will be working in pairs or small groups, as appropriate, using photocopiable sheet 136. Remind the class briefly of the previous story, hand out the sheets and read the first paragraph with the children up to the gap; then set them off to fill the spaces with their own

words, describing what happened in the babysitting story that they heard in Session One. Once the children have completed their sheets, gather the whole class together again to share finished work and respond to each other's suggestions.

You could word-process all the different versions, with or without the children's assistance (depending on their keyboard skills), and display the whole collection.

Session Three: Matching captions to pictures
Read and discuss *Here Come the Babies* by Catherine and Laurence Anholt (Walker Books, 1993) with the children in the class. Ask them what events they can remember from their own babyhood – or perhaps about a younger sibling at home.

Give out copies of photocopiable sheet 137. Explain to the children that they will work in pairs, and that their task is to match the pictures with the appropriate captions. When they have done that, they can share their results with another pair and justify their choices.

Finally, join together as a class to play a quick word recognition game – for instance, to find two captions that begin with the letter j.

Session Four: Preparing a taped reading with musical accompaniment

Tell the children that they are going to be radio personalities and make a broadcast reading of a children's story.

Read and discuss another book on the babysitting theme: *Mr and Mrs Pigs' Evening Out* by Mary Rayner (Piccolo Picture Books, 1976). Encourage prediction as you read, drawing on children's prior knowledge of the relationship between pigs and wolves from the classic tale of the Three Little Pigs.

Then invite the children to respond spontaneously to the story. Comment on how sensible the pigs were to act together, as none of them could have managed to trap the wolf single-handed. Ask the children what they would have done to trap Mrs Wolf. List their suggestions in the form of a poster, as hints for pigs that might get wolves as babysitters!

Now begin preparations for the 'broadcast' version of the story, with you as narrator and a confident reader as Mrs Pig. Give groups of children a choice of parts: the piglets, the babysitter and Mr Pig. Give out the ready-made scripts to the children.

Discuss the voice that would be appropriate for each character, so that listeners can tell the difference between them. Run through a first rehearsal together. With the children, decide on music for the start and end of the story reading. Which instruments would be suitable to capture the particular moods? Consider whether to have sound effects during the course of the story – for example, to represent groans, gasps, splashing in the bath, the doorbell, yawning, stairs creaking and the final landing in the river.

Recommend that the children rehearse their reading parts, their music and their sound effects during the week to ensure a competent performance. Later, record the performance on tape and play it to another class before adding it to the bank of resources in the listening corner.

Session Five: Counting songs and rhymes

Introduce the song book *Ten Pink Piglets: Garth Pig's Wall Song* to the class. The children will recognise the link with 'Ten Green Bottles' very easily. See if the children spot the visual clues as you sing your way through the book and the tension builds: the puff of smoke, the exhaust and the wheel, the sleeping wolf – until the wolf finally races along the wall in an attempt to catch one of the piglets!

Sing the song again together, encouraging the children to count down from ten with their fingers as they sing.

Continue with the next song: *Garth Pig's Rain Song*. Do the children see the storm clouds coming? Ask if they notice anything special about the words (they rhyme with the numbers each time – point out each rhyming pair). Sing the song together.

Finish off with a quick quiz based on the rhymes – for instance, what number is Sarah if she swings about on the *gate*? Ask the children to suggest other words that rhyme with numbers.

Encourage the children to share the two song books, to read and sing along with their friends during the week.

In subsequent storytimes, you could show the words on an OHP or a flip chart and encourage the children to read the words as they sing.

Session Six: Making inferences

Read *All in One Piece* by Jill Murphy (Walker Books, 1987), encouraging children to comment on the chaos in the house, Mum's mood and the children's feelings. Watch to see if they spot the mistake when Mum sits down in the paint box, and why the author says 'Just as well really'.

Go back through the book and take a closer look at the illustrations. Draw the children's attention to the expressions on the elephants' faces, and any other details they might have missed on a first reading.

Discuss the children's own experiences of being naughty or demanding. Ask them about their parents' reactions and feelings. What will they do if they ever become parents?

Suggestion(s) for extension

After completing photocopiable sheet 136, some children might like to have a second go and change the names of the characters to fit their own or an invented family. They can then rewrite the story, supplying different unfortunate events that might happen to a new babysitter.

Experienced readers could read the other books by Jill Murphy, such as *A Piece of Cake* (Walker Books, 1989) and *Five Minutes' Peace* (Walker Books, 1986). *A Piece of Cake* could lead to discussions about diets, healthy eating and stereotypical gender images. Fluent readers might like to read other Mary Rayner books and make tapes of readings for less experienced readers to listen to – for example, *Garth Pig and the Ice Cream Lady* (Macmillan, 1994), *Garth Pig Steals the Show* (Pan Macmillan, 1993) or *Mrs Pig's Bulk Buy* (Macmillan, 1989). You might also suggest that they read another pig versus wolf story: *Suddenly* by Colin McNaughton (Andersen Press, 1994).

Confident writers could write reviews of the books, and could write to the authors to express appreciation of their books. They could set up an author's visit, with your help, writing the letter of invitation, a letter to the parents, a list of questions to ask the author and a thank-you letter afterwards. Photos taken of the visit, together with the children's written accounts, could be incorporated into a class publication.

Suggestion(s) for support

Some children may need to work co-operatively in a small group, with a teacher to scribe for them. Others may well be able to work with a more experienced partner from the class.

To encourage close observation, you could play 'Kim's game' with a small group, based on the 'What's on the table?' picture in *Five Minutes' Peace*: one minute to look, then close the book and ask them to name ten things that were out of place (for example, recorder, knife, book, spoon, eggcup, eggshell, honey, lid, cereals, cup, toy car, teddy).

To reinforce letter-sound association, you could discuss the names of the family in one of the stories (for example, Mr and Mrs Large, Laura, Lester, Luke and the little ones). Ask the children what these names have in common, and then collect as many other names as possible beginning with L. Explain to the children that the names can be those of people (real or in books) or those of places or shops. You could move on to verbs and adjectives beginning with L. Scribe the suggestions on a large sheet of paper, so the children can refer to them at leisure. They could use this sheet to play 'I Spy' during the week.

Assessment opportunities

Children's talk when recalling events, retelling stories, commenting on illustrations, making suggestions and comparisons, making inferences and expressing feelings will indicate their developing reader response. Note correct sound-symbol associations for the letter L, and reading strategies used for matching words and pictures and for completing cloze procedures. Note the children's level of confidence when reading print with the support of a partner or a large group.

Opportunities for IT

In Session Two, children could work in pairs or small groups to complete the cloze exercise actually at the computer. The teacher could type in the text and replace the deleted words with stars. If the text is then saved as a file, each group of children can load it into the word processor and then fill in the spaces, printing out their solutions and saving the file to disk under another name so that it does not overwrite the original text. The children will need to be shown how to position the cursor where they want to put a word, then delete the stars and type in their word. They may also need support to load the starting text into the word processor and save their completed version. The teacher could prepare different texts for different ability groups, deleting more or fewer words, or selecting more difficult words to be replaced.

In Session Four, the children can use the tape recorder to record their sound effects, which could be made with musical instruments, the actual sounds themselves or even be taken from the sound synthesiser part of an electronic keyboard. They should be shown how to record, play back and edit their recorded soundtrack.

If the children are inviting an author to visit, the letter of invitation could be word-processed, with children shown how to lay out a letter in standard format using format commands such as 'right justify' for the address, 'centre' for 'Yours faithfully' and 'right justify' to even out the right-hand margin.

Children could also word-process their list of questions with each child, or pair of children, adding their question to the list which should be saved and then retrieved later for other children to use. Older or more able children might be shown how to arrange the list into a particular order using the 'cut' and 'paste' commands.

Display ideas

You could make an initial stimulus display of books by an 'author of the week', such as Mary Rayner or Jill Murphy.

The children could help you to create an interactive display, with photos of the class as babies on flaps with current photos hidden underneath. These could be interspersed with covers from books on the theme of babies, children's personal accounts of their experiences with babysitters, retellings of familiar stories on the same theme and wanted posters about a dangerous wolfish babysitter.

A multimedia display could include children's writing about exercise routines for Mrs Large and paintings or drawings of the Large family (before and after!) alongside healthy eating posters, adverts for leisure pursuits, special clothes for working out and tapes of exercise routines.

Other aspects of the English PoS covered

Speaking and listening – 1a, b, c; 2a, b; 3a, b.
Writing – 1a, b, c; 2a, b, c, d, e; 3b.

Reference to photocopiable sheet(s)

Photocopiable sheet 136 is a cloze procedure based on a story read in Session One. Photocopiable sheet 137 requires children to match pictures to words (verbs).

PETS

For the children to:
▲ **predict possible outcomes when reading;**
▲ **become involved in stories by making comparisons with their experiences in real life, and with situations and characters in other books they have read;**
▲ **face difficult situations, such as illness, old age and death, through fiction;**
▲ **explore linguistic features such as 'doublet' words, repetition used for emphasis and onomatopoeia;**
▲ **use the structural pattern of a familiar book to create a new story.**

†† *Session One: whole class; Session Two: whole class, then pairs; Sessions Three and Four: whole class, then groups; Session Five: working in pairs; Session Six: whole class.*

🕐 *Session One: 25 minutes; Session Two: 30 minutes; Session Three: 35 minutes; Sessions Four and Five: 30 minutes each; Session Six: 25 minutes.*

Previous skills/knowledge needed

It is preferable for these sessions to be set in the context of a general class topic on pets or animals.

Key background information

The crucial role of stories in helping children to come to terms with complex emotions is at the heart of these activities. Pets are of the utmost importance in many children's lives, and provide a strong motivation for reading and writing both fiction and non-fiction.

Preparation

Collect a range of artefacts to do with pets (collar, leash, dog biscuits and so on), as well as written materials such as pamphlets about the care of pets and adverts placed by vets. Arrange a visit from a vet to talk about caring for pets.

Resources needed

A tape recorder; writing, drawing and book-making materials for zigzag and flap books; a glass tank, soil, pebbles and worms for starting a wormery; copies of *Freckle and Clyde*, *Dear Zoo*, *Cat and Dog*, *The Worm Book*, *The Julian Stories* and *I'll Always Love You* (see below for details); one copy per child of photocopiable sheet 138.

What to do

Session One: Introduction to the topic

Tell the children that they will be reading a lot of books about different pets by a variety of different authors in connection with the class topic. Show them the first book that you have chosen, which could be *Freckle and Clyde* by Patricia Cleveland-Peck (Collins, 1992). Read the story to the children

take several sessions to complete, from the initial ideas stage to the finished product including drawings, cover, title page, blurb and author biography. When the books are completed, share them in whole-class sessions with the children reading their own texts. Praise specific points – such as effective vocabulary, eye-catching illustrations, careful attention to detail – in order to develop children's awareness of what readers appreciate.

Finally, the children can present the books to the Nursery in paired-reading conferences with the Nursery children.

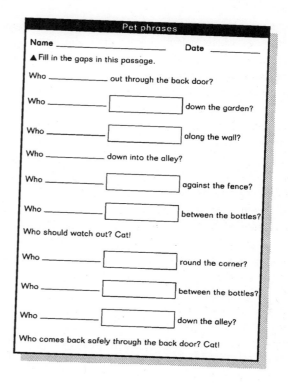

and discuss their favourite parts, not forgetting the splendid illustrations. Mention the allusion to Jekyll and Hyde in the title, and comment on the rhyming features of the text.

Ask the children if they felt sorry for the owners when their cat went missing. Find out what they thought had happened. Had anyone predicted the ending? Invite their suggestions for ways of solving the problem.

Then encourage the children to talk about their own pets. Find out who has what kind of pet, how many, what they live in, what they eat, what they do, how they exercise, problems they have had, visits to the vet and so on. In subsequent writing sessions, the children can write their own 'pet' stories and you can use them to create a class anthology of pet stories, a collection of zigzag books about pets or a set of non-fiction books about how to take care of various pets.

Session Two: Patterning on a known text

Read *Dear Zoo* by Rod Campbell (Picture Puffin, 1982), encouraging the children to predict on every page what the hidden animal might be. Ask for any suggestions that might fit, using the shape of the crate, the descriptive words on the crates and other hints in the illustrations to work out the solution.

Children may need added support for the basket page, depending on their previous experience; so be ready to prompt by reading out the written text and stressing the word *scary*, or by giving spoken hints if necessary (such as 'Do you think it will bite us? Will it sting us? Will it poison us?' or 'I think I can hear it HISSSSing ...') before you look under the flap. Encourage the children to read the book on their own or with a friend during the week.

Then explain to the children that they are going to write their own version of *Dear Zoo* with a partner, as a flap book to offer to the nursery unit or local playgroup. They will use the same structure as the original, but will choose different animals (with different crates as necessary to fit their animals); they will need to think of different adjectives to describe their animals, such as *too fat, too bulky*... This will

Session Three: Vocabulary extension and word recognition

Read *Cat and Dog* by David Lloyd and Clive Scruton (Walker Books, 1983). Encourage the children to join in, and to predict what will happen next at the end of each page. Ask them why they think the book is so easy to read (repetitive pattern, rhythm). Draw their attention to the question form (*who* and a question mark), and to the doublet words such as *pitter-pat*. Ask for their opinions about the repetition of *getting closer* and why it's there. Praise them for recognising the words *cat* and *dog* each time.

Then explain to the children that they can make the book even better by replacing the *1p words* – the ordinary, over-used, everyday verbs such as *walk* and *run* – with *£1 words*: more expressive verbs... Invite their suggestions, such as *trot, prance, frolic, leap* or *scuttle*.

Organise the children into small groups and give out copies of photocopiable sheet 138. Ask them to read through the sentences and then set to work to supply the missing phrases. The aim is to increase the children's vocabulary of expressive verbs; so tell them not to stop at just one

suggestion each time, but to think of as many options as they can before making their final choice. As you circulate, praise thoughtful choices that sound good to the ear.

The next task is for the children to find alternative versions for the doublet words: *pitter-pat* might become *hippity-hop*, and so on.

To conclude, the groups will report back to the whole class and make final choices from all the offerings to put on an OHP for a joint class version, which they can read aloud together. Each group can publish its version in a book shaped like a dog or a cat. Call on the help of older members of the school or parents to translate the texts into all the languages spoken by the class, using transliterations if necessary.

Session Four: Writing a dictionary

Discuss as a class the possibility of having a worm for a pet and setting up a class wormery.

Working with small groups to allow close inspection of the illustrations, an adult helper can read the *Worm Book* by Janet and Allan Ahlberg (Picture Lions, 1989) one section at a time like a diary over a few days, encouraging the children's spontaneous responses and involvement (especially with all the humorous touches).

Each group then has to make a dictionary of worms. Deaf worms, shy worms, overweight worms, invisible worms, square worms and ghost worms are mentioned in the book, so the children could start by putting these into alphabetical order. Then they can work their way through the alphabet, thinking of other sorts of worms to complete the list. Encourage the children to supply adjectives that fit the humorous tone of the book. In subsequent sessions, they can write a definition for each type of worm.

Session Five: Playing with words

Read the short story 'Catalogue Cats' from the collection *The Julian Stories* by Ann Cameron (Fontana Young Lions, 1981). Listen and respond to the children's immediate reaction to the story. Discuss the main issues with the children: What is the difference between telling lies and making up imaginative stories? Should Julian do such things? Was Huey hurt? Was their Daddy cross? Encourage the children to recount their own experiences of leading people on... and the consequences.

Then look at the joke element in the story: how the author plays with the word *cat*. Tell the children that they are going to have fun playing with words too. Working in groups, the children will make a 'words within words' *cat*alogue by finding as many words as possible with *cat* in them. Share just a few suggestions of specific words to get the children going (catch, cater, caterpillar, cattle, catastrophe, catapult, catfish, scatter, category, cathedral, Catherine, catkin, catmint, Catholic, catamaran, scathing, catarrh, catchment, catty), and discuss where they might look for extra ideas when they run out (dictionaries, thesauri). The groups will report back

to the class to share their catalogues and have a grand count-up of their wordbank. The children can illustrate the examples and make a class book.

Session Six: Emotional growth

Read *I'll Always Love You* by Hans Wilhelm (Knight Books, 1986) to the children. Listen and respond supportively to their immediate reactions. Sensitive subjects such as burial, cremation and belief in an afterlife will no doubt arise, as well as the emotional themes of loss, grief and pain. Children will also be likely to move on from thinking about animals to thinking about people, especially grandparents, and will need reassurance that they will always have their memories to keep with them forever.

There will almost certainly be gender issues too about boys being tough and never crying; so do make it clear that it is acceptable for everybody to cry in such circumstances – boys, girls, men and women.

Other useful books that cover the same theme are: *Goodbye Max* by Holly Keller (Julia MacRae Books, 1987); *Badger's Parting Gift* by Susan Varley (Picture Lions, 1985); *Grandpa* by John Burningham (Picture Puffin, 1992), and 'Burning the Tree' from *Stories by Firelight* by Shirley Hughes (Bodley Head, 1993). The last of these has an accompanying tape of Anna Massey reading the text.

Afterwards, some children might like to write personal accounts and draw or paint portraits of loved relatives or pets who have died; but others may prefer not to.

Suggestion(s) for extension

Confident readers could have regular group bookshare sessions to recommend books about pets that they have read during the week. Here are some suggestions to get the group started: *The Patchwork Cat* by Nicola Bayley and William Mayne (Julia MacRae, 1991); *Our Cat Flossy* by Ruth Brown (Beaver Picture Books, 1987); *Whistle for Willie* by Ezra Jack Keats (Picture Puffin, 1986); *John Brown, Rose and the Midnight Cat* by Jenny Wagner (Picture Puffin, 1986); *My Cat Likes to Hide in Boxes* by Eve Sutton and Lynley Dodd (Picture Puffin, 1993); *Arthur* by Amanda Graham (Picture Puffin, 1988); *When Willy Went to the Wedding* by Judith Kerr (Picture Lions, 1977) and the *Mog and Bunny* series (Collins); *A Dog Would Be Better* by Carolyn Dinan (*Cartwheels* series, Hamish Hamilton, 1987); the *What-a-Mess* series of books by Frank Muir (Picture Corgis); *Sam's Cat* by Sarah Garland (Walker Books, 1987).

Children could write detailed descriptions of their pets as if for the 'missing' column of a local newspaper. They could organise a pets visiting week for the class (one at a time) to 'show and tell' and take questions from peers. Observational drawings of the visiting pets could be incorporated. A survey of pets round all the classes of the school could be made and then recorded on a graph.

Suggestion(s) for support

Some children will need adult support, pairing with a more experienced partner or mixed-ability grouping for generating ideas, for scribing and for book-making. Instead of writing a worm dictionary, less experienced readers and writers might benefit from more experience of making books patterned on familiar texts. They could, for instance, make a pop-up or flap book based on David Carter's *How Many Bugs in a Box?* or *More Bugs in Boxes* (Orchard Books, 1987). Similarly, they could write a story about what their cat likes to do patterned on *My Cat Likes to Hide in Boxes*.

Children who need more reinforcement of letter-sound association could work with an adult and read *The Minister's Cat* by Lynley Dodd (Picture Puffin, 1994), which would also reinforce alphabetical order. To extend vocabulary they could play the Minister's Cat game with their group, taking turns to supply a different adjective each time.

Assessment opportunities

Note the children's involvement with books when they are responding in storytime and bookshares, and when they are expressing their feelings about sensitive issues. Note their confidence and cueing strategies when they are reading aloud in a group or individually to the Nursery, and when they are predicting outcomes in storytime. Note their growing vocabulary, their phonological awareness and their word recognition when they are hunting for words within words, playing the Minister's Cat game and making books patterned on familiar texts.

Opportunities for IT

In Session One, the children could collect information about their pets and the number and sorts of animals that they have. This could be presented using graphing software.

The children could use a word processor to write and draft their own personal pet stories to create a class anthology. They could also bring in photographs of their pets, which could either be stuck on to the final printed version or scanned into the computer so that the scanned picture can be included in the written account.

Groups of children could work together to word-process a mini-book about looking after pets. Individual children could write about different aspects of pet care. Each part of the book could be written as a separate file, and the files could then be combined to make a single file for the whole book. Alternatively, each part of the book could be printed out separately and the printouts combined to make a book. The children might also like to explore ways in which the pages of the book can be numbered using page format commands.

With support, older or more able children might be able to make a multimedia presentation of their book using simple authoring software. They could set up a title page for their book and a list of options, so that when the reader clicks on the title word 'feeding' they will be taken to a section about feeding their pet. The presentation could include text and pictures drawn by the children and scanned into the computer, drawn using an art package or taken from clipart sources. The children could also include sounds recorded through the computer.

In Session Two, the children could use a word processor to type and print out the text for their version of *Dear Zoo*. They could either create the whole book on the word processor, adding the flaps later, or alternatively stick their text on to the flap book. They could experiment with different sizes of text, different font styles or even different colours to represent their animal.

The children could use electronic thesauruses in Session Three to help them look for new words. They could use a thesaurus which might be a part of their word processing program, one which is a stand-alone piece of software, or the thesaurus on a hand-held computer (such as a PSION or Franklin electronic thesaurus).

If the original text is presented to them on a word processor, the children can actually use the thesaurus to replace words in the text. They will need to be shown how to set up the search, select the word they want and replace the original word in the text.

In Session Five, after the children have exhausted their own ideas for 'cat' words, they could use an electronic dictionary such as those on word processors, hand-held computers or spelling checkers. They will need to be shown how to set up the search and possibly print out the results. They could also explore search facilities which allow them to search for 'cat' within a word as well.

In Session Six, the children could create their own epitaph for a loved pet using a word processor or simple desktop publishing package. This could be set up so that there is a border around the text. They should discuss the information to be included and how the text is to be laid out. This might be a good opportunity to introduce the centring command, so that the children do not have to position their text using the space bar.

Display ideas
Create an 'Our pets' art gallery with drawings and the descriptive pieces of writing on each picture, attractively presented with handwriting patterns for borders. Set up a 3D display of an Ideal Home Exhibition for pets, designed and made by the children with accompanying instructions and perhaps an interactive quiz game about 'who lives in which house'. The class poetry corner could be converted into a churchyard with epitaphs for pets.

Other aspects of English PoS covered
Speaking and listening – 1a, b, c; 2a, b; 3b.
Writing – 1a, b, c; 2a, b, c, d, e; 3a, b.

Reference to photocopiable sheet(s)
Photocopiable sheet 138 requires children to find appropriate adverbial phrases to relate the movements of a cat, using their imagination to build on the story they have heard.

HOLIDAYS

For the children to:
▲ *read 'between' and 'beyond' the lines;*
▲ *feel confident enough to recount their own experiences and represent them in a 'published' book;*
▲ *express their own worries and fears in response to a story;*
▲ *extend their vocabulary and develop their language awareness.*

†† *Sessions One and Two: whole class; Session Three: group work; Sessions Four and Five: whole class; Session Six: group work; Session Seven: whole class, then groups.*

🕓 *Session One: 20 minutes; Session Two: 35–45 minutes; Session Three: 35–40 minutes; Session Four: 20 minutes; Session Five: 30–35 minutes; Session Six: 30 minutes; Session Seven: 45 minutes.*

Key background information
These sessions provide contexts for children to write and read about personal experience of special moments that live in the memory. There are opportunities for taking on a role, and for reading and writing poetry. These activities could link with class projects on Holidays, Journeys, the Seaside, Weather, Water, Leisure and Sports.

Preparation
Collect books, fiction and non-fiction, dealing with the seaside, shells, caves and water sports. Collect natural objects from the seashore. Write out the poem 'Waves' by Eleanor Farjeon (*Ginn Goes Home Collection*, 1987) on an OHP or a very large sheet of paper. Set up the Home Corner as a travel agent's office.

Resources needed

Musical instruments; writing, drawing and book-making materials; copies of *The Big Big Sea*; *Lost*; *Magic Beach*; *Wish You Were Here* and *Come Away From the Water, Shirley* (see below for details).

What to do

Session One: Introduction to the topic

This is purely an oral session, to encourage the children to respond fully to a story. Read *The Big Big Sea* by Martin Waddell (Walker Books, 1994). Listen and respond to the children's first reactions to the story. Comment on how the endpapers establish the mood, with shimmering light on water; and how the tones of the illustrations all the way through the book convey the atmosphere of a moonlit night.

Discuss with children their own memories of holidays, gradually focusing in on actual seaside visits or coastal scenes in TV programmes they have seen. Prompt, if necessary, by mentioning waves, shells, caves, rocks, the fun-fair, ice-creams, sun, rain, wind and journeys. (As always, use discussions to extend the children's vocabulary.) If you have memories of your own to share with the children, this sign of trust will increase their confidence to respond in a personal way. Invite the children to recall memories of holidays they have shared with their families or friends, and to try to pinpoint what it was that made these times special.

Session Two: Choral reading

Recap with the children the discussion from Session One, then read the Eleanor Farjeon poem 'Waves' to the class. Show a large written version on an OHP or chart, and encourage the children to join in on the second and third readings. Suggest that they could make a studio recording, with appropriate sound effects, to add to the class resources. Discuss the sounds they need to represent: splashing, whooshing, crashing and so on. Look around the classroom for suitable articles to use for this, including parts of the body. Then try out a reading with sound effects; record it on tape, then play it back and assess the results.

Ask the children if they think the sound effects could be improved with real instruments. Discuss which instruments would best represent each sound, and try them out until you are all happy with the result. Tape a choral reading of the poem with the new sound effects. Play it back and evaluate the result. Make any changes the children deem necessary (perhaps combining body and instruments?)

When you are satisfied with the reading and the sound effects, add the tape and the book to your class collection, ready for use. You could also perform the poem in an assembly for the whole school to enjoy.

Session Three: From reading to writing

Organise the children into small groups and tell them that they are going to be poets today, writing about a day at the

seaside (either real or imagined). Give them the following headings on large sheets of paper, to help them organise their thoughts:

What they saw
What they heard
What they smelt
What they touched
What they did

Tell them to start by listing everything they can remember (or can think of) under those headings. When they have done that, the group will choose the most important item from one section and every child will then write one sentence about it. Put all their sentences together to make the first verse of their poem. Next, look back at their list and repeat the same routine for the next section, until they have finished them all and the first draft of their poem is complete.

Groups can read out their poems to the class, and make constructive suggestions for improvements to each other's work. Draw the children's attention to linguistic features such as vocabulary choice, rhythmical patterns and alliteration. You might discuss whether the poems would benefit from a refrain at the end of each verse (such as 'On the day I went to the seaside') or from an onomatopoeic line of wave noises. Remind the children to think of a title as well.

When the children have made any changes they feel are necessary, they can publish their poems in a wave-shaped book with illustrations to enhance the text.

Session Four: Making predictions, expressing feelings

Introduce the book *Lost* by Anthony Kerins (Dent, 1990) to the children as a holiday story with a warning message. Read the title to the children and ask them to predict what will happen in the book. Encourage them to make more specific predictions on the way through the book, altering their initial ideas as they derive more information from the text. Compare the events in the story with the children's own experiences before going on to debate the issues involved. Discuss how unwise Callie was to go off on her own, and ask the children if they think she would ever do that again. Discuss with the children other crowded places where they should be extra careful, such as shopping centres, fairgrounds, football pitches, Saturdays in town, bus stations, railway stations, fireworks displays, large parks and strange places where they don't know their way around. Talk about how they can keep themselves safe. Discuss what to do if they ever do get lost, and stress that they must never go with anyone they don't know.

In the next writing session, children could design posters to prevent other children from getting lost.

Session Five: Reading between the lines

Explain to the children that you will read two books that have something special about them, and you want the children to listen and look very carefully to detect what that is.

After you have read *Magic Beach* by Alison Lester (Puffin, 1993) to the class, ask if the children spotted anything unusual about the book. See if the children can explain the two different strands in the book (the reality and the 'magic' episodes). Do the children think the latter are magical or imagined episodes? Discuss how the illustrator signals to the reader the difference between the two strands: the imagined episodes are presented in a round frame, like a thought bubble.

You could also draw the children's attention to the rhymes and the language used, and find out which words the children specially liked and why. Comment on the use of alliteration and assonance.

Next, read *Come Away From the Water, Shirley* by John Burningham (Jonathan Cape, 1993). Did the children notice the similarity with *Magic Beach* (another book that presents two different stories happening at the same time)? How does the illustrator make that clear in this book?

Invite the children to say why they feel Shirley needs to imagine things. Ask them what they might imagine in her place. Go through Shirley's pages again, and discuss what she might be thinking or saying to herself or the dog or the pirates.

Congratulate the children on their observational powers as readers, and let them know that they can put their ideas to good use as writers in the next session.

Session Six: Providing text for pictures

Organise the children into groups to write the text to go with Shirley's tale. They will have to discuss among themselves and make decisions about what Shirley is saying or thinking during her adventures in the book – when she is: looking out to sea; rowing out to the galleon; getting her first view of the pirates; walking the plank; having a sword fight; diving off into the sea to escape; trying to follow the map; digging for treasure; opening the box and finding the jewels; and sailing home in the moonlight with the crown on her head.

Several sessions will be necessary to finish this work, as the children will need to draw the scenes on to sheets of paper and incorporate their chosen words in bubbles on each page, then design a cover and write a publisher's blurb for their new publication about Shirley's adventures at sea.

The groups can read their finished books in assembly.

Session Seven: From reading to writing

Before you read the story, ask if any of the children have older siblings who have been away on a school holiday. Listen and respond to what the class has to say, and discuss what children might worry about the first time they go away from home – for instance, being sick on the bus, making friends,

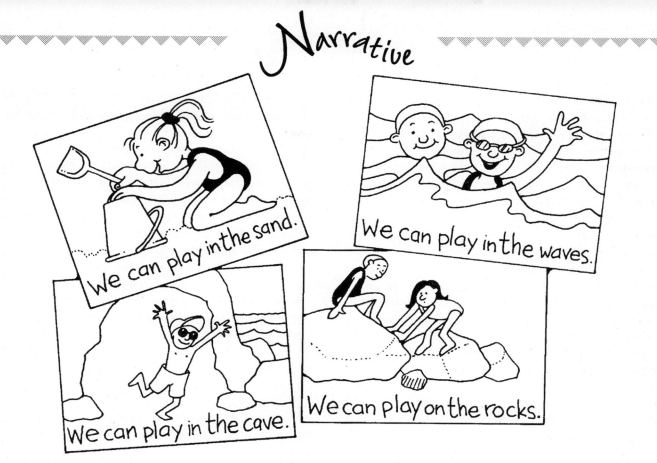

We can play in the sand.

We can play in the waves.

We can play in the cave.

We can play on the rocks.

not liking the food, getting lost, hurting oneself, wetting the bed, being frightened at night, minibeast problems, being told off, losing your money, missing your mum and dad and wanting to come home. Write their ideas down on a flip chart.

Introduce the book *Wish You Were Here* by Martina Selway (Hutchinson, 1994) and tell the children to note Rosie's feelings in a similar situation. After the reading, recall with the children all the things that Rosie didn't like, such as the other girl being sick, the rain, the smelly hut, the runny egg, the long walk, Danny licking her bun, the rope swing, falling in the water and the creepy-crawlies in the tents.

Check how Rosie's experiences compared with the class list. Ask the children what they would have felt in Rosie's place. What do they think made her change her mind? Talk through all the possibilities.

In small groups, in pairs or individually according to preference, the children can now compose the postcard home that Rosie might send home on the next day of her holiday. Tell the children to bear in mind what they already know from the text about the holiday programme and about Rosie's state of mind. When they have finished, the children can read their postcards to the class, explain the reasons for their choices and note the similarities and differences between the various versions.

Suggestion(s) for extension

Experienced writers could design a brochure for a seaside holiday resort, and/or write a non-fiction book about things to do in water: paddle, swim, catch fish, snorkel, dive, row, sail, windsurf, surfboard, water-ski, build sand castles. Drawing on their real or imagined holiday experiences, they could make books about transport around the world, coins

and currency in different countries, markets and shopping in different countries, or food abroad.

Suggestion(s) for support

Less experienced writers could make an easy reading book about the seaside for the Nursery, with a repeating language pattern such as *We can play...* (in the sand, in the waves, in the cave, on the rocks), and provide illustrations to match the text. Children with limited writing stamina could carry out a survey of favourite kinds of holidays. There are diverse opportunities for emergent writing in role through a drama centred on a journey: listing what to take, making a map of the route, drawing a street plan of the place, making passports and sending letters home.

Assessment opportunities

Note the children's responses when they are expressing their feelings, recounting their own personal experiences or expressing their opinions about books. Note also their ability to make deductions and to read between the lines. Note their confidence when reading back their own writing to different audiences.

Opportunities for IT

In Session Three, once the group has written its different verses, the children could type their particular lines into the word processor. This would only involve the children in relatively short typing tasks. The group could then re-read the poem and decide whether it would sound better if they moved some of the lines around to get a better rhythm or rhymes. Children could then be shown how to mark lines of text and move them from one place to another, either by

cutting and pasting them or by using the drag and drop facility available on some word processors.

In Session Four, the children could use an art package to design their poster, incorporating pictures and text and experimenting with different font styles, sizes and colours, and in Session Six, they could use an art package to design the cover for their book about Shirley's adventures at sea. They could also word-process the publisher's blurb for the back of the book.

As an extension activity, the children could work in small groups to publish a holiday brochure using either a word processor or a simple desktop publishing package. They could experiment with different layouts to produce an A4 sheet, or a two-fold or three-fold design. With appropriate support, children could scan in pictures taken from their own holiday photographs, postcards or actual holiday brochures.

Alternatively, the children could word-process and print out the various parts of the brochure and then use a traditional cut and paste approach to put the final brochure together. They may need to reprint parts of the work to make them smaller or larger – which would necessitate saving and retrieving the text, and experimenting with different print styles and sizes.

Display ideas

The children could create a frieze of a seaside scene, surrounded by the collection of their holiday brochures, their postcards from Rosie, posters from travel agents, photos and their personal writing about holidays.

The books the children have written about Shirley's adventures could be displayed in the reading corner to encourage everyone to read them.

Other aspects of the English PoS covered

Speaking and Listening – 1a, b, c, d; 2a, b; 3a, b.
Writing – 1a, b, c; 2a, b, c, d, e; 3a, b.

EXPRESSING FEARS

For the children to:
▲ *visualise events from a narrative;*
▲ *use chapter headings to predict outcomes;*
▲ *relate a character's experiences to their own fears and express these openly to a group;*
▲ *understand that everyone is afraid at some time or other, and that it is nothing to be ashamed of;*
▲ *discuss ways of coping with fear.*

Also to enhance children's self-image as readers and increase their stamina by introducing a book with chapters, necessitating recall from day to day of what has happened previously and prediction of outcomes that might follow.

†† *Session One: whole class; Session Two: whole class, then small groups.*

🕑 *Session One: 20 minutes; Session Two: 45 minutes.*

Previous skills/knowledge needed

It would be helpful if the children were already used to expressing their feelings openly to a large group.

Key background information

Within the supportive environment of storytime, these activities will increase the demands made on young listeners and early readers in terms of retaining information over a period of time, without the support of visual clues to help them to internalise meaning. They also provide a safe environment in which children can acknowledge and talk about feeling afraid.

Preparation

Assemble a collection of books that deal with feelings of fear, such as *I'm Coming To Get You* by Tony Ross (Picture Puffin, 1986); *The Monster Bed* by Jeanne Willis and Susan Varley (Andersen Press, 1986); *The Owl Who Was Afraid of the Dark* by Jill Tomlinson (Chivers, 1994); *Going to Playgroup* by Laurence and Catherine Anholt (Orchard Books, 1991); *Moving Molly, The Visitors Who Came to Stay* and *Willie the Wimp* by Anthony Browne (Magnet Books, 1988).

Resources needed

Large sheets of paper and felt-tipped pens; *There Are No Bears on Hemlock Mountain* by Alice Dalgleish and *The Trouble with the Tucker Twins* by Rose Impey (see below for details).

What to do

Session One: Introducing books in chapters

Compliment the children on how experienced they are as readers. Tell them you are now going to read a story in chapters instead of a picture book. Stress the need for them to listen carefully and make their own mental pictures of the people and events in the story.

During the week, read one chapter of *There Are No Bears...* per session and encourage the children to use the chapter titles as sources of information. As well as commenting in the usual way on the children's reaction to events (comparing them with incidents in their own lives or in other books), ask the children to work out where and when the story is set and to give their reasons.

Invite the children to join in the chant 'There – are – no – bears – on – Hemlock Mountain', keeping to the steady rhythm of Jonathon's footsteps.

Session Two: Focusing on feeling afraid

Talk with the children about Jonathon's fear of meeting bears when crossing the mountain, and ask them if they would have been scared of the bears too. Reassure them that everyone is afraid of something at some time or other. Brainstorm together the likely fears, such as spiders, the dark, being left alone, falling, hurting oneself, being ill, losing a special toy, a best friend moving away, getting told off, getting things wrong at school, changing schools, a pet dying, a relative going to hospital and parents getting divorced. Share one of your own experiences from childhood, and encourage the children to talk about things they have been afraid of. Discuss the things that can help us to overcome fears, and talk about what we can do to help other people.

Read *The Trouble with the Tucker Twins* by Rose Impey (Picture Puffin, 1992). Together, talk through all the unkind things that the twins did to hassle the little boy. Ask the children what they thought of his mum's suggestions. Ask if they had predicted the ending. What did they think was going to happen to change the situation?

Discuss what they would do if this happened to them in school. What do they think their mums might say? What do they think you would do? What could be done in school to stop this happening?

Working in small groups with a large sheet of paper, the children can make a poster providing a set of rules which help people to treat each other kindly. Children could make another list of suggestions for what to do if things start to go wrong. These can all be posted in the school entrance hall, and children in other classes (as well as parents and teachers) can contribute ideas to add to the lists. Check each day for new suggestions, and watch them mushroom.

Suggestion(s) for extension
Confident readers could read a range of books on the same theme (perhaps from the reading list suggested) independently, and report back in bookshares. Confident writers could write book reviews.

Suggestion(s) for support
An adult helper could support less experienced writers when they are making their posters; or the children could tape their ideas instead.

Assessment opportunities
Note the children's ease in admitting fears and talking about their feelings. Note also their ability to listen to a short novel and understand its meaning without the support of illustrations. Note their confidence and their use of a range of cueing strategies when they are reading back from their posters.

Opportunities for IT
In Session Two, children could use a word processor to present their rules to be displayed around the school. They could experiment with different font styles, sizes or colours to make their rules more eye-catching. They could also be introduced to simple commands like centring or underlining to make the display more interesting. Borders or even pictures could be added to their posters.

Display ideas

Children's personal stories about what they are afraid of, together with their drawings and paintings, could be displayed with appropriate books of poems and stories alongside posters with suggestions for coping with fears.

Other aspects of the English PoS covered

Speaking and listening – 1a, b, c; 2a, b; 3b.
Writing – 1a, b, c; 2a, b, c, d, e; 3a.

TRADITIONAL TALES

For the children to:
▲ *learn how traditional tales are structured and recognise the patterns of language used;*
▲ *show increasing critical awareness and an ability to discuss the moral issues they encounter;*
▲ *recognise similarities and differences between tales from various sources;*
▲ *use prediction skills, reading on and back, for cloze procedures;*
▲ *develop vocabulary and alphabetic knowledge.*
†† *Sessions One to Five: whole class; Session Six: whole class, then pairs.*
⏲ *Session One: 25 minutes; Session Two: 35 minutes; Session Three: 20 minutes; Session Four: 35 minutes; Session Five: 40–45 minutes; Session Six: 35–40 minutes.*

Previous skills/knowledge needed

It would be helpful if the children were already used to a wider-world approach to the curriculum, and were interested

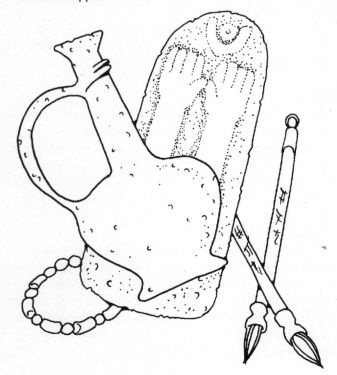

in languages and cultures other than their own. It would also help if they were acquainted with the most well-known Western fairy tales, such as 'Cinderella'.

Key background information

A wider-world heritage allows children to explore common themes and note similarities and differences across time and space, and to engage with moral issues in the world of the book and relate them to their own world. Links can be made with class projects on Metals, Treasure, Money, Patterns and Reflections.

Preparation

Prepare a collection of tales from around the world (which the children can add to), together with artefacts and clothes connected with the various cultures encountered in the tales. Assemble a range of postcards, pictures, posters and books on art from the Middle East, the Far East, the Indian sub-continent and Australia, plus examples of Islamic and Chinese calligraphy, Hindi script and special calligraphic pens and brushes. Arrange for dual-language storytelling whenever possible. Arrange for traditional Indian dancers and musicians to visit the school as a link with the tale from India. Set up the Home Corner as a Chinese restaurant, with authentic utensils, to link with the Chinese tale. Encourage writing in role: signs, menus, cheques, bills.

Resources needed

A computer, software packages based on traditional folktales or fairy tales, taped versions of the tales in a variety of languages and dialects (if commercial ones are not available, arrange to tape the stories in school with the help of the local community), taped music from Indian and Chinese traditions, a flip chart, one copy of photocopiable sheets 139 and 140 for each child.

What to do

Session One: Introduction to the topic

Explain to the children that people have always loved telling and listening to stories, even before any of them were written down. Storytellers all over the world used to go from village to village, telling stories that gradually became very well-known traditional tales and were eventually written down for us to read today. Tell them that over the next few weeks, you are going to be travelling on a magic carpet around the world in search of traditional stories.

So, close your eyes and off we go! First stop: the Middle East.

Introduce the popular collection *The Arabian Nights*. Tell the children that these tales are supposed to be the ones that the famous Queen Scheherazade told to her husband every night for a thousand and one nights.

Show them the different versions from your display, and discuss the different styles of illustration. Show them some

Mogul miniature paintings and books of Islamic patterns that link with the illustrations in the texts. Draw the children's attention to the detail: the tiny brushstrokes, the gold paint, the patterns on clothing, the accoutrements, jewellery, furnishings, tableware. Point out the evidence of the skilled craftworkers of the East: the embroidery, the woven blankets and carpets, the delicate copperware and silverware, the decorated tiles and plates. Compare these with genuine artefacts from the class display, if possible. Mention how important Islamic calligraphy is and show some examples, together with the special calligraphic pens. Encourage the children to browse through the books and the artefacts during the weeks that follow, and to try writing with the special pens.

Then read one of the most famous tales to them: *Ali Baba and the Forty Thieves* as retold by Walter McVitty (Cambridge University Press, 1988). Listen and respond to the children's initial reactions. Discuss with them the typical features of traditional tales, noting the language used: the hero and heroine; the wise and the devious; greed; disguises; faithful servants; virtue rewarded and evil overcome. Remind them to look for such features in other traditional tales.

Session Two: Comparing different versions of tales

Explain to the children that over the years, traditional tales like *The Arabian Nights* were written down by different people, all of whom changed them a little bit, so that now we have several different versions of them. Tell them that during the day, you are going to read three different versions of another Arabian Nights story that they will probably know already. They have to decide which one is best, and explain why.

Then read *Aladdin and the Wonderful Lamp* – firstly by Carol Carrick (Scholastic, 1990), then by Michael Rosen (*Tell Tales* series, Firefly, 1989), and then the Ladybird Disney (1993) version.

Ask the children to comment on the quality of the illustrations and the language, and then to vote for their favourite.

Encourage the children to compare these books with other media, as they are likely to have seen a corresponding film, video, TV series and/or pantomime. Talk with them about which things work better on the page and which on the screen or the stage. Why is this?

Finish off the session by asking the children what they would wish for if they had a magic lamp. Play the alphabet game around the class: In my treasure chest I found an amazing amethyst, a beautiful bracelet, etc. In a subsequent writing session, the children can write out their sentences and draw the appropriate items to make up an alphabet book, which can be added to the classroom resources.

Session Three: Introducing computer software

On to the magic carpet again, and we're on the way to Germany. Read *Rumpelstiltskin* – for example, the version retold by Paul O. Zelinsky (Aurum Press, 1986) – to the class; then ask the children to comment on features of previous tales that recur in this one.

Do the children find it easy to tell who is good and who is evil this time? What about the miller and the king? In their opinion, should the heroine have promised her child to Rumpelstiltskin in the first place? Ask the children how they feel about keeping promises.

Encourage the children to retell the story to each other during the week, and to compare this version of the tale with others from the class collection.

Invite the children to work in pairs or threes at the computer throughout the week, using *Fairy Tales* software (RESOURCE) to create their own version of a traditional story and choosing pictures from the 'library' provided. More

unkind sisters, a weak father, a special event, magic help, a king and a lost slipper.

Then list the differences, such as: *Wishbone* is set in China; the characters have different names; a different celebration; a magic fish, not a fairy godmother; no chiming of the clock at midnight; a greedy king after the wedding (who soon learns his lesson, though, so that in the end they can live 'happily ever after'). Ask the children for their views on who the old man is, and discuss his role in the story.

Session Five: Rewriting a traditional tale

Tell the children that you are flying on your magic carpet from China to India today, to collect an Indian traditional tale. Play a tape of traditional Indian music to set the scene.

First of all, draw the children's attention to and comment on the exquisite artwork; then read *The Wizard Punchkin* by Joanna Troughton (Picture Puffin, 1994). Afterwards, discuss together the characteristics that conform to a traditional tale, such as: a captured princess, a poor man to the rescue, the good outwitting the wicked, the hero winning the hand of the princess. Ask the children what is unusual about the hidden treasure in this tale: not gold or jewels, but the soul of the evil-doer that will break the spell and release the princess. Encourage the children to reread the book in paired reading times during the week. You could tell them the very similar Russian tale about Koshchei in *The Encyclopaedia of Myths and Legends* edited by Stuart Gordon (Headline, 1993). Suggest that they read it in paired reading times during the week and bring it to a bookshare session.

Invite the children to consider what a present-day version of this story might be like. In a multi-racial school, the children may be able to draw comparisons with Asian films (seen in the cinema or on video) which feature romantic stories where problems are overcome by an heroic figure who wins the hand of a beautiful young woman.

As a class, you could create a co-operative story with an adult scribing on a flipchart and each child providing a sentence which has to link with the one before and take the narrative forward.

If possible, ask older children or parents to record stories in Hindi, Punjabi and other languages on tape (with translations) for the class collection.

In subsequent writing sessions, children can work in pairs or threes at the computer on *Ramayana Tales* software (Longman) to create their own version of the most famous of Indian stories, the tale of Rama and Sita. This story is the basis of the Diwali celebrations.

Session Six: Text completion

Tell the children that you are off on the magic carpet again in search of more traditional tales, and this time you are going to Australia.

Read *What Made Tiddalick Laugh* by Joanna Troughton (Picture Puffin, 1994). Discuss the words used in the book:

confident readers can work in pairs or threes on *Selective Software Part 1: Red Riding Hood* (ESM). They will have to read the text, make deductions and answer questions in order to solve the problem of the obstacles that get in Red Riding Hood's way.

Session Four: Comparing across cultures

Tell the children to settle down on the magic carpet for the long ride to China.

Explain that in different parts of the world, very similar stories were being told by storytellers long ago. You will be reading a Chinese story to them, and you want them to think hard and see if it reminds them of a story they already know.

Play a snippet from a tape of traditional Chinese music to introduce the reading. Read *Wishbones: A Folk Tale from China* by Barbara Ker Wilson and Meilo So (Frances Lincoln, 1993). Invite the children to tell you straight away which story it reminded them of. *Cinderella* is the likely answer.

Together, list on a flip chart or board the points that the two stories have in common, such as: a stepmother, two

READING

Nabunum's special dance

Name _____ Date _____

▲ Fill in the gaps in this passage.

At first, his dance was slow and

graceful, like _____

_____

_____

He _____

his long, thin body.

He _____ twirled.

He sh_____

He fl_____

He did _____

Making Tiddalik laugh

Name _____ Date _____

▲ Complete these jokes, then write some of your own on the back of this sheet.

Why do birds fly south in the winter?

Why do bees hum?

When is water like a kangaroo?

What did the mouse say when he broke his tooth?

140, the children can work in pairs or small groups to complete the missing chunks of text that Tiddalik has swallowed, using their skills of prediction and rereading to create a meaningful paragraph. Finally, they can share their different versions with the class.

Suggestion(s) for extension
There is no shortage of traditional tales linked to the theme of treasure, gold and silver or riches; examples are *Jack and the Beanstalk*, *Puss in Boots*, *Molly Whuppy* and *King Midas*. Fluent readers should be encouraged to read as many as they can, remembering to compare and contrast stories from different cultures and eras and to relate the moral issues that arise in the stories to their own situation today. They should keep a record of their reading to talk about in weekly reading conferences.

Some children may wish to write more jokes to make up a class anthology *Let's Make Tiddalik Laugh*, which can be published and added to the class collection.

Suggestion(s) for support
Some children will need the support of an adult or a more experienced reader when working with the photocopiable sheets or with the computer software.

wilted and withered, *slurp*, *gurgle*, *swoosh* and so on. You will probably need to explain Australian terms that are outside the children's language repertoire, such as *billabong*, *wombat* and *platypus*.

Invite the children to recall everything the animals tried in order to make Tiddalik laugh: jokes, tricks, pulling faces, silly dances and songs. Encourage them to suggest other ideas for making people laugh. What makes *them* laugh?

Suggest that in paired reading times during the week, the children read *Tiddalik the Frog* by Susan Nunes (Hodder & Stoughton, 1990) and compare the two versions of the tale.

Using photocopiable sheet 139, the children can work in pairs to complete the jokes. Then, using photocopiable sheet

Assessment opportunities

Note the children's increasing use of a range of reading strategies when completing cloze procedures and jokes. Note also their developing involvement in responding to stories, and their increasing awareness of language use. Note the language of books appearing in children's own writing, and their increasing range of vocabulary and syntax.

Opportunities for IT

In Session Two, children could word-process their alphabet game contributions, with each child typing his own sentence into the class alphabet.

In Session Three, children could use software like *Fairy Tales* in which they can write their story and then add their own pictures from a library of different fairy-tale characters and objects. Alternatively, they could use a word processor or simple desktop publishing package and select fairy-tale characters from clipart sources, or make their own pictures using a simple art or graphics package.

Children could write their co-operative story from Session Five using a word processor, with an adult scribing on the keyboard for the sake of speed. Children could then make printouts and work on them in pairs to improve and redraft the original story. Each pair could then return to the computer, reload the original file and make their alterations to create their own version of the story.

Display ideas

You could create a 3D display of Aladdin's cave, with shiny objects that reflect light, jewellery made by the children and silky fabrics. The children's alphabet poem, letter by letter, could be hung as mobiles from the cave roof.

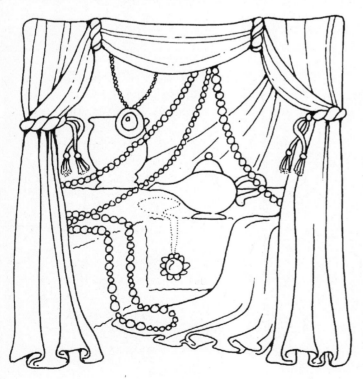

The children could gradually assemble a large frieze centred on a picture of Ali Baba, with their individual retelling of a favourite tale on each basket.

Other aspects of the English PoS covered

Speaking and listening – 1a, c; 2a, b; 3a, b.
Writing – 1a, b, c; 2a, b, c, d, e; 3a, b.

Reference to photocopiable sheet(s)

Photocopiable sheet 139 invites children to write the punchlines to jokes, and/or to tell riddles/jokes of their own. Photocopiable sheet 140 is a cloze procedure based on a text read out in class.

AFRICAN FOLK TALES

For the children to:
▲ *become acquainted with folk tales from Africa;*
▲ *become familiar with the conventions of folk tales;*
▲ *appreciate poetic language and the effects of alliteration;*
▲ *be able to retell familiar stories orally and in writing;*
▲ *be able to dramatise known stories;*
▲ *identify words through graphophonic clues and sentence syntax, and from the sense of surrounding text;*
▲ *recognise the digraphs* sh, ch *and* th *and the blends* fl *and* fr.
†† *Session One: whole class; Session Two: small groups.*
🕐 *Session One: 30 minutes, followed by workshops; Session Two: 35 minutes.*

Previous skills/knowledge needed

It is preferable if these sessions can be placed in the context of a class topic where children will have the experience of hearing African drummers, of using African artefacts as a stimulus for artwork (making patterns and prints, dyeing fabric, weaving), of taking part in African cookery sessions and of recipe writing. This might culminate in a class celebration: a feast day when the children could be dressed in fabrics from Africa, greet each other in at least one African language, listen to visiting storytellers and musicians and watch visiting dancers.

Key background information

Through exploring folk tales that read aloud well and capture their interest, the children will learn the typical ingredients of folk tales and the ways in which they differ from modern story books. These sessions can link with class projects on Animals, Camouflage, Food, Pattern, Weather, Storytelling, Traditions and Celebrations.

N.B. Refugee children who have fled from areas of conflict will need very sensitive care to counteract the traumatic experiences they might have been through.

Preparation

Assemble a collection of books (both fiction and non-fiction), posters, maps, fabrics and artefacts from Africa, ensuring that urban as well as rural images are included. Arrange for African storytellers or musicians to visit the school. Arrange a trip to the African village in Bishop Stortford, if possible. (Contact 'AKLOWA', Takeley House, Brewers End, Takeley, nr. Bishop Stortford, Herts CM22 6QR.) Learn basic greetings, such as 'Jambo' in Swahili.

Resources needed

A tape recorder, taped African music, materials for mask-making (such as card, glue, scissors, paper, string, wool, paints, pieces of fabric), percussion instruments, writing and drawing materials, one copy per child of photocopiable sheet 141.

What to do

Session One: Introduction to the topic – preparing for an assembly

Tell the children that they are to prepare an assembly presentation to link with the theme of Africa, and that you have brought one of your favourite African folk tales to share with them as a basis for the assembly.

Point out that Fiona French is an artist as well as a writer, so they are to pay particular attention to the artwork in the book. Then read the story of *Aio the Rainmaker* by Fiona

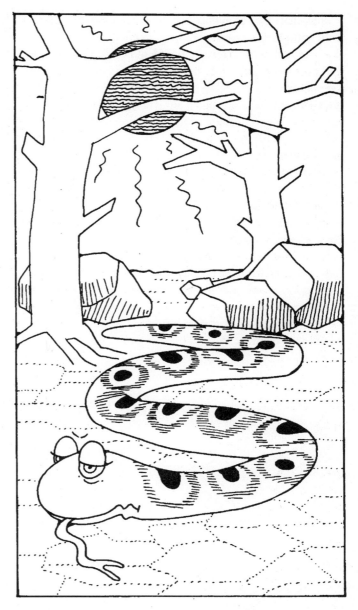

French (Oxford University Press, 1975), encouraging the children to respond spontaneously at the end. Comment on the melancholy tone and the rhythmic, poetic use of language. There may be some vocabulary that the children are not sure of – such as *baobab tree, torrents, rivulets, orchids, ancestors* and *scorpion* – and which you could explore with them.

You will need to counteract stereotypical views of Africa that the children may have picked up from the media, by referring to recent droughts in England when water was rationed, garden hoses were banned and some communities had to rely on street pumps.

Reread *Aio* and help the children to decide on the work to be done in preparation for the assembly, such as mask-making workshops, music-making workshops, a whole-class dance session for the ceremony to thank the ancestors and individual animal dances to link with the text of the story. Individuals will also have to rehearse the reading of their parts of the text.

African folk tales

Name _____

▲ Fill in the blanks from this passage.   Date _____

Many years ago, the rain did not fall at the end of the _ _ y season. The _ _ ops died and the rivers turned to dust. Aio called to the ancestors to send rain. 'The leopard is so _ _ irsty, he has no _ _ rength to _ _ ase the antelope. All he can do is sit in the _ _ ade of the baobab _ _ ee. The antelope has lost his streng _ _ . He is so thir _ _ y, he ju _ _ sits all day under the baobab _ _ ee.

'The _ _ ameleon has no strength to _ _ ange his colour. The parrot cannot _ _ y. The monkeys sit in silence in the bran _ _ es. The _ _ ogs sing no more in the evenings. Even the py _ _ on has no strength to _ _ ed her _ _ in. The _ _ orpion cannot carry her _ _ ildren.'

'Aio, we hear your song. If you remember us, we will _____

_____

_____

READING

Plan the order of events with the children, for instance:
▲ an introductory musical composition;
▲ a reading of the story with masked children performing the sequence of animal dances in turn, to a rhythmical accompaniment;
▲ Aio's pleas to the ancestors;
▲ a musical composition to usher in the celebration;
▲ a grand finale – thanksgiving dance with musical accompaniment.

When all is ready, perform to the whole school in assembly.

Session Two: Reading strategies

Arrange the children into groups and give a copy of photocopiable sheet 141 to each child. Explain to the children that they will have to read the text carefully and to discuss together what the missing initial blends or digraphs might be – using the meaning of the rest of the sentence, the syntax of the sentence and the other letters in the word as clues.

Then they have to decide how they would reply if they were the ancestors. Remind the children to bear in mind the

tone and language of the rest of the story, and also how they think respected people like ancestors would speak.

Gather together as a whole class to share results and discuss any difficulties. Ask the children to tell you which cues they used to make their decisions. Draw the children's attention to interesting features such as the *ch* in *choose* and *chameleon*.

In subsequent sessions, revisit in turn each of the initial digraphs that appeared in the text (*sh, ch, th*). Following the same pattern each time, broaden the children's vocabulary by brainstorming as many words as possible that have this initial digraph. Encourage the children to suggest connections: names of people and places; dialect words, borrowings, slang words; different parts of speech (nouns, verbs, adjectives).

Then revisit the blends from the text (*fl* and *fr*) in the same way.

The children could make a class mini-dictionary with their collection of words.

Suggestion(s) for extension

More experienced readers could investigate the different sounds in English that are represented by the letters *ch*. They could brainstorm as many words as possible beginning with *ch* as in cheese (choose, chocolate, Chester, China, chicken, chortle, chubby and so on). They could sort these words into sets of adjectives, verbs and nouns, and make up alliterative sentences using words from their list.

They could then repeat the task with *ch* as in chameleon (Christmas, chaos, chemistry, chemicals, choreographer, chrysalis, chorus, choir, chiropractor, chiropodist), and again with *ch* as in Charlotte (Charmaine, chauffeur, chef, chassis, chateau, choux pastry). You would need to explain to the group afterwards the different language roots that have led to these variations.

They could read *The Hunter* by Paul Geraghty (Hutchinson Books, 1994) to give a different slant to African animal stories, and discuss the message behind this story.

Confident writers could write out instructions for making a mask, and give these to other classes in the school after the assembly. They could make up and 'publish' their own versions of an African animal story (such as 'How the camel got its hump') and read them aloud to the class in storytime.

Suggestion(s) for support

Some readers will need adult support when preparing their reading for the assembly, when rehearsing their opening paragraphs for taping, and when working on the photocopiable sheet.

Assessment opportunities

Note children's understanding of the folk tale form, their recall of events in stories, their appreciation of poetic language and their use of a range of cues when providing the missing initial letters.

Narrative

Opportunities for IT

In Session Two, children could work in small groups or pairs to word-process their part of the class mini-dictionary of initial blends or digraphs. Each group could use a common page format to provide a consistent approach. Children could also print out larger versions for display in the classroom.

As extension work, children could be introduced to electronic dictionaries – either hand-held ones or those found on word processors. They could search for other words with particular blends, jotting down those they already know from words that are new.

Confident writers could use a word processor to draft and redraft their instructions for making a mask.

Display ideas

Paintings of the animals in the *Aio* story could form the centre of a display, with the children's comments and retellings along with the masks they have made.

A 'wake up to language awareness' type display with children's work on *ch* – the lists they have made, what they have found out about derivations, their alliterative sentences – would promote children's interest in language.

Other aspects of the English PoS covered

Speaking and listening – 1a, b, c, d; 2a, b; 3a, b.
Writing – 1a, b, c; 2a, b, c, d, e; 3a, b.

Reference to photocopiable sheet(s)

Photocopiable sheet 141 requires the children to supply the starts of words (blends or digraphs) in a passage and compose an ending.

ANIMAL TALES

For the children to:
▲ further develop their understanding of the characteristics of the folk tale genre;
▲ extend their range of cueing strategies when reading;
▲ develop their skills in reading aloud.
†† Reading session: Whole class. Subsequent sessions: individual or pair work. Reading interview: individual children with teacher.
🕐 Reading session: 20 minutes. Subsequent sessions: 5–10 minutes each. Reading interview: 10–15 minutes.

Key background information

Children will need to be familiar with the folk tale genre, and will need previous experience of taping themselves reading in order to avoid reluctance and confusion. Teachers need to be familiar with miscue analysis.

Preparation

You will need enough tapes to record each child reading.

Resources needed

A collection of folk tales featuring animals, a tape recorder, cassettes.

What to do

To introduce this activity, read *Tortoise's Dream* by Joanna Troughton (Picture Puffin, 1994) to the class. Ask the children

which parts of the story they liked best, and whether they believe that the story really happened. If *not*, why not? Can they recall the events in the right sequence – for example, the lion, elephant, hyena, ostrich, baboon, giraffe, tortoise? What happened to each one? Did the children notice the pattern of how each animal avoided the previous animal's downfall but was then caught by a new obstacle? Ask the children to think of other African animals that might have been involved in the story, and what they think might have happened to them.

Then recall with the children all the fruits on the tree – bananas, dates, coconuts, melons, millet, yams, cassava, maize, pineapples, oranges. Ask the children which of these fruits they like and which ones they haven't tried. Do they know of any other tropical fruit that might have been on the tree – for example, mangoes, avocados, papayas, breadfruit? What strange-sounding names can they dream up to give to this tree?

Reread the story and encourage the children to join in whenever they can. Invite them to read the book in pairs during the week.

Explain to the children that over the next week or two, their task will be to choose a favourite African tale and to prepare a reading of the opening passage on tape, to use as a publicity advert to make other children want to read the book. Show the class a few books that might help them to choose their favourite tale, such as: *Crafty Chameleon* by Mwenye Hadithi (Picture Knight, 1988); *Hot Hippo* by Mwenye Hadithi (Knight Books, 1987); *Who's in Rabbit's House?* by Verna Aardema (Bodley Head, 1980); *Elmer* by David McKee (Piccolo Picture Books, 1968) and the subsequent *Elmer* books; *The Day the Tide Went Out and Out* by David McKee (Blackie Picture Paperbacks, 1985); *Two Can Toucan* by David McKee (Beaver Books, 1985). Don't forget stories about the most famous of African tricksters, Anansi, the spider man – for instance, 'Anansi and the Phantom Food' from *Misoso, Once Upon a Time Tales of Africa* by Verna Aardema (Hamish Hamilton, 1994).

Explain to the children that they can choose books that have already been read in class. Timetable short individual reading sessions, during which the children have access to a tape recorder.

When the children have made their choices, photocopy the relevant passages so that you can mark off their miscues as you listen to their taped reading or observe them preparing their reading. Analyse each child's miscues and check substitutions for a balance of cueing strategies across graphophonic, syntactic and contextual processes, and note self-corrections. This could be included as a summative assessment in the child's longitudinal portfolio, with recommendations for future teaching.

In individual follow-up reading interviews, you could ask the children why they chose a particular book, and question them about the events in the story, encouraging them to relate it to real-life situations and/or other books they know, and to comment on any interesting language use or repetitive refrains. These comments could be added to the children's literacy profile.

Suggestion(s) for extension
More experienced readers could read *The Hunter* by Paul Geraghty (Hutchinson Books, 1994) which gives a different slant to African animal stories, and discuss the message behind the story.

They could also make up and 'publish' their own versions of an African animal story (such as 'How the camel got its hump') and read them aloud to the class in storytime.

Suggestion(s) for support
Some readers will need adult support when preparing their 'appetite-whetters' for taping, in which case the adult concerned would need to keep notes about the child's reading strategies throughout the rehearsals.

Display ideas
Children's paintings of the animals from the stories could form the centre of a display, alongside the children's descriptions and retellings of stories.

Other aspects of the English PoS covered
Speaking and listening – 1a, b; 2a, b, c.
Writing – 1a, b, c; 2a, b, c, d, e; 3a.

Poetry

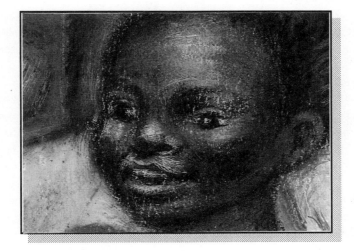

At the heart of children's early language development lie their experiences at play when they take on the issues of adult society in their own way, challenging conventions and addressing taboo subjects like sex, birth and death. Such language play provides the opportunity for them to subvert the status quo and incorporate audacious ideas — for instance, with girls in powerful roles. This linguistic play is expressed in the children's own voices, in dialect and in community languages; it resonates with the rhythms of the pop music of the day, with double meanings, puns and wordplay of every sort. Children control the language they use in these situations, and it is more lively than many classroom experiences! It is our responsibility as teachers to celebrate this in school and not stifle it, to raise a cheer for playground culture with its manifestations in clapping, skipping, chanting, juggling and ring games.

It is a short step from the music of the vernacular to the music of the poet. Children need to be exposed to a wide variety of poetic voices, to experience a whole-body response to the rhythms of language, to learn poems by heart and to hold 'memorable speech' in the mind.

It is generally agreed that there is a connection between children's understanding of rhyme and their success in the early stages of learning to read. This should be seen as an added bonus rather than a chief aim, as there are far wider implications in the teaching of poetry to children from a very young age. It is the richness of a child's experiences in oracy that drives literacy forward.

73

GAMES, RHYMES AND SONGS

For the children to:
▲ enjoy responding to the rhythms of language;
▲ increase their repertoire of action songs, rhymes and singing games;
▲ resequence chunks of known text or reassemble scrambled text;
▲ learn songs in a variety of languages and dialects in celebration of language diversity.

†† Session One: whole class in a large space; Session Two: whole class or small groups; Session Three: whole class or small groups.

🕐 Session One: 20 minutes; Session Two: 5–10 minutes; Session Three: 10–15 minutes.

Previous skills/knowledge needed

It is preferable, but not essential, for the children to be familiar with working in a large space.

Key background information

A series of learning experiences centred on ring games, action rhymes and songs that will immerse the children in the rhythmical aspects of language.

Preparation

Collect a range of books, tapes, records and videos related to the topic. For example: *This Little Puffin* edited by Elizabeth Matterson (Puffin, 1985); *Hand Rhymes* and *Play Rhymes* by Marc Brown (Picture Lions, 1992); *Stamp Your Feet* by Sarah Hayes (Walker Books, 1989); *Brown Gal in de Ring* edited by Olive Lewin (Oxford University Press, 1974); *Dandy Shandy* edited by Olive Lewin (Oxford University Press, 1975).

Learn the words and tunes to any unknown songs so that you are ready to teach them to the children.

Resources needed

Copies of photocopiable sheets 142 and 143 (one for each child), writing, drawing and bookmaking materials, musical instruments, a tape recorder, a video recorder.

What to do

Session One: Ring games

Tell the children that you are all going to play some games which they might have played at parties. Ask them if they have any suggestions for what sort of games they could play.

Introduce 'Here We Go Round the Mulberry Bush', which children may already be familiar with. Sing it through, and encourage the children to listen for the beat and join in with the words if they can. Join together in a circle and as you sing, encourage the children to feel the beat through their bodies and keep in time with it by hopping, skipping or walking to the beat, one step at a time. They should also do the miming actions in time with the beat. After the usual actions of getting ready to go to school (put on our clothes, clean our teeth, wash our face, brush our hair, come to school), ask for the children's suggestions for things to do – play the piano, play the flute, bang the drum.

Introduce a second ring game of the same type and to the same tune:

> What shall we do when we go out to play?
> We shall play with a skipping rope
> We shall play with our bicycles
> We shall play with our brand new ball
> We shall play with our friends next door (swing in a pair).

In subsequent sessions, continue to expand the children's repertoire of ring games, always remembering to praise them for moving to the music so well and keeping the beat.

The following are suggestions for other ring games which all involve singing while moving to a definite beat: 'Ring a ring o' roses' (explain the historical connection), 'The farmer's in his den', 'Here we go gathering nuts in May', 'The Grand Old Duke of York', 'The big ship sails on the Ally Ally O', 'Oranges and lemons', 'Here we go Looby Loo', 'The Hokey Cokey', 'We can play on the big bass drum'.

Include games in other languages, for example, in French: 'Sur le pont d'Avignon' (Verses: 'Et les belles dames font comme ça' (curtsey); 'Et les messieurs font comme ça' (flourishing bow); and any others you care to mention and know the French word for! – 'les jeunes filles', 'les garçons', 'les bébés').

Other games and movement rhymes you could include are given below.
▲ Introduce the children to:

> I can hear two soldiers marching in the street,
> Left right, left right,
> Listen to their feet.

Build in two more children at a time (for example, 'I can hear four soldiers', and so on) until the whole class is involved

in marching to the beat with the correct foot, up and down the hall.

Variations might include finger clicking, humming, clapping, quiet and loud parts, quick march versions.

▲ Introduce the children to:

'All around the kitchen, cock a doodle doodle do' (repeat twice for the chorus with the children strutting/hopping round in a circle virtually on the spot, with elbows moving like a chicken flapping its wings, in time to the beat).

For the verses the children could make up different actions in time to the beat, for example:

'Now rub your tummy, cock a doodle doodle do, Now rub your tummy, cock a doodle doodle do, Now pat your head... Now touch your toes...' Repeat the chorus after each verse. Carry on *ad infinitum* or until exhausted. The children's stamina will far outlast your own!

▲ Introduce the children to 'Brown gal in de ring' from Jamaica. Perform the ring game together, all copying the action demonstrated by the child in the centre of the circle. Let a different child take a turn in the centre with each new action. Discuss the interesting language differences afterwards: for example, she 'like' sugar and I like plum; 'Den yu skip across de ocean'; 'Den yu show me yu motion'.

▲ Introduce the children to 'The bear walked over the mountain', developing different kinds of movement such as he ran to another mountain, hopped, skipped, marched, tiptoed, climbed, jumped, stamped, crawled and any alternatives the children can think of.

Session Two: Using parts of the body

Rather than keeping the beat with the whole body, encourage the children to use particular parts of their bodies. The following suggestions lend themselves to the odd few minutes here and there during the day, as they do not demand a large space to work in.

▲ 'Peter hammers with one hammer' – keeping the beat with a fist on the knee; two hammers – two fists; three hammers – two fists and a stamping foot, and so on.

▲ In French: 'Savez-vous planter des choux à la mode, à la mode, Savez-vous planter des choux à la mode de chez nous?'

'On les plante avec le doigt (finger)... le coude (elbow), le nez (nose), le genou (knee), le pied (foot)...' and so on, with the appropriate action to accompany the planting. (This is very similar to 'We are going to plant a bean', but offers the opportunity to celebrate language diversity.)

▲ Hand-clapping the beat or the rhythm can be introduced to accompany any song the children know. (For instance, a short song that the class has adopted as a signal to gather on the carpet at the end of the day, such as: 'Something inside me says, Time for my tea, time for my tea, time for my tea.') First of all, keep the beat, then try the full syllabic rhythm.

As the children's confidence grows, you can move on to play 'traffic lights' using a red and green lollipop signal. When the green signal shows, the children *clap and sing*; but when the red signal shows, they have to *clap only* and carry the song in their heads. Children need a lot of experience before they can do this well, but they all get there in the end.

Hand clapping, body movements and musical accompaniment can all be used to develop children's sense of rhyme and rhythm in language. 'Keyman' (based on the story of Noah's Ark) from *Dandy Shandy* is one example of a song that can be used for this purpose: drums and tambourines suit its insistent rhythm well.

Children can use appropriate instruments to represent particular animals in songs such as 'Old MacDonald had a farm' or 'I went to the animal fair'. Finger clicks, claps, fists on chest and hands on knees can add to the overall effect.

▲ More complicated opportunities can be offered to children when you feel they can cope. Miss out words and replace them with actions (more and more in successive verses), and encourage the children to carry the words and the beat in their heads. You can easily tell as you watch which children can and which cannot yet carry the song in their heads when you see whether they join in, or fail to join in, or indeed never stop singing in the supposedly silent parts! Suitable rhymes for this activity include 'Head, shoulders, knees and toes', 'My bonny lies over the ocean', 'Underneath the spreading chestnut tree' and 'John Brown's baby has a cold upon its chest'.

Session Three: Finger rhymes and counting songs

All cultures have a repertoire of these activities, and it is important to encourage all children to teach examples that they have learned at home in their first language to the rest of the class.

Children can use their fingers for counting or do the actions as appropriate to fit in with the words in the following songs and rhymes:

Counting – 'Five little ducks went swimming one day', 'Five currant buns', 'Five little speckled frogs', 'Five little peas in a pea-pod pressed', 'Ten fat sausages sizzling in the pan', 'There were ten in the bed', 'Ten green bottles' (children often know this song in their first language, so do check and teach it to the whole class) and '1 2 3 4 5, Once I caught a fish alive'.

Traditional rhymes

▲ Cut out the word strips and arrange them in order to make nursery rhymes.

| We all fall down. |
| A pocketful of posies. |
| Ring-a-ring o' roses. |
| Atishoo! Atishoo! |

| So are you! |
| Hark don't you, |
| I'm wet through. |
| I hear thunder, |
| Pitter patter raindrops, |
| Hark don't you? |
| Pitter patter raindrops, |
| I hear thunder. |

Out came
Down c
Incey Wincey Spider
and washe
and drie
So Incey Wincey Spid

Bits and pieces

▲ Someone's broken the teapot! Can you put the pieces back together to make a well-known rhyme?

short   I'm

Tip   stout

teapot   up   little

and   the   my   I

spout   out   a   me

me   and   my

When   me

hear   shout

Here's   handle   see

here's   pour

teacups

Doing the actions – 'I'm a little teapot', 'Incey Wincey Spider', 'Piggy on the railway', 'Two little dicky birds', 'I hear thunder', 'I love to row in my big blue boat' and 'The wheels on the bus go round and round' (but without the sexist images of chattering women). A pop-up book version of this song by Paul Zelinsky (Orchard Books, 1990) is available.

Suggestion(s) for extension

Record the class reciting and singing the different types of rhymes on tape, and video the class playing ring games.

More confident children can work in pairs on photocopiable sheet 143 to cut out and reassemble the scrambled text of 'I'm a little teapot', using word recognition, initial sounds and punctuation cues together with prior knowledge of the rhyme.

Make a book of songs and action rhymes for the Nursery which the children can illustrate, design a cover for, and so on. Evaluate the end product and reflect on what might be done differently next time – size, shape, borders, cover, list of illustrators, contents page.

Present it to the Nursery. Children can work in pairs and take it in turns to read parts of the book aloud to the Nursery class.

Suggestion(s) for support

In small groups with an adult to help, less experienced readers can work with photocopiable sheet 142 to cut out and resequence chunks of text from a familiar action rhyme into the correct order, using word recognition, letter recognition and punctuation cues together with their prior knowledge of the rhyme.

Assessment opportunities

Observe the children when they are dancing, singing, clapping and hearing 'internally', in order to assess their awareness of rhythmical patterns.

Listen to the children's conversation when they are planning and evaluating the book made for the nursery, and their cueing strategies when they are reading aloud to the Nursery children.

Discuss the quality of illustrations in the children's book and the way these work alongside the text.

Opportunities for IT

The sequencing activity could be carried out using a word processor. The teacher could prepare the original text and jumble the order of the lines in the rhyme. Children could then be shown how to move pieces of text around, using either 'cut' and 'paste' commands or drag and drop facilities to reorder the text. Different files could be prepared for children of differing abilities.

An alternative approach would be to use a concept keyboard linked to a word processing package. The concept keyboard overlay would contain the lines in jumbled order. When the child presses on any word in the line, it will be displayed on the computer screen. The final version can be printed out. It would be useful to include a set of arrow keys and a 'rub out' command, so that the children can move the cursor where they want to on the screen and use a rub out line to rectify any mistakes they might have made.

Display ideas

Children could mount displays featuring work based on scenes from songs and counting rhymes from one to ten (including entries in other languages and dialects).

Other aspects of the English PoS covered

Speaking and listening – 1a, c; 2b; 3a, b.
Writing – 1b, c; 2a, e; 3a, b.

Reference to photocopiable sheet(s)

Photocopiable sheet 142 (rearranging lines of rhymes) can be used as a support activity. Sheet 143 (rearranging scattered words in a rhyme) can be used for extension work.

NURSERY RHYMES

For the children to:
▲ *increase their repertoire of nursery rhymes known by heart;*
▲ *sort nursery rhymes according to a set of basic criteria;*
▲ *develop phonological skills and recognition of rhyme;*
▲ *make rhyming associations;*
▲ *respond from a safe distance to suggestions of violence and cruelty mixed with humour;*
▲ *compare alternative versions of nursery rhymes and discuss their cultural and historical origins.*
†† *Sessions One, Two, Three and Four: whole class; Session Five: working in pairs; Session Six: whole class.*
🕐 *Session One: 25 minutes; Sessions Two, Three and Four: 20 minutes; Session Five: 30 minutes; Session Six: 25 minutes.*

Previous skills/knowledge needed

It would be helpful if some of the children already knew some nursery rhymes and could recognise rhyming words; but it is by no means essential.

Key background information

Throughout the series of sessions, it is expected that nursery rhymes will be recited and enjoyed by the whole class/group regularly (at least once every day), with new rhymes being introduced and old favourites revisited. It is also envisaged that the children will be encouraged to read Big Book versions of rhymes in paired and shared reading sessions.

Preparation

Collect and display a wide selection of nursery rhyme books, including a variety of types of book such as treasuries and pop-up books, and tape selections. Don't forget Moslem rhymes and Caribbean collections, for example *The Kiskadee Queen* edited by Faustin Charles (Picture Puffin, 1991) or *The Rebus Treasury* by Jean Marzollo (Methuen, 1986). Also write out poster-sized alternative versions of rhymes to use for class reading in Session Six.

Resources needed

A tape recorder, 'big book' versions of nursery rhymes, copies of photocopiable sheet 144 (one for each child).

What to do

Session One: Introducing the topic

Recite a favourite nursery rhyme to the class and ask which children know it already and where they learned it. Highlight the rhyming words. Discuss briefly why they think nursery rhymes are easy to remember – for instance, strong rhythms, tune, rhyme, actions, frequency, fun element. List the first lines/titles of all the other rhymes they know on a flipchart. You will probably end up with quite a lengthy list, so praise the children for their extensive repertoire.

Working from the list, ask the children to sort the rhymes into four sets: those about animals, those centred around boys, those centred around girls and those centred around grown-ups. Then choose one category at a time to look at more closely. If you start with animals, rhymes in this category might include: 'Hickory Dickory Dock', 'Pussy cat, Pussy cat, where have you been?', 'Ding dong bell, Pussy's in the well', 'Baa, baa, black sheep', 'Sing a song of sixpence', 'Hey diddle diddle', 'Ride a cock horse to Banbury Cross', 'Old Mother Hubbard went to the cupboard', 'Mary had a little lamb', 'Incey Wincey Spider', 'Little Bo Peep has lost her sheep', 'Three blind mice', 'Higgledy piggledy, my black hen', 'Tom, Tom, the piper's son', 'Goosey goosey gander'.

Discuss the rhymes in this category. For example, discuss the plight of some of the animals in the rhymes; historical factors; reality and fantasy. You can then let the children take turns in choosing rhymes from the list of titles to recite together. Encourage the children to spot the rhyming words after each one.

Session Two: Boys in nursery rhymes

Start this session by looking at the list of nursery rhymes the children compiled in the first session, and then look more closely at the rhymes in another set, for example nursery rhymes that are centred around boys. Rhymes in this category could include: 'Georgie Porgie', 'Wee Willie Winkie', 'Diddle diddle dumpling, my son John', 'Little Jack Horner',

'The Queen of Hearts', 'Little Boy Blue', 'Simple Simon', 'Ding dong bell', 'What are little boys made of?'

Recite some of the rhymes with the children and help them to learn any that they do not know. Discuss the images of boys in these nursery rhymes. Are they always naughty or silly? Are there any exceptions? Are boys like this in real life? Are all boys the same? Are the rhymes set now or in the past? How have boys' lives changed over the years?

Session Three: Girls in nursery rhymes

Look at the list of nursery rhymes again and then focus on another category, for example nursery rhymes centred on girls. Rhymes in this category might include: 'What are little girls made of?', 'Mary had a little lamb', 'Mary, Mary, quite contrary', 'Little Polly Flinders', 'There was a little girl and she had a little curl', 'Little Miss Muffet', 'Little Bo Peep', 'Polly put the kettle on', 'Roses are red'.

Recite some of the rhymes in the list together and help the children to learn any new ones, so that they will increase their repertoire. Discuss the image of girls as presented in these rhymes – is it a one-sided image? Do they always appear to be incompetent in these rhymes? What are girls really like? Is there only one accurate answer to this question? Ask the children to think about all the girls they know. What are they like? Do they fit the image of girls in the nursery rhymes? Are the rhymes about girls today or girls in the past? You might then like to talk with the children about how girls' lives have changed over the years – for instance, what they wear, what they can do, where they can go, what they can say, how they behave.

Session Four: Grown-ups in nursery rhymes

Focus on the last category of nursery rhymes drawn up in the first session, in this case rhymes centred on grown-ups. Read out the list of rhymes together. Rhymes in this category might include: 'There was an old woman', 'Doctor Foster went to Gloucester', 'I do not like thee, Dr Fell', 'Goosey Goosey Gander', 'Jack Sprat could eat no fat', 'Old King Cole', 'As I was going up the stair', 'Pat-a-cake, pat-a-cake, baker's man', 'Lavender's blue, dilly dilly', 'Peter, Peter, pumpkin eater', 'There was a crooked man', 'One fine day in the middle of the night'.

Then recite some of them together. Discuss the images of adults and adult life as portrayed in these nursery rhymes. Ask the children to compare it with what they know about adults from their own families, and note down the similarities and differences on the flipchart.

Session Five: Identifying nursery rhymes

Give each child a copy of photocopiable sheet 144. Explain to the children that it is quiz time and that they must pretend to be detectives to work out the answers to the picture clues on the photocopiable sheet. Each picture on the sheet represents something that belongs to a character in a nursery

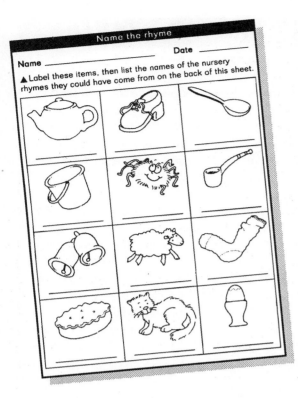

rhyme. Their task is to identify the object, label it and then work out which nursery rhyme character(s) would have such an object and which nursery rhyme(s) they appear in. They should then write the title(s) of the rhyme(s) for each picture. The children should work together to make these decisions. Encourage discussion and thoughtful reasoning rather than wild guesses and instant answers.

Session Six: Alternative versions

Introduce to the children the notion that there are often alternative versions of songs and rhymes – for example, 'Happy Birthday to you, Squashed tomatoes and stew...' or 'Here comes the bride, forty inches wide...' Sing a few of the alternative versions together and then ask the children if they know any alternative versions of nursery rhymes. Below are just two versions the children may come up with:

> Humpty Dumpty sat on a wall
> Eating ripe bananas.
> Where do you think he put the skins?
> Down the king's pyjamas.
> or
> Roses are red,
> Violets are blue,
> Onions stink
> And so do you.

If offensive versions are offered, you can use the occasion to develop children's knowledge about language: discuss the appropriateness of language; when, where and with whom we use different types of language; and what is acceptable in school. If racist or sexist versions are offered, the underlying attitudes need to be discussed.

If the children do not know any, recite some alternative rhymes to the class and show a poster-sized version on a flipchart to read and learn together.

Introduce to the class alternative versions of nursery rhymes that you have found in books from the library. Tell them to the children or show them enlarged versions. For example:

> Hickory Dickory Dock
> The mice ran up the clock.
> The clock struck one ...
> And the cat got the other two!

Read them together and encourage the children to use the enlarged versions of rhymes for paired reading during the week.

Tell the children that you want them to conduct a survey over the next couple of weeks to find out how many alternative versions of nursery rhymes are known in your school. Let them work in pairs to collect as many alternatives as possible from all the other classes. At the end of the survey, the children should share their findings and discuss the differences between the alternatives as well as between them and the originals. Encourage them to look for any common pattern emerging, such as alternatives often being humorous or subversive, and talk about this with the children.

Finally, the children can make posters of their favourite alternative rhymes, and then these can be used for paired or independent reading.

Suggestion(s) for extension

Experienced writers could create a quiz game by writing out questions about particular characters in nursery rhymes on pieces of paper or card and then putting them into a hat. Each child in the class could then pull out and read aloud a question for the others to answer, for example: Who jumped over the moon? Who fell asleep at work?

Provide cut-up text from two – or more, as appropriate – different nursery rhymes all muddled up together, for children working in pairs to unscramble.

Suggestion(s) for support

Record some rhymes on tape and set up a nursery rhyme listening corner for children who may not be familiar with many of them.

An adult could read the 'big book' version of *Each Peach Pear Plum* by Janet and Allan Ahlberg (Viking, 1991) to inexperienced readers, helping them to identify the nursery rhyme characters involved.

Some children will need adult support to prompt them and scribe for them when working on the photocopiable sheet, and when playing the games described above.

Assessment opportunities

Note in particular children's contributions when discussing issues, reading and chanting, interviewing peers for the school survey, enjoying the humour of alternative versions of rhymes and working on photocopiable sheet 144.

Opportunities for IT

In Session Six, children could word-process their own favourite alternative rhymes to make posters for display or use in the classroom. They could experiment with the font style and size to make the poster eye-catching.

Display ideas

Ask the children to write out their favourite nursery rhymes and illustrate them. These could then be displayed alongside the quiz questions and some of the posters of alternative versions of rhymes.

Work with the children to produce a frieze based on one rhyme, showing each event in sequence like a storyboard.

Other aspects of the English PoS covered

Speaking and listening – 1a, c; 3a, b.
Writing – 1a, b; 2b, c, e; 3a, b.

Reference to photocopiable sheet(s)

Photocopiable sheet 144 requires children to identify drawn items and state what nursery rhymes they have come from, relying on memory and reasoning rather than guesswork.

RHYMING STORIES

For the children to:
▲ *further develop their 'ear for language';*
▲ *recognise rhyme and produce rhyming words of their own;*
▲ *predict text by using rhyming features as cues;*
▲ *join in reading with an adult, taking over parts of the text by recalling the line endings that carry the rhyme;*
▲ *engage in shared reading activities;*
▲ *use rhyming techniques and rhythmical patterns to invent new names.*

†† *Session One: 20 minutes, then 20 minutes follow-up; Session Two: 20 minutes; Session Three: 25 minutes; Sessions Four and Five: 30 minutes; Sessions Six, Seven and Eight: 20 minutes.*

🕐 *Session One: whole class, then pairs or small groups; Sessions Two and Three: whole class; Session Four: working in small groups; Sessions Five, Six, Seven and Eight: whole class.*

Previous skills/knowledge needed

It is assumed that the children will already be familiar with rhyme, probably in the form of nursery rhymes, and that they will not be inhibited by the presence of a tape recorder.

Key background information

By providing texts with strong rhyming and rhythmical patterns, these activities allow children to engage in successful and enjoyable reading experiences. The security of choral reading also builds children's confidence in themselves as readers. Children's ability to recognise and supply rhyming words will also be developed.

Preparation

Write out large-print versions of couplets from *Bringing the Rain to Kapiti Plain* by Verna Aardema (Picture Mac, 1986), and cut them up to support children's reading on to tape.

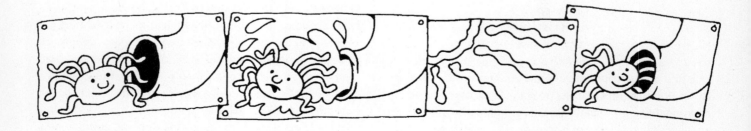

Resources needed

A collection of stories that rhyme, for example, the Lynley Dodd *Hairy Maclary* books such as *Hairy Maclary From Donaldson's Dairy* (Picture Puffin, 1986) and *Hairy Maclary's Rumpus at the Vet's* (Spindlewood, 1989), *Bringing the Rain to Kapiti Plain, The Giant Jam Sandwich* by John Vernon Lord (Pan Piper Paperbacks, 1988); one copy per child of photocopiable sheet 145, a tape recorder, musical instruments, writing and drawing materials, a flip chart.

Question and answer

Name _____ Date _____

Can you remember who caused the rumpus?

Who had a troublesome beak and gave Hairy Maclary a tweak?

Who had a bottlebrush tail and jumped over the rail?

Who came from Parkinson Place and joined in the chase?

Who forgot he was sore and clattered all over the floor?

Who, in a thundering rage, crashed into a cage?

What to do

Session One: Introducing Hairy Maclary

Read one of the *Hairy Maclary* books, such as *Hairy Maclary From Donaldson's Dairy*, to the children. Encourage them to respond to the story and listen to their spontaneous reactions. You can then help the children to discuss particular aspects of the story, such as the dogs' antics (compare them with children's own pets) or the choice of names for the dogs (what do the children think is unusual and appealing about these? Do they tie in with each dog's character or appearance? What are the children's own pets called? Encourage the children to make comparisons with the pets in the book.)

Ask the children whether they noticed how easy it was to guess what was coming next as you were reading the story. Can they see why? Introduce the term *rhyme* to them if they do not know it already. Reread the story to the children and encourage them to join in with you on the rhyming words.

During the week, read another story in this series: *Hairy Maclary's Rumpus at the Vet's*. Highlight the rhyming patterns once again, as well as enjoying the humorous incidents in the plot.

In the follow-up session, distribute a copy of photocopiable sheet 145 to each child and ask the children to work in pairs or small groups. Draw their attention to the rhymes in the questions, then ask them to recall the events in sequence to help them answer the questions.

Session Two: Guessing games

Reread the *Hairy Maclary* story used in the previous session; but as you read, pause to leave gaps so that the children can provide the missing text. The first time you read it, miss out one rhyming word (for instance, 'Bottomley Potts, covered in _____'). On a subsequent reading, miss out the whole rhyming phrase; for example, read 'Bottomley Potts', then pause for '____ ____ _____'; 'Muffin MacClay _____ ____ ____ ____ ____'. Then miss out the whole couplet

on turning the page, and use the picture clue to prompt the children. You can then play an oral game of 'I spy', giving the rhyme as a clue and asking the children to supply the name of the character. For example, 'I spy a dog with a very low tum. Who am I?... I am a dog who looks like a bundle of hay. Who am I?'

Explain to the children that you are now going to make the game more fun by asking questions using a different word that rhymes with the one in the book, so they will need to think very carefully. For example, 'I am a dog that has got no mum. Who might I be?' or 'I am a dog that was born in May. Who might I be?' You could brainstorm possibilities with the class before you start the game; so for 'Muffin MacClay like a bundle of hay', you could have bay, day, May, pay, play, say, gay, way, and so on.

Session Three: What's in a name?

Recap the unusual names of the dogs in the *Hairy Maclary* story and look at them together one at a time. For example, why is Hercules Morse a good name for a dog as big as a horse? Do any of the children know who Hercules was? Explain if necessary. Hercules was the Roman name but the same man was called Heracles by the Greeks... so the dog could have been called Heracles Morse. Show how the name still fits the rhythm of the line – clap three beats for Hercules and three beats for Heracles.

Can the children think of any other names with three beats, such as Timothy, Anthony, Jennifer, Nicholas, and so on? Ask them to test each name by putting it together with Morse. Do these new names sound like suitable names for a dog? How about some more creative ones with three beats, for example, Appleby, Pommely, Rhapsody... Clap out the

Poetry

rhythms of the new names together. What about using words that suggest size but aren't really people's names, such as Tidalwave Morse, Towerblock Morse, Juggernaut Morse? Collect as many of these humorous ideas as you can.

Now suggest that the children change the second name – let them use both made-up and real names, as long as these still rhyme with Morse and horse. Allow the children two minutes' 'buzz' with the person sitting next to them; then write down all their suggestions on a flip chart in alphabetical order. Ask them how they worked out their rhyming names, and show on the flip chart how the *end* of the word stays the same and only the initial letter or blend is changed. Go through the alphabet together to see if any possible rhymes have been missed.

Session Four: Rhyming alternatives

Divide the class into groups to work in the same way as in the previous session. Ask the children to brainstorm as many alternative first and second names as possible for the other dogs in the *Hairy Maclary* story. Encourage the children to clap the beats of each name to make sure that it fits the rhythm of the name (for instance, Bitzer Maloney: two claps plus three claps).

Allow about 20 minutes for this; then gather together as a whole class. Ask each group in turn to present their list of alternative names, and encourage the response of the other children. Which names do they prefer? Which don't work very well? Why don't they work very well? Consider such factors as the quality of the rhyme, the effect of the combination of sounds, whether it 'sounds like' the name of a dog. Praise the children's efforts.

Session Five: Introducing a new book

Before reading *Bringing the Rain to Kapiti Plain*, show the cover to the children. Point out how the front and back covers operate as a double-page spread. What does the illustrator tell us here? Where do they think the book is set? What do they think is the author's attitude to the animals? How can they tell? Ask them to look at the title too. What does it tell us? Draw on the children's prior knowledge about Africa – has anyone been there, lived there, seen programmes on television about it, read anything about the continent; does anyone have family living there?

Now read the story to the class and discuss the cumulative pattern: how each event is linked to the next and to the conclusion. Remind them of other stories structured in a similar way that they already know – for example, the old woman who swallowed a fly, or *The House That Jack Built* by Emily Bolam (Macmillan Children's Books, 1992). Were their predictions about this story correct?

Comment on the artwork, the poetic use of language, the expressions or vocabulary that were particularly memorable. Consider made-up words like 'green-up', and the effect of the rhyme and rhythm on the reader.

Finally, reread the story and encourage the children to join in as and when they can.

Session Six: Clapping the rhythm

Discuss the traditions of dance and music in Africa with the children, and introduce the idea of the talking drum (which is used to send messages from village to village). Read the story of Kapiti Plain, and ask the children to clap the beat as you read.

Read a small section again while the children clap the full syllabic rhythm instead of just the pulse-beat. Then reread the book with the children alternating between clapping the beat and clapping the full rhythm for each couplet in turn. For example: Clap the beat only for the first couplet – *It fell near Kipat* (one clap while saying that), *Who watched the herd* (again one clap), *As he stood on one leg* (one clap),

Like the big stork bird (one clap). For the next couplet, clap the full rhythm with a clap for each syllable – *Kipat whose cows were so hungry and dry* (10 claps of varied length to fit the words), *They mooed for the rain to fall from the sky* (10 claps again). For the next couplet, clap the steady beat only; and for the next couplet, clap the full syllabic rhythm.

After several accompanied readings or when the children are comfortable with this pattern, split the class into two groups so that each group claps a different accompaniment as you re-read the story.

Session Seven: Preparation for a choral reading

Tell the children that they are going to perform a choral reading of *Bringing the Rain to Kapiti Plain* to the rest of the school. You can act as the narrator to get the tale going; then seven different pairs, trios or quartets of children, depending on the size of the class, will be needed to take on the recitation:

This is the *cloud* all heavy with rain
That shadowed the ground on Kapiti Plain.

This is the *grass* all brown and dead
That needed the rain from the cloud overhead.

These are the *cows* ...

This is *Kipat* ...

This is the *eagle* ...

This is the *arrow* ...

This is the *bow* ...

The whole class will recite the final stanza together: *This is the shot* to the end of the story.

NB Point out the subsequent variations after the very first introduction of the different elements. For example, 'This is the cloud' becomes 'The big black cloud' in the repeats.

Let the children choose the parts they would like to recite and form themselves into groups. They will need the large-print couplets you have prepared to help them practise. Several rehearsals will be needed for the collective reading, so that there are no awkward gaps between couplets. However, it is important to make the reading fun and not a chore – with emphasis on enjoyment of choral chanting, not on a prize-winning performance.

The children can include musical accompaniment to suggest the shimmering heat, the mooing of the cows, the twang of the bow, the flight of the arrow, the clap of thunder and the deluge of rain; and you can use a tape of African music to lead the children into the assembly.

Session Eight: From story to drama

Introduce *The Giant Jam Sandwich* by J.V. Lord and J. Burroway (Cape, 1972) to the class, telling them that this is another story told in rhyme. Ask the children to pick up clues as to what the story could be about from the front cover and the blurb on the back cover.

Then read the text and encourage the children to respond to the story, enjoying the humour and sympathising with the plight of the town.

In subsequent sessions, structure a narrative based on the events in this story. Working in role, the children will have to negotiate, make decisions and solve problems. There will be letters and newspaper articles to write, speeches to be made, interviews to be held, and so on.

Suggestion(s) for extension

Encourage the children to read and enjoy with their friends the other Lynley Dodd books about Hairy Maclary and his gang. Remind them to continue trying to predict as they read.

Some children may like to retell the story of *The Giant Jam Sandwich* in a storyboard format, using a maximum of eight pictures.

More experienced readers could be asked to investigate whether words that rhyme have to be spelt the same way. Working in pairs, they could go through the list the class have compiled and suggest alternative spellings (such as Morse/Maughs) by making comparisons with other words they know already .

Suggestion(s) for support

Some children will need the support of an adult to provide cues for reading and clues to prompt recall when using the photocopiable sheet. They may also need help with recognising and suggesting rhyming words. It may benefit some groups to read or hear the *Hairy Maclary* story again, with attention focused on the hunt for particular answers, before they tackle the task. Try to avoid open access to the book, question by question, to eliminate straight copying without any discussion.

Assessment opportunities

Note children's contributions when offering rhyming words, joining in with the stories, reading on to tape, and so on. Look for confidence, understanding of purpose and ability to make appropriate rhyming suggestions.

The children's involvement when making lists of names, storyboarding, writing speech bubbles and retelling the tale gives a good indication of their level of interest, perseverance,

pride in their work and level of independence in transferring ideas to paper.

Opportunities for IT

In Session Three, children could write their description of one of the dogs using a word processor. This could be printed out for display along with the picture.

Display ideas

Display work from these sessions could feature a vet's surgery including drawings of animals, notices about illnesses, posters, adverts for pet food, opening hours, and so on; Cruft's Dog Show; a frieze of Kapiti Plain, or a baker's shop window complete with written labels for the varieties of bread on sale (for making sandwiches).

Children could also display their work on rhyme and the writing arising from the various roles in the drama.

Other aspects of the English PoS covered

Speaking and listening – 1a, c, d; 2a, b; 3a, b.
Writing – 1a, b, c; 2a, b, c, d, e; 3b.

Reference to photocopiable sheet(s)

Photocopiable sheet 145 requires children to answer questions based on a rhymed story they have heard, developing their feel for rhyme and rhythm by recalling names from the story.

CHILDREN'S PLAYGROUND GAMES

For the children to:
▲ *enjoy playing with language;*
▲ *enjoy the surreal language of nonsense verse;*
▲ *respond to the rhythmical patterns in language;*
▲ *recognise rhyme;*
▲ *compare the various versions of songs or chants found across areas of Britain and abroad;*
▲ *discuss feelings and issues involved in rhymes;*
▲ *complete partially obliterated text by using a range of reading strategies;*
▲ *experience other languages than English.*
†† *All sessions: whole class.*
🕐 *Session One: 15–20 minutes; Session Two: 20 minutes; Session Three: 25 minutes; Session Four: 20 minutes.*

Previous skills/knowledge needed

It will be helpful if an atmosphere of trust has already been established in the classroom, with children feeling free to take risks; and if talking about language is an integral part of classroom life.

Key background information

The importance of socialisation should not be underestimated: we all need to feel that we belong. Playground games have a crucial part to play in this process, and these sessions provide an opportunity for teachers to contribute to it. By celebrating the vernacular, they also bring a welcome breath of fresh air into the classroom.

Preparation

Display a collection of books about rhymes, skipping, ball games, clapping games, dipping games and rhymes from children's folklore. *Rhymes about Fun Times* edited by C. Hurst (DLM, 1989) and *Inky Pinky Ponky* edited by Michael Rosen and Susanna Steele (Picture Lions, 1982) are both useful sources of rhymes. Read *The Lore and Language of Schoolchildren* by Iona and Peter Opie (Paladin, 1977), *I Saw Esau* by Iona Opie (Walker Books, 1992) and *The People in the Playground* by Iona Opie (Oxford University Press, 1993).

Resources needed

One copy of photocopiable sheet 146 for each child, a tape recorder, a computer, writing and drawing materials.

What to do

Session One: Introducing the project

Explain to the children that they are going to work on a project about the games they play in the playground. Hold a class brainstorming session to identify as many games as possible, and write these on a flipchart – for example, skipping, clapping, ball, dipping, tag, jokes, team games, hide and seek. Discuss which ones they play most, what they used to play in the past, and whether some games are played more in winter or in summer.

Session Two: Collecting playground rhymes

Remind the children of the list of games they drew up in the previous session, and then focus on the games that involve talking or singing – using language in some way. Ask them for examples and add some from your own childhood. Write down the first line or title of each one and then discuss the range of topics they cover, such as:

▲ Growing up – 'When Suzy was a baby'.

▲ Girls in charge – 'My boyfriend gave me an apple'.

▲ School – 'No more Latin, no more Greek, we're off school for potato week!' or 'We break up, we break down, we don't care if the school burns down.'

▲ Adults – 'Mrs White had a fright in the middle of the night'.

▲ Nonsense – '1 2 3, Mother caught a flea, put it in a teapot and made a cup of tea' or 'It's raining, it's pouring, the old man is snoring'.

▲ Well-known characters – 'I'm Popeye the sailor man, full stop' or 'Cinderella dressed in yella'.

▲ Shock value – children will almost certainly suggest rhymes such as 'Batman and Robin in the batmobile'.

Session Three: Rhyming games

Recap the rhymes suggested by the children in the previous session and talk about the range of playground games they cover.

▲ Skipping – 'I'm a little girl guide dressed in blue, these are the actions I must do, salute to the King and curtsey to the Queen, and show your knickers to the football team' or 'Down in the kitchen doin' a bit o' stitchin', in comes a burglar and knocks you out'.

▲ Dipping for games of tag or other purposes – 'One banana two banana three banana four'; 'Ip Dip Battle Ship'; 'One potato two potato...'

▲ Clapping – (pairs) 'Down by the bramble bushes' or (circle) 'I've got the German measles'.

▲ Scissor-jumping – 'The cat's got the measles'.

▲ Juggling with two balls – 'One two three a lairy, me Mam's gone down the dairy, gone to fetch me Auntie Mary, one two three a lairy'.

Discuss what the children like about these games, and where they learned them. How hard is it to learn to skip? What about the variations – backwards, crossing over the

READING

rope, and so on? How easy is it to turn a long rope with someone else at the other end? Who do they play all these different games with – boys, girls, older children, younger children, their own class? Is it easy to join in the games in the playground? If not, why not? How do they feel if they are left out? How do they help new people to join in? How do they feel if they don't do something very well or let their side down?

Why are the rhymes so easy to remember, even when they are very long? Do the children always know what the words mean, for instance in 'High Low Dolly Pepper...'?

Session Four: Rhymes in other languages

Encourage bilingual children to teach the class some chants in their first language. Take the opportunity to teach some variants from other parts of the world yourself, if none are forthcoming – for example, the Barbados version of 'Down by the bramble bushes':

Down by de bamboo bushes
Down by de sea
Johnny break a bokkle and he blame it ahl on me
I tell my mama
I tell my papa
An Johnny get a lickin'
With a ooh, aah, cha cha cha.

Or the French dipping chant:

Am stram gram
Pic et pic et colégram
Bour et bour et ratatam
Am stram gram pic!

Discuss similarities and differences between these rhymes and British rhymes the children know.

Suggestion(s) for extension

Invite an expert to visit the school to talk about how playground games originated and to introduce to the children some older versions of rhymes that they can learn. Take photographs during the visit, and encourage the children to write about it and the things they have learned afterwards for inclusion in a display.

In groups, the children can then decide on a particular category of rhymes to investigate further and can hunt through books in the school library, the local library and from the class collection. Assemble as many variants of particular rhymes as possible. Photocopy the children's favourites and enlarge them to poster size, so you can all read them together and learn them by heart. Compare and contrast the various versions.

Invite a parent or grandparent into the school to talk about the playground games they played when they were young. Encourage the children to ask questions to extend their learning. Children could then interview their own parents or grandparents about their favourite rhymes, and report back to the class. They could bring tape-recorded versions of any

unusual rhymes they discover back to school for everyone to hear.

Suggest to the children that you all write to a school in a different area or in another country that you or they might have connections with, to enquire about their playground traditions. Compose a communal letter together and enclose an illustrated anthology of favourite rhymes from your area.

Contents page

Name _____ Date _____

▲ Something's gone wrong at the printers. Can you finish off the Contents page from a book of playground rhymes?

1. The cat's got the measles
2. It's raining, it's pouring, the old man's snoring
3. I'm Popeye the sailorman full stop
4. Cinderella dressed in yella
5. Mrs White had a fright
6. I'm a little girl guide dressed in blue
7. When Susy was a baby
8. 1 2 3 mother caught a flea
9. Cowboy Joe(s) from Mexico
10. Batman and Robin in the batmobile

When responses arrive – a very exciting moment for the class – compare the two sets of rhymes. This could be the beginning of a twin-school arrangement that could prove very fruitful in other areas of the curriculum as well.

The children can work in pairs or small groups to decipher the names of the rhymes on photocopiable sheet 146, where the text is printed with only one half of the letters showing. The children will need to use graphophonic clues, in conjunction with contextual cues and knowledge of the rhymes, to puzzle this out.

Suggestion(s) for support
Less experienced readers and writers can select their favourite rhymes to include in an anthology for the school. With the help of an adult, the work can be word-processed and 'published'. Decisions about fonts and layout can be taken jointly. Then, as a group, the children can read the rhymes aloud and record them on tape for the class listening corner.

When working with photocopiable sheet 146, some groups will need the support of an adult to prompt their use of the various reading strategies.

Assessment opportunities
Observe the children's conversation during their work on rhymes and games. This gives a good indication of their understanding and recall, opinions and feelings about outdoor play, ability to compare different versions of rhymes and prediction skills when working on the photocopiable sheet.

Opportunities for IT
Children could use a word processor or simple desktop publishing software to write and produce a class anthology of playground rhymes. They could also print out some larger versions of rhymes for display in the classroom. Children could explore the use of different font styles and sizes and the use of colour to make the displays more interesting.

If the school has access to electronic mail through CAMPUS or the Internet, children could write to schools in other parts of the country, or the world, to ask for examples of playground rhymes. These could be added to the class anthology and displays.

Display ideas
Favourite rhymes can be written out neatly or word-processed and then illustrated and mounted on to coloured card with decorative borders. These can be incorporated into a class display featuring playground scenes with captions. The work resulting from the expert's visit, accompanied by photographs, would also make an effective display. Other possibilities include: letters, maps, drawings and photos from a school in another area/country; and what the children have found out about childhood rhymes and games that were popular in the past.

Other aspects of the English PoS covered
Speaking and listening – 1a, b, c; 3a, b.
Writing – 1a, b, c; 2e; 3a, b.

Reference to photocopiable sheet(s)
Deciphering the half-printed lines of text on photocopiable sheet 146 requires children to combine memory of playground rhymes with letter and word recognition.

PLAYING WITH LANGUAGE

For the children to:
▲ *enjoy word play;*
▲ *build on their knowledge of sound-symbol associations;*
▲ *recognise, enjoy and produce alliterative phrases;*
▲ *recall and make up jokes;*
▲ *increase their experience of riddles;*
▲ *develop their skill at rhyming;*
▲ *use similes effectively and create similes of their own.*
†† *Sessions One and Two: whole class; Session Three: whole class, then small groups; Session Four: whole class, then pairs or small groups; Sessions Five, Six and Seven: whole class.*
🕐 *Session One: 30 minutes; Session Two: 20 minutes; Session Three: 20 minutes, then 25 minutes; Session Four: 15 minutes, then 20 minutes; Session Five: 20 minutes; Session Six: 25–30 minutes; Session Seven: 25 minutes.*

Previous skills/knowledge needed
It will be helpful if the children have already been encouraged to take an active interest in letters, words, phrases and meanings.

Key background information

These activities encourage children to look carefully at (and listen carefully to) words and their meanings and usage. They will not only extend children's vocabulary, but also ensure that children start to enjoy learning about language and become keen to develop the range and sophistication of their own language use.

Preparation

Provide a collection of books on all forms of word play – puns, jokes, riddles, limericks. *The Lore and Language of Schoolchildren* by Iona and Peter Opie (Paladin, 1977) will come in handy as a reference text for examples of all kinds of word play. *Knock Knock Pop-up Book* by Colin and Jacqui Hawkins (Walker Books, 1990) and *Sky in the Pie* by Roger McGough (Puffin, 1985) are other popular titles.

Write out poster-sized versions of tongue-twisters for shared reading.

Resources needed

Writing and drawing materials, a tape recorder, a computer, a copy of photocopiable sheet 147 for each child.

What to do

Session One: Focus on alliteration

A simple way to tackle alliteration is to concentrate on one letter each week. For example, brainstorm all the proper nouns, other nouns, verbs and adjectives beginning with B that the children can think of – with some prompting from you, if necessary. Write them on a flip chart in columns according to their language function (all the verbs together, and so on).

Explain to the children that you are now going to play a game based on *alliteration*, by making up sentences with as many words as possible that start with the same letter – in this case, B.

Each child can pick one word from each column to make an alliterative sentence. For example:
Betty bought a bunch of blue begonias.
Billy baked a batch of big biscuits.
Bryony borrowed a birthday bangle.
Baby blew bubbles in bed.

Read these out aloud and arrange them into verses on the flip chart, looking for the best rhythmical effect. When you are satisfied with the result, supply a title (again selected from the wordlist) and recite the whole as an alliterative poem. Later in the day or week, children can work in pairs or groups to create a similar poem of their own.

Session Two: Focus on tongue-twisters

Introduce tongue-twisters to the children as alliteration taken a step further. You could begin with an old favourite which the children may well know already, 'Peter Piper picked a peck of pickled pepper', and read it together slowly from your prepared poster. Try to speed up on subsequent readings without tripping up!

Use the range of tongue-twisters you have written out on posters for the children to read along with you. Try them in turn over the week. For example:
'She sells sea shells on the sea shore.'
'Sister Susie sews shirts for sailors.'
'How many cookies could a good cook cook, if a good cook could cook cookies?'
'The sixth sick sheik's sixth sheep's sick.'
'Swan swam over the sea.'
'I saw Esau sawing wood.'
'Betty Botter bought some butter.'

The children can have fun timing each other with stopwatches to see who can recite a tongue-twister the most times in one minute.

Encourage the children to practise reading the posters during the week.

Session Three: Focus on similes

Read *A Dark Dark Tale* by Ruth Brown (Red Fox, 1992) and listen and respond to the children's reactions.

Focus on darkness. Discuss with the children how we can often get a more accurate picture if we make comparisons between things. Ask the children to think of *similes* that describe darkness by comparing it with something else – for example, as dark as night.

Move on to consider other similes they know: as black as coal, soot; as white as snow, a sheet, chalk; as cold as ice, as the grave; as warm..., snug..., light..., heavy..., good..., clever..., kind..., brave..., quiet..., pretty..., busy..., handsome..., keen..., old..., safe..., plain..., deaf..., wise..., quick..., sharp..., proud..., hungry..., clean..., bright..., strong..., weak..., cool..., blind..., happy..., miserable... Write them all down on a large poster-sized sheet or flip chart.

Tell the children that these similes have been in use for a very long time and have become over-used, so they have lost some of their power – their impact on the listener or the reader – and are in need of a new lease of life. Brainstorm a few fresh ideas for similes, then introduce similes focusing on the feelings of a new boy or girl in the school playground. For example:

My first day at a new school

In the playground
I felt as lost as an abandoned teddy
As lonely as the last person on earth
As miserable as a king without a kingdom
As awkward as a fish without a tail.

Talk with the children about the choices made in this verse and how effective they are. Encourage them to suggest alternatives.

Explain to the children that, in small groups during the day, they will use photocopiable sheet 147 to share ideas and compose a second verse to the poem. They will need to think carefully in order to provide innovative and accurate comparisons which convey the feelings of the new child when he has been in school for a term and has made some friends.

Ask the children how the new child might be feeling by then, and brainstorm possible adjectives: happy, excited, elated, ecstatic, delighted, glad, cheerful, thrilled, exuberant, bubbly, terrific, and so on. Encourage them to think of comparisons to make good similes that capture the feeling exactly.

At the end of the day the groups can present their poems full of vibrant similes to the rest of the class for constructive comment and suggestions for further improvements.

Session Four: Other aspects of similes

Introduce the children to another type of simile, using *like* instead of *as;* this is generally used to describe how somebody does something or how somebody feels. For example: like a scalded cat..., like a cat on hot bricks..., like a cat on a hot tin roof..., like a bear with a sore head..., like a bull in a china shop..., like a child with a new toy..., like a ship in full sail..., like a ship without a sail..., like a boat without a rudder..., like a dog in a manger... Discuss what these similes mean and what mood or manner they are describing.

Talk to the children about how they feel on special occasions such as their birthday, Christmas, Eid, Diwali, New

Year or any other special time. Ask them to think of any similes to describe those feelings, using *like...*

Introduce a poem starter, such as the one given below, and organise the children into groups or pairs to complete the poem using a simile for every alternate line:

My special day
The doorbell rings.
Like a dog with two tails
I dart for the door
Like a...

A workshare and review session at the end of the day will offer a further opportunity to reinforce children's appreciation of similes.

Session Five: Focus on jokes

Ask the children which comedians they watch on television, and which ones they have seen in pantomimes or on other occasions. What do they like about them especially? Would they like to be a comedian when they grow up? Do they know enough jokes to be a comedian? Who knows some jokes already? Share a few of them with the class.

Discuss with the children what makes jokes funny. Ask whether they think that jokes are sometimes cruel or hurtful. Do the children feel that it is all right to make jokes about anything and anyone? If not, why not?

Suggest that the children make a class collection of good jokes. Where can they look to find jokes? Who can they ask? Discuss how to go about collecting and presenting the jokes. The project might include the following:

▲ In a class library session, children can hunt for joke books to take back to the class for browsing and paired or group reading.

▲ Children can interview their families at home to bring back jokes for the class collection.

▲ Children can interview other classes in the school and add their contributions to the class collection.

▲ Children can work in pairs to invent some jokes of their own.

▲ As a class, the children can then choose favourites from each category of jokes – for example, elephant jokes, doctor jokes, knock-knock jokes, lightbulb jokes, 'what's the difference between' jokes – to put in the class joke book.

▲ In turn, children can read out, say, three jokes per 'carpet session' from the class joke book once it has been published.

▲ The class could write to a well-known comedian enclosing a copy of the class joke book. Children would need to decide which questions they would like to ask the comedian about his or her job and how he or she thinks up new jokes and prepares for telling them to a large audience.

Session Six: Focus on limericks

Read a selection of limericks to the children from the class book collection (there is a selection in the *Young Puffin Book of Verse*) and talk about the rhyming pattern and the set rhythmical pattern. Ask the children if they know any others.

Look at a limerick together – for example, one of Edward Lear's limericks:

There was an old man on the border
Who lived in the utmost disorder.
He danced with the cat
And made tea in his hat,
Which vexed all the folks on the border.

Write out a large version of the limerick on a board or flipchart for the children to read with you, then work on an alternative version together. Ask the children how it can be done so as to keep the rhyme and the rhythm. You will need to keep reading it aloud to check whether their new ideas sound attractive to the ear.

For example, *on the border* in the first line could become *called Phil Corder*. What other words might fit there? Write down all the possibilities. What else could he dance with that rhymes with cat? Where else could he make tea that rhymes with hat? Write down every suggestion that would fit, then make final choices together and perhaps create several different versions. The children could write these out later for a display.

Little Nancy Netticoat wears a white petticoat, the longer she lives the shorter she grows. (A candle.)

First I am as white as snow,
Then as green as grass I grow.
Next I am as red as blood,
Lastly I'm as black as mud. (A blackberry.)

Give children clues to help them solve the riddles if they are stuck.

Point out that there is a close link between the structure of riddles and the structure of jokes, and that the children probably know a lot of both. They both rely on playing with language. For example, with jokes: Why did the chicken cross the road? Why did the cow look over the wall? Why does the Duke of Edinburgh wear red, white and blue braces? With riddles: What holds water yet is full of holes? (*A sponge.*) What goes up when the rain comes down? (*An umbrella.*) What goes up but never comes down? (*Age.*) What grows with its roots upwards? (*An icicle.*)

Ask the children to carry out a riddle hunt over the week, and encourage them to make a personal collection of favourite riddles to read aloud to the class at the end of the week. Encourage them to work co-operatively to try to make up some riddles of their own to share with the class as well. Remember to allow plenty of time for the riddle exchange to take place!

Assessment opportunities

Observe the children's contributions when making suggestions for alliteration and similes; during shared reading sessions; when planning answers using the photocopiable sheets; and when writing poems and riddles. Look for understanding of language use and word play, and creative use of language. Check handwriting skills in the copying out of jokes and riddles for display.

Opportunities for IT

The work in Session One lends itself well to the use of a word processor. The amount of text to be typed is limited, and as children's ideas develop they can easily add extra words to their sentence to make it longer and more complicated. The final result can be printed out in large type for display in the classroom, or for inclusion in a class anthology.

In Session Three, children could be presented with the first verse of the poem on a word processor and then complete the second verse at the keyboard; while in Session Four, groups of children could write their poem using a word-processor. Some groups might need an adult to scribe for them and channel their thoughts and ideas.

In Session Five, children could word-process their own anthology of jokes, making them more interesting by using a variety of fonts, type sizes and colours. Each child could be

Session Seven: Focus on riddles

Children love riddles and delight in copying them out and collecting them, and their interest can be channelled into this topic.

Explain to the children that riddles date back for centuries. Share a few very old ones with the children. For example: 'How deep is the ocean?' (a stone's throw) or 'How many balls of string will it take to reach the moon?' (Only one, if it's long enough.)

Introduce the following James Reeves riddle poem (which can be found in many anthologies) to the children without telling them the title, and ask them to listen carefully as you read it out. At the end, ask them to solve the riddle and supply a title for the poem.

I can get through the doorway without any key
And strip the leaves off the great oak tree.
I can drive storm-clouds and shake tall towers,
Or steal through a garden and not wake the flowers.

Sea I can move and ships I can sink,
I can carry a house-top or the scent of a pink.
When I am angry I can rave and riot;
And when I am spent, I lie quiet as quiet.

Discuss the children's ideas about possible answers, the clues they found in the words, and so on. Tell them that many riddles are much shorter than that. Offer alternatives for the children to solve. For example:

Riddle me, riddle me, riddle me ree, I saw a nutcracker up in a tree. (A squirrel.)

responsible for one page of the joke book, which could be written over a period of time. If a simple desktop publishing package is used, each child could have a page with three frames on it – one for each joke. It might also be possible for children to illustrate their jokes by scanning in their hand-drawn pictures.

Children could word-process their own favourite riddles in Session Seven to make a class anthology, or present them in larger print to make a display of riddles for the classroom wall or another part of the school. Children could also use a word processor to write their own riddles.

A simple authoring package could be used for children to make an interactive riddle game. Each page could present the reader with the riddle, which is linked to another page that contains the answer. The child clicks on to the answer icon and is taken to this page. It would also be possible for children to record themselves speaking the riddle and the answer, and include this in the presentation. This would enable non-readers to enjoy the riddles. Bilingual children could record the spoken riddle in their own language.

Display ideas

The children could contribute to a 'Let's celebrate word play' display, featuring a mixture of all the different forms they have enjoyed. This display can be added to gradually as the weeks go by. The answers to riddles can be presented in a 'lift the flap' format, and children can provide paintings to illustrate similes.

Other aspects of the English PoS covered

Speaking and listening – 1a, b, c; 2a, b; 3b.
Writing – 1a, b, c; 2a, b, c, d, e; 3b.

Reference to photocopiable sheet(s)

Photocopiable sheet 147 invites children to continue a poem based on emotive similes, developing their capacity for imaginative use of language as well as their awareness of human emotions.

🖥 POEMS

For the children to:
- ▲ *enjoy hearing poetry read aloud;*
- ▲ *read familiar poems to each other;*
- ▲ *learn new poems by heart;*
- ▲ *become more confident, competent and independent readers by following the print in 'big books';*
- ▲ *recognise rhyme;*
- ▲ *provide words that rhyme;*
- ▲ *recognise rhythm patterns in words;*
- ▲ *complete modified texts;*
- ▲ *broaden their knowledge about language and their awareness of language diversity.*

†† *Sessions One to Five: whole class; Session Six: whole class; Session Seven: whole class, then pairs or small groups; Session Eight: pairs or small groups; Session Nine: pairs, groups or whole class.*

🕐 *Session One: 20 minutes; Session Two: 25 minutes; Session Three: 30 minutes; Session Four: 20 minutes; Session Five: 20 minutes; Session Six: 30–35 minutes; Session Seven: 40 minutes; Session Eight: 30 minutes; Session Nine: 30–35 minutes.*

Previous skills/knowledge needed

It is preferable if the children are used to listening and responding to others and to expressing their opinions in a large group. It is expected that there will be a positive attitude throughout the school towards language diversity. It would be beneficial if a class visit to the local library could be arranged to evaluate the children's poetry collection. A class visit from a poet, to talk about his/her work or run a workshop with the children, would be of enormous benefit.

Poetry

Key background information

These activities develop children's 'ear for language' and their appreciation of the rhythms of language, as well as increasing their phonological awareness and their ability to recognise and supply rhyming words. They also extend the decoding strategies and critical responses of young readers, and encourage the use of children's own writing as valid reading material.

Resources needed

A wide selection of 'big books' and sets of smaller versions for the children to take home to share with the family (most reading schemes now include 'big books' covering a broad range of songs, rhymes, stories and non-fiction).

A collection of poetry books, including work by such poets as Ahlberg, Rosen, McGough and Nichols but also ensuring a variety of poets, both male and female, from all around the world writing in different dialects of English. Useful titles include *Mother Gave a Shout, Poems by Women and Girls* edited by S. Steele and M. Styles (A & C Black, 1990); *Stop That – An Anti-bullying Rap* by L. Simeon and R. Clifford (Blackie, 1994); *A Caribbean Dozen* edited by John Agard and Grace Nichols (Walker Books, 1994); *Come Into My Tropical Garden* by Grace Nichols (Young Lion, 1992); *Singing Down the Breadfruit and Other Poems* by Pauline Stewart (Red Fox, 1994).

Also required are posters, book covers, brochures for poetry festivals, pictures and biographies of poets to create an initial stimulus display; a tape recorder, musical instruments, paints and drawing materials, writing materials and a computer.

What to do

Session One: Working with 'big books'

A daily 'storytime' devoted to poetry is invaluable, especially if you use 'big books'. Here are a few suggestions.

Focusing on a familiar theme such as Ourselves is a useful way to introduce children to poetry. *Here Are My Hands* by Bill Martin Jnr. and John Archambaut (DLM, Bobber Books 1987) is one book that concentrates on this theme. The rhyme and rhythm of the text will support young readers, and the 'big book' format allows you to finger-point to the print as you read and enables children to follow the text with their eyes at the same time as following it with their ears.

As well as the support for decoding offered here, there are interesting points for discussion too. The two main areas of thinking and feeling represented in the book provide plenty of scope for talk; it cannot be stressed enough just how important it is for young children to be encouraged to express their emotions verbally.

Down by the Bay (Macmillan/McGraw Hill, 1993) is a traditional rhyme, with illustrations by G. Ancona that show a child in a wheelchair amongst a group of friends romping on the beach. The rhyme, rhythm and humour, together with the repetitive pattern, offer great support for young readers. Encourage prediction as you read, and talk with the children afterwards about the features that make the book so easy to read. Encourage the children to suggest extra creatures that you might add to the list to extend the rhyme.

Leave the book out, as usual, for paired reading during the week, and very soon the children will be reading it successfully on their own.

This is the Bear by Sarah Hughes (Candlewick Press, 1986) has a running link all the way through the story which children will pick up: the bear who fell in the bin, the dog who pushed him in, and so on. The speech bubbles provide an added point of interest that you can talk about with the children after you have read the story.

With the emphasis on prediction and use of picture clues as well as the rhyming features of the text, the Bobber Book version of the traditional rhyme *Susie Moriar*, with illustrations by Mark Foreman (1977), is another story that children can read quickly and independently. They are forced to make predictions as a rhyming word is replaced by a picture each time. For example, 'This is the story of Susan Moriar, It started one night as she sat by the [picture of a fire].' You can always increase the level of difficulty by covering the picture, if appropriate.

Session Two: What is a poem?

Read a few of your own favourite children's poems to the class from any anthology you particularly enjoy. Your

enthusiasm in this session will be crucial in helping the children to enjoy the poems too. Listen and respond to the children's immediate reaction to the poems, then shift the emphasis of the discussion so that they begin to try to define what is special about poetry. To help them, ask questions such as:

▲ Do they like poetry – why/why not?

▲ How is a poem different from a story book?

▲ Are poems as long as or shorter than story books?

▲ How could they change a story into a poem?

▲ Is it the way a poem is written on the page with shorter lines that makes the difference?

▲ Is it the sort of words that are used in poems?

▲ Are all poems about certain particular things, or can they be written about anything?

▲ Do poems always rhyme?

▲ Do they have a special rhythm?

▲ Are there refrains and repetitions, or a set pattern of words?

▲ Why do poems stick in the memory?

▲ Who writes them?

Try to end the session by concluding that poems are usually economical with words, with redundant words being deleted and the words that remain being carefully chosen. Children should also realise that musicality is important in poems – a definite rhythm and sometimes rhyme, which you need to hear read out aloud to get the full flavour of the 'memorable speech', and which feels good on the tongue as well as to the ear.

Session Three: Making a class anthology

Tell the children that they are going to make a class anthology of favourite poems with an accompanying tape. First, however, you are all going to the library to hunt for some poetry books. Once in the library, ask the children if they know the name of a poet. Has anyone seen one on television or heard one on the radio? Is there someone whose work they especially want to look out for? Do they want to look for anthologies and/or books of poems by a single author? Do they want poems on any particular theme?

Remind the children about the features that are designed to help us choose a book: cover and blurb, contents page and index. After browsing and making choices, gather the children in a circle to share findings and comment on each other's books. Read one or two poems before returning to the classroom to whet children's appetites for future poetry bookshares.

Once in the classroom, the children will need several short sessions when they can browse through the books before they will be ready to select a favourite poem to work on with a friend. Tell the children that they are going to make a taped reading of their poem when they feel ready. They will also write a short piece justifying their choice. This will appear alongside their poem in the class anthology. The anthology will need a contents page, a list of 'editors' or 'critics', an index and an enticing cover, as well as the selected poems written out neatly or word-processed, with attractive patterned borders to the pages and, perhaps, some illustrations – all of which will take several sessions to complete.

Session Four: Reading rhymes aloud

Help the children to feel confident about reading aloud by introducing short easy-to-learn poems with a very strong sing-song rhythm. Keep a regular daily slot for this purpose, so that the children rapidly build up their stock of known poems. Children will very quickly be able to join in at the ends of lines as you read, because of the support of the rhyme and

the rhythm; and soon they will know the whole poem by heart. Encourage paired and shared reading of the known texts during the week, and encourage the children to read with gusto and feeling. Before very long, the children will be reading these poems independently and successfully.

The following suggestions from the *Young Puffin Book of Verse* are popular choices for children at KS1. For the most part, they are centred on themes close to the children's early experiences and do not make too many demands too soon: 'Jeremiah Obadiah, puff, puff, puff' (this poem appeals to children because the central character flouts the conventions of behaviour normally imposed on children by adults); 'One-eyed Jack the pirate chief' (this appeals for similar reasons and is another great favourite); 'I'm looking for a house, said the little brown mouse'; 'Clink clink clinkety clink, the milkman's on his rounds I think'; 'When I grow up I'd like to be a window cleaning man'; variations on 'The old woman who lived in a shoe'; 'Bidderly-do, Bidderly-do, I'm on a train and I'm off to Looe' (with a wonderful rattling steam train rhythm); 'Jemima Jane, Jemima Jane, loved to go out and splash in the rain'; 'What is the matter with Mary Jane, she's crying with all her might and main'.

Children also enjoy playing with nonsense verses that stretch words and language to the limit in a humorous way. The work of Edward Lear is a popular example of such verse, and is a good place to start. *The Owl and the Pussy Cat* illustrated by Louise Voce (Walker Books, 1991) and *The Quangle Wangle's Hat* illustrated by Helen Oxenbury (Heinemann, 1985) will delight children, who always revel in the fascinating made-up words – the Crumpetty Tree, the Fumble Fowl, the Pobble who has no toes, the Dong with the luminous nose, the Aterry Squash, the Bisky Bat, the Mulberry Moon.

Another poem that is eagerly soaked up by young children is John Rice's 'Bears Don't Like Bananas' in the collection *Ten Golden Years* (Walker Books, 1989).

Session Five: Extending the range

Children cannot, of course, learn every poem by heart, though they will always remember half-phrases and snippets throughout their lives. As the children's appreciation develops, read longer and more complex poems about more serious issues to them and allow plenty of time to talk about the ideas represented as well as the language patterns.

Encourage the children to find their own favourites, share them with friends in regular bookshares and take them home to read with the family.

Use of the vernacular is commonplace in poetry, and this is one area where children can read and enjoy works in a range of dialects. Below are listed some titles particularly suited to this purpose.

▲ *Albert and the Lion* by Mariott Edgar (Methuen, 1978) is a fun way to generate discussion, and the language can be compared with your local dialect. If you have children in your class with connections in a variety of different areas of the country or parts of the world, you could perhaps try rereading the poem in other accents and dialects to see what changes would have to be made for Cockney, Geordie, Brummie, Creole, and so on.

▲ Grace Nichols' 'Wha Me Mudder Do' from *The Song That Sings the Bird* (Collins, 1989) carries a strong rhythm and a recurring refrain, enabling children to pick up and join in with the reading quickly. Gender issues can be discussed as children consider what everyone's mother can do if she wants to (or has to); and there are a range of linguistic features for the children to analyse. Which words are new to the children? Do they know the exact meaning of *fufu*, for instance, and *calaloo stew*? Does it matter what the exact meaning is? Compare the language with Standard English forms and local dialect forms.

Children could perform the poem with hand-clapping and drumming accompaniment in assembly.

▲ Adrian Mitchell's 'Rattin' It Up' from *Ten Golden Years* (Walker Books, 1989) lends itself perfectly to rapping sessions with feet stomping, body movement, hand clapping and a persistent drum beat. Again, there is plenty to discuss about the language used and the laid-back attitude of the town rats!

▲ More experienced readers will enjoy reading the humorous verses in Colin Hawkins' *The Granny Book* (Fontana Lions, 1984). Written mainly in rhyming couplets, the text reads aloud well, so inexperienced readers can benefit from hearing you read it before moving on to read it themselves. Children of all ages will have fun poring over the illustrations. An Author Bank video (Children's Book Foundation, Harper Collins) on Colin and Jacqui Hawkins is available.

Session Six: From reading to writing

Explain to the children that they are now going to be poets themselves and write a poem together. Use a shared experience or a stimulus such as a picture, an artefact or a story as a focus for ideas, then follow these steps:

▲ Quickly capture the children's initial ideas on to a flipchart.

▲ Narrow the focus, picking the most interesting parts to write about.

▲ Write the ideas out in whole sentences composed by the children, making decisions as you go by asking them questions and taking a vote if disagreement arises about wording or emphasis.

▲ When you have finished, ask the children why the text they have created is not a poem yet.

▲ The next step is to dispose of redundant words and lay the text out on the page in a different format. As you change things, check for ways to improve vocabulary, punctuation, and so on. Keep reading the words aloud to hear how the poem sounds – this is a very useful tool to help poets make a choice.

▲ Write out a finished, agreed version and read the poem aloud together.

▲ Different sections could be read by groups, pairs or solo voices, for greater effect.

▲ Encourage the children to word-process their work for publication and to co-operate on decisions about illustrations, book format and page decorations.

Session Seven: Question and answer poems

Read the story 'Frederick' from *Frederick's Tales* by Leo Lionni (Andersen Press, 1986) to the children and discuss different aspects of the story before drawing the children's attention specifically to Frederick's poem:

Who scatters snowflakes? Who melts the ice?
Who spoils the weather? Who makes it nice?
Who grows the four-leaf clover in June?
Who dims the daylight? Who lights the moon?

A series of questions provides the first verse of a poem, then the second verse provides us with the answers.

Suggest to the children that they write their own question

and answer poem, but that they do it in a slightly different way – by asking a question, then providing an answer straight away. You could keep the seasons theme and capture on paper children's impressions of the current time of the year – and their personal associations with particular times of the year (for example, in winter: frosty mornings, the nip in the air, the bands of fog at their door, frost patterns on the car windows…)

Then divide the children into pairs to work on the questions they would like to ask about these natural phenomena. Encourage them to ask questions along the lines of: *Why? Who? When? What? Where?* Try to make the questions interesting: *Why does the fog swirl in circles? What makes the icicles sharp? Where does the frost go in summer?* They can then pass their questions to another pair, who try to think of unusual answers. Emphasise that these should not be the first ideas that spring to mind – they can jot ideas down, then think more carefully about them before deciding.

You can amalgamate the work of the two pairs and arrange it as a question and answer poem, possibly alternating different voices all the way through or performing it as a choral reading. Finally, each group of four can present their poem to the class.

Session Eight: Like-loathe poems

Divide the class into pairs or groups of four and ask the children to choose a theme on which to base a poem. It is more productive if this is an issue that is important to them – for example, television, football, weekends, holidays, my big brother, and so on. Ask them to write down five sentences saying why they like the chosen topic. Then ask them to take an opposing view and to write down five sentences saying why they don't like it. Put the two together to make two verses, or alternate the two line by line to make a poem.

Alternatively, one pair could work on the 'Why I love…' aspects of the theme while the other pair work on the 'Why I loathe…' aspects. The two strands can then be amalgamated to make the poem.

As always, gather as a class at the end of the session to share the work.

Session Nine: Stretch-elastic poems

The children can work in pairs, individually, in small groups or communally as a whole class, as appropriate to their level of experience, confidence and competence. The poems can be about any subject chosen by the children, or suggested by you if the children are vacillating. Offer a range of possible alternatives, if necessary – but not too many, or that will confuse them.

The basic idea behind this activity is for the children to write one line first and then to keep on doubling the number of lines until they have a poem! Probably eight lines will be enough for most children initially; but this could be as low as four for some, or as high as sixteen for others.

For example:

One line: *I lift up my pencil.*

Two lines: *I lift up my pencil*
                and suck on it.

Four lines: *I lift up my pencil*
                and suck on it.
                I close my eyes
                and think hard.

Eight lines: *I lift up my pencil*
                and suck on it.
                I close my eyes
                and think hard.
                No thoughts come a-running
                to flood my head.
                No words rush down
                to the page.

Sixteen lines: *I lift up my pencil*
                and suck on it.
                I close my eyes
                and think hard.
                No thoughts come a-running
                to flood my head.
                No words rush down
                to the page.
                I just can't do it
                I tell you.
                It's no good, Miss,
                I just can't.
                I'm not a poet
                and we all know it.
                So let's just leave it,
                All right?

This series of activities could culminate in a 'poetry festival' where each child reads her own work. The whole collection of children's poems could be 'published' on a word processor and presented to the school library.

Suggestion(s) for extension

Experienced writers would benefit from further opportunities to write poems – individually, with a partner or in a small group, according to preference. Encourage them to try some of the following:

▲ Acrostic poems – perhaps on children's names to begin with, for example:

> **M**y very special friend
> **A**nd a whole heap of fun
> **R**eally makes me chortle
> **Y**es, she's number one.

▲ Shape poems – for instance, the sun is a simple one to start with. Word associations form the rays and make a sun very easily. A shape poem called 'My mum, the ray of sunshine in my life' could have the word *mum* in the centre, with all the words the children can think of in relation to their mums as the rays emanating from the centre (kind, funny, smiling, and so on).

▲ Choral chants arising from group work. Noises are a good focus for this – gather snippets overheard at the shops, on the way to school, on the bus. Organise them to form a poem using repetition for emphasis, or a refrain to give an insistent beat.

▲ Poems from the five senses – sights, smells, noises, touches, tastes. Children can choose any suitable topic to write about, such as a class trip to a local wood. Divide a page into five areas and tell the children to jot down thoughts in each of the sections; then the poem is already organised as five separate verses, or they could use a line from each section as part of each verse.

READING

Suggestion(s) for support

Inexperienced readers may need adult encouragement when reading their favourite poems on to tape. For some children, the question/answer and like/loathe poetry sessions may be more appropriate as oral activities; or an adult could act as scribe.

Assessment opportunities

Observe the children's contributions when reciting, joining in as you read and spotting rhymes and rhythms; when comparing and contrasting dialect features; and when preparing their writing. Note their ability to read aloud with expression.

Children's poems will reveal their vocabulary awareness, sense of rhythm, ability to rhyme, confidence in tackling writing in different forms and growing competence in secretarial skills.

Opportunities for IT

In Session Six, children could work in pairs or small groups to complete the poems at the computer. The teacher could type in the poems and replace the deleted words with stars or leave gaps. If the poem is then saved as a file, each group of children can load it on to the word processor and fill in the missing rhymes, printing out their work and saving it to disk under their own name so that it does not overwrite the original text. The children will need to be shown how to position the cursor where they want to put a word, delete the stars and type in their word. They may also need support to load the starting text on to the word processor and save their completed version.

The teacher could prepare other poems for different ability groups, deleting more or fewer words, or selecting easier or more difficult words to be replaced. Some children might like to prepare their own poems in a similar way for other groups to work with.

In Session Eight, if the school can link their computer to a large television screen or can borrow an OHP computer tablet, this exercise can be conducted on the computer so that the class can all see the poem developing on the screen. As the composition of the poem progresses, the teacher or another adult can draft and edit the original version. Printouts of the completed poem can be made and given to different groups, who could use them to practise for a performance or as a starting-point for further refinement or extension. In the latter case, the group could return to the original computer version and redraft this.

In the extension section, the poems could be written using a word processor; in this case, pieces of text can be positioned on the screen using the space bar or other formatting commands. Alternatively, the children could use a simple graphics package which would enable them to move the text around the screen in a wide variety of ways. The children will need to be shown how to key in the text, select it and move it around the screen to wherever they want it to be. More experienced users might want to rotate the text to make, for example, a ray pattern.

The poems that the children write could be typed into a word-processor or simple desktop publishing program and presented in the form of a book for display in the class, library or school display area for others to read.

Display ideas

The initial stimulus display can be extended by adding a selection of children's work alongside some work by their favourite poets, plus the children's views on what a poem is alongside the views of established authors such as Ted Hughes and Michael Rosen. Children's 'work in progress' on their various poems would validate the process of writing; and paintings of scenes and people encountered in poems could add a different dimension. The work of a particular child could be featured as 'poet of the week'. You could highlight language diversity by displaying poems in a variety of different dialects.

Other aspects of the English PoS covered

Speaking and listening – 1a, b, c; 2b; 3a, b.
Writing – 1a, b, c; 2a, b, c, d, e; 3a, b.

CLOZE PROCEDURE

For the children to:

▲ *use their knowledge of rhyme and rhythmical patterns in language to reconstruct incomplete texts.*

†† *Children working in pairs or small groups. Final session(s) as whole class.*

🕐 *30 minutes per sheet. Feedback sessions: 30–35 minutes.*

Key background information

Cloze procedure activities encourage children to use a range of reading strategies – linguistic, contextual, graphophonic – to complete a text. They are particularly effective if the children subsequently talk about their reasons for making choices. It is helpful (especially with inexperienced readers) for the children to have some prior knowledge of the text in order to use contextual clues more successfully. Any texts connected with the work you are doing in class can be used in this way.

Here, two different cloze procedure activities will be used to provide evidence of children's reading strategies using the support of rhyme and rhythm. The first activity will provide either observed or taped evidence, and in the second children will read their versions of the poem and justify their choices in a reporting session to the class. The children will need to be familiar with cloze procedure and being recorded on tape while they are working.

Resources needed

One copy of photocopiable pages 148, 149 and 150 for each child, tape recorders, writing materials.

What to do

Read 'The Dark' by Adrian Henri (from *Ten Golden Years*, Walker Books, 1989) to the class and discuss any feelings the children have about darkness. Then note the simple structure of the poem, and the powerful effect it has on the reader. Tell the children that they can now write a poem of their own about the dark. They can follow the same structure, keeping the same rhythm with the same number of beats, but supplying their own words. Clap out the rhythm with the children until they are sure of it; then recap their ideas about how they feel in the dark.

Divide the class into pairs and give out photocopiable sheet 148 for the children to complete the poem. If you are not directly observing the groups as they complete the activity, leave a tape recorder on the table where they are working, so that you have access to their conversation and thinking processes in order to assess their strategies for deciding which words they wished to use. Allow 15–20 minutes, then gather the class together for the children to read their poems in turn.

Because we are focusing on rhyme and rhythm, and because the theme of dinosaurs seems to have universal appeal, we suggest using *Tyrannosaurus Was a Beast* by Jack Prelutsky (Walker Books, 1988) as an exemplar for the second activity. Over the week, read the poems from the book to the class, so that the children are familiar with the poems but do not know them by heart.

Then divide the class into small groups and distribute copies of photocopiable sheet 149 (about Ankylosaurus). Explain to the children that they will have to read the poem through and then supply the missing words – remembering that the poem has to make sense and keeping to its rhythmical and rhyming pattern. Allow about 15 minutes for

READING

this; then reassemble as a class for the children to read their offerings. Talk about possible alternatives that would work well, and about problems (words that rhyme but don't make sense, or vice versa).

In a subsequent session, follow a similar format for photocopiable sheet 150 (where every tenth word has been nibbled by a Brachiosaurus).

These activities will provide evidence of children's learning in the tangible form of the completed photocopiable sheets, and in spoken form as children talk and explain their vocabulary choices. This can be used for a summative assessment not only of what children know about rhyme and rhythm at the end of this chapter, but also of what knowledge and skills they can put to effective use. It will also provide general information about their developing reading strategies when they read their versions of the poems aloud to the class.

Suggestion(s) for extension
Experienced writers may like to write their own poems about a different dinosaur.

Suggestion(s) for support
Some children will need an adult to read the text through with them before they can suggest ideas for completion.

Display ideas
Children's paintings and clay models of dinosaurs can be displayed alongside the completed cloze procedures and the children's own poems. Artwork and poems based on the children's fears of the dark can also be included.

Other aspects of the English PoS covered
Speaking and listening – 1a, b, c; 2a, b; 3a, b.
Writing – 1b; 2a, b, c, d, e; 3a, b.

Reference to photocopiable sheets
Photocopiable sheets 149 and 150 are cloze procedures based on poems the children have listened to. Photocopiable sheet 148 is similar, but invites a creative response.

The Dark

Name _____ Date _____

▲ Fill in the gaps to make your own version of this poem.

I don't like the dark coming down on my head

It feels like _____

I don't like the dark coming down on my head.

I don't like the dark coming down over me

It feels like _____

I don't like the dark _____

I don't like the dark coming _____

It feels like _____

Adrian Henri

Clankety clank

Name _____ Date _____

▲ Fill in the gaps to complete the poem.

Clankety, clankety, clankety clank

Ankylosaurus was built like a _____

its hide was a fortress as sturdy as _____

it tended to be an inedible meal.

It was armoured in front, it was armoured _____

there wasn't a thing on its minuscule _____

it waddled about on its four stubby _____

nibbling on plants with a mouthful of pegs.

Ankylosaurus was best left _____

its tail was a cudgel of gristle and _____

Filling the gap

Name _____ Date _____

▲ Brachiosaurus has been nibbling again! Please fill in the gaps to finish off the poem.

Brachiosaurus had little to do

but stand with its _____ in the treetops and chew,

it nibbled the leaves _____ were tender and green,

it was a perpetual eating _____

Brachiosaurus was truly immense,

its vacuous mind was uncluttered by _____

it hadn't the need to be clever and wise

_____ beast dared to bother a being its size.

Brachiosaurus was _____ and slow,

but then, there was nowhere it needed _____ go.

if Brachiosaurus were living today,

no doubt it _____ frequently be in the way.

Jack Prelutsky

Information & instructional texts

Most children's earliest acquaintance with books and reading is through stories, poems and rhymes learned by heart. They quickly learn the characteristic features of narrative texts, and draw on their prior knowledge to set up predictions that help them to read new, unfamiliar books in the same genre. However, information books (and data banks on CD-ROM) operate in a different way, and children need to become accustomed to the conventions of this genre before they can use them with confidence.

Teachers have a role to play here by ensuring that during storytime, children become familiar with information books as well as narrative and poetry, so that non-fiction can be enjoyed as an area of interest in its own right and not just as an aid to topic work. This may prove particularly important for boys, since research shows that more boys than girls underachieve in reading and that they seem to prefer non-fiction books to fiction.

This section focuses on ways of supporting young children as they read non-narrative texts by providing activities that will guide their reading and help them to locate information, list questions to interrogate a text, select appropriate information, organise new information and communicate their findings. Learning to take advantage of the supporting features in information texts is crucial, so due emphasis is placed on the use of structural guides such as headings, index, contents, glossary, subheadings, captions, illustrations and diagrams.

Information books provide ideal opportunities for reading across the curriculum; many of the activities have strong links with topics in science, history, art and geography.

READING

EVALUATING INFORMATION BOOKS

For the children to:

▲ *be aware of structural reference guides in non-fiction texts;*

▲ *know and understand the important role these features play for the reader;*

▲ *evaluate a range of non-fiction books using these features as criteria.*

†† *Sessions One, Two and Three: whole class; Session Four: small groups.*

🕐 *Session One: 35 minutes; Session Two: 20 minutes; Session Three: 25 minutes; Session Four: 45 minutes.*

Key background information

These activities are most effective if they are based around a class topic you are currently working on, in order to provide a meaningful purpose. Alternatively, they could be linked with a survey of the school library or resources in general. This will lay the foundation for supporting children in the early stages of reading for information, and start the process of learning to read non-fiction texts effectively – that is, selectively and reflectively.

Preparation

Make a collection of non-fiction books on a current class theme. Read *How It Looks* by Sue Walker and *Desktop Publishing for Teachers*, both published by the Reading and Language Information Centre at Reading University.

Resources needed

Materials for small groups to draw up charts when recording findings; one copy of photocopiable sheet 151 per pair of children.

What to do

Session One: Introduction to information texts

Tell the children that they are going to be working as researchers, finding out how useful the non-fiction books in the class collection or in the school library are, whether they are helpful to readers looking for information, whether they could be improved and if so, how.

To begin with, explain to the children that they will be allowed two minutes to survey a book to find out everything they can about it. They can then tell the rest of the class what the book is about. Give every child a book and start the stopwatch! After the two minutes are up, give each child a chance to report what they found out from the quick survey of the book to the class.

Next, ask the children what they did in those two minutes to learn as much as possible about their book. Who started reading from the beginning? Who looked at the pictures? Who looked at the title/contents page/index? What did they think was most helpful and why? What was not very helpful? What would they have done if it had been a story book? Explain to the children that non-fiction books are different from story books, so they have to be read in a different way. Tell them that they will be carrying out further investigations during the rest of the week.

Session Two: Development

Recap what was learned in the introductory session before moving on to take a closer look; then, working with a few non-fiction texts as exemplars, talk through all the main features of books in turn, using the proper terms:

▲ *The front cover:* What information does a front cover offer – for example, the title, the author, the illustrator? Note whether there are any borders, whether photographs or drawings are used, the style of lettering that has been chosen, whether the cover is in colour or black and white. Ask for the children's opinions about the choices made. Will the cover appeal to readers? Does it set a tone or a mood? Can you tell from the cover that this is an information book and not a story?

▲ *The back cover:* Point out the blurb. Ask the children what this tells them. Compare it with an advert that is trying to 'sell' the book to the reader. Point out the ISBN number and explain that this is like a passport number for this particular book – no two are the same.

▲ *The spine:* Check what information is provided here.

▲ *The endpapers:* In some books, these pages provide clues as to what the book is about.

▲ *The half-title page, then the title page:* Check what information is provided.

Remind the children to make use of these supports when they are reading for information, and tell them that they will carry on with their investigation of features of books that help readers during the next few days.

Finally, allow 15 minutes' silent reading with a selection of non-fiction books, so that the children can put their new-found knowledge to good use.

Session Three: Fine details

Using a selection of non-fiction books, continue investigating different ways of obtaining information as quickly as possible. Tell the children that together, you are going to look very closely all the way through a book to find every feature that might be helpful.

Point out chapter headings, chapter openings, page numbers, sub-headings, illustrations, photographs, diagrams, captions, bold type, summaries and any other details, and discuss each one as you come across them with the children to show how much can be discovered without reading the whole of the book.

Remind the children of the two-minute stopwatch game, and ask how much more they think they could find out in two minutes now that they know about all these helpful clues. Try the game again, making sure each child has a different book from last time!

Session Four: Evaluating books

Explain that you are now going to evaluate a selection of non-fiction books from the school library in readiness for your next classroom topic, to make sure that they have all the features that help readers to find the information they need.

A book record sheet			
book title			
contents			
chapters			
page numbers			
headings			
pictures			
photographs			
diagrams			
captions			
index			
glossary			
bibliography			

▲ *The title verso page:* Ask the children what information can be found on this page. Children are often fascinated by copyright logos, and sometimes incorporate them when they are writing their own books!

▲ *The contents page:* Discuss how useful this is, and when we would use it.

▲ *The index:* Draw the children's attention to this feature (and ask the children for instances of when and how they would use it). Note the alphabetical order of entries.

▲ *The glossary:* Point out some of the words listed, and encourage the children to comment on how useful they might find a glossary.

▲ *The bibliography:* Discuss with the children when this could be of help.

Together, recap the features found in Sessions Two and Three and write them on a flip chart or board to serve as the left-hand column of a chart, allowing two other columns for book titles and a space for a tick should the book indeed have the required feature. Evaluate one book together, using this chart to model the process of locating and recording findings for the children (allow about ten minutes for this).

Now take the children to the school library to work in pairs on evaluating the books. Each pair will need a copy of photocopiable sheet 151 to record the names of the book titles they evaluate and to mark ticks as appropriate in the boxes. Each pair can report their results back to the class, using their chart and the books evaluated as evidence. The children can then decide whether there are enough resources for your next class topic, or whether you need to find more from elsewhere.

Look at the books again to find out which publishers usually offer readers proper support and which do not. Encourage the children to write to those that do not, pointing out the lack of these features and the reasons why they need to rethink their policy. You could do this as a communal activity, or invite each pair to write to their own offending publisher.

Suggestion(s) for support
More able readers could be paired with less able ones. Alternatively, some children could be paired with an adult to help in the search for structural guides, to channel discussion and to help with recording findings.

Assessment opportunities
Note how well children use the structural guides as they survey the books. Which ones were able to remember new terminology, to read titles and other features confidently, to record findings independently on the chart, to copy titles quickly and accurately?

Other aspects of the English PoS covered
Speaking and listening – 1a, c; 2a, b; 3b.
Writing – 1c; 2a, b, e; 3a, b.

Reference to photocopiable sheet(s)
Photcocopiable sheet 151 is a book record sheet which the children can use for recording observations about the books they investigate in the library.

GROWTH

For the children to:
▲ *develop their strategies for retrieving information from non-fiction books by using structural guides to find out specific information;*
▲ *use a range of cues to sequence and match labels and pictures;*
▲ *recognise and use an appropriate format for writing instructions.*
†† *Session One: whole class; Session Two: working in pairs; Session Three: whole class and group work; Session Four: working in pairs.*
🕐 *Session One: 25 minutes; Session Two: 25 minutes; Session Three: 30 minutes; Session Four: 30 minutes.*

Previous skills/knowledge needed
Before the sessions, arrange for a keen gardener to visit the class to talk about gardening; or alternatively, take the class to visit a nearby garden centre, so that the children are familiar with the special vocabulary associated with the topic.

Key background information
Children will locate, retrieve and put to use information from non-fiction texts within the context of a class theme, and will use their skills to resequence sets of cards, match captions to illustrations and devise instructions for planting seeds of various sorts.

These activities could equally well be linked to human or animal growth.

GARDEN CENTRE

Preparation

Assemble and display a collection of books on seeds, plants, gardens, germination, flowers, fruit and vegetables. Collect seeds and stones from a variety of fruits, for example avocado, apple, carrot tops, beans, cress, alfalfa.

With the children's co-operation, convert the home corner into a garden centre with an emphasis on writing in role – signs showing opening hours, directions, plant categories, sale notices, adverts, receipts, cheques, labels for plant pots detailing care of plants, and so on.

Resources needed

A copy of photocopiable sheets 152, 153 and 154 for each child, materials and tools for planting and caring for plants – trays, plant pots, a trowel, compost, labels, seeds.

What to do

Session One: Formulating questions

Begin by finding out what the children already know about growing plants. Ask whose family has a garden, a window garden, an allotment. What do they grow in them? Who has planted anything before? What happened to it? Who has seen programmes on television or read anything about how plants grow? What do they remember about the needs of a plant when it is growing? How does it start to grow? Scribe all the information the children provide on to a flipchart or a large sheet of paper for everyone to see.

Tell the children that they are going to put on their gardeners' gloves and plant some beans in school. Discuss what else they think they need to know before they can begin.

Remind them about the range of question words – What? When? Where? Why? Who? How? – to stimulate their questions, and note down all the questions they feel they need to find answers for. For example:

▲ What do they need to do first?

▲ What will they plant the beans in?

▲ Where should they put the beans while they grow?

▲ What do they have to do to make sure the beans do not die?

▲ Who exactly will take the responsibility for looking after the beans?

▲ How often do they have to do anything to the beans?

Session Two: Selecting texts

Explain to the children that the object of the task is to select those books from the class collection that will be of use for their project on planting beans and to reject those that will not, so that they do not waste time searching carefully through books that have nothing to offer. Make sure before the session that there are plenty of helpful books in the class collection, as well as some that would be of no use for the subject of growing beans.

Here are some suggestions you might find useful:
My First Gardening Book (Dorling Kindersley, 1992); *Seeds, Bulbs and Spores* by Jane Walker (Franklin Watts, 1993); *The Plant Cycle* by Nina Morgan (Wayland, 1993); *Sow and Grow* by Gabrielle Woolfitt (Wayland, 1994); *What Is a Flower?* by Robert Snedden (Belitha, 1993); *What's Inside Plants?* by Anita Ganeri (Simon & Schuster, 1993); *Grow Your Own* by Thompson Yardley (Cassell, 1992); *The Visual*

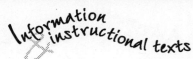

Dictionary of Plants (Dorling Kindersley, 1992); *My First Look at Nature* (Dorling Kindersley, 1991); *How Nature Works* by David Burnie (Dorling Kindersley, 1991); *Flowers* (Harper Collins, 1994); *Broad Bean* by Christine Back and Barrie Watts (A&C Black, 1991); *My Science Book of Growth* by Neil Ardley (Dorling Kindersley, 1992).

The children should work in pairs, and each pair will need a chart with the questions generated during the previous session written down one side.

Book title	Plants in school	Growing seeds	Beans
What potting material should we use?			
Where should we leave the beans to grow?			

At this point, it may be useful to remind the children of the structural guides that will tell them whether or not a particular book will be useful to them. They can then go through the books, using structural guides to pick out the books that will be of help in answering their questions and to discard those which are of no use for this particular topic. They can fill in the details of their findings on the chart as they do this.

The children can then report back to the class, reading from their charts, and finally create a display of the books that are of use for this topic, returning the rejected books to the school library.

Session Three: Locating information

Point out that now that the children know which books will be useful, they can do their research. Introduce them to 'jigsawing' techniques, whereby 'expert' groups each research one area, then individual 'experts' report back to their 'home' group. This way, every child has the chance to be an 'expert' and report back to their group, and everyone learns what the others have found out.

Divide the class into, say, four 'expert' groups. Each group can then take a selection of the books found to be useful and research its own set of questions from the children's list. For instance, one group might search for information on the growth cycle of a bean; one group might search for information on experiments/tests they can carry out to determine what factors are needed for growth; another group might list all the tools and materials needed to carry out an experiment on growth; while another group might list all the jobs to be done in an experiment on growth. Armed with a range of books so that they are able to check across sources, each group then sets about the task of finding answers to their particular questions. Encourage the children to use the structural guides to find the appropriate details in each book.

The class can then reform into 'home' groups of four, with a representative from each of the 'expert' groups in every small group. Each 'expert' gives an account of what was discovered in their group.

Round off the session with a class discussion of how easy it was to record the information found in the books. List any factors that made recording difficult – for example, too much text, too hard to read, too much to remember, too much to write down. Ask what the children actually did when recording the information found in the books. Do they think it is necessary always to remember every word? How do they know which are the important words and which words do not matter so much?

Suggest to the children that they continue this work the next day to improve their research tactics even further.

Session Four: Retrieving information

Organise the class into pairs and give each pair a copy of photocopiable sheet 152. Explain to the children that they have to underline the words they think are the most important – that is, the ones that will help them to remember the main message of this piece of text. Tell them that they can underline no more than ten words. Encourage each pair to read the piece carefully as many times as they like and to talk about the various possible words they could underline before making their final decisions. Once they have done this, the children should then represent what they have learned in picture form.

Come together again as a whole class to give the children the chance to explain and justify their choices.

It is important for children to put new information to use and evaluate it. These activities should, therefore, go hand

Planting seeds (1)

Name _____ Date _____

▲ Read the captions below carefully with a friend, then match the captions to the pictures on 'Planting seeds (2)'.

1. Fill the seed trays and flowerpots with compost, and water so that it is moist but not soaking wet.

2. Plant the big seeds in the flowerpots about 1cm below the surface of the compost. Label the pots with the names of the seeds.

Spray the trays

Planting seeds (2)

Name _____ Date _____

▲ Use this sheet with 'Planting seeds (1)'.

Underlining important words

Name _____ Date _____

▲ Decide with a friend which are the most important words in this passage. You can choose no more than ten! Underline the ones you have chosen.

Roots and shoots: how a bean starts to grow

When a seed starts growing. water enters the seed. The growing parts of the new plant begin to swell. First, the root breaks through the seed coat and starts to grow downwards. Next, the shoot pushes through and begins to grow upwards. Tiny hairs grow on the root and take in water and minerals from the soil. When the shoot has pushed through the surface of the soil, green leaves appear.

▲ Now draw pictures on the back of this sheet to show what you have learned about how a bean starts to grow.

in hand with science experiments that involve growing plants from a variety of seeds, pips and stones in a variety of different conditions.

Suggestion(s) for extension

Encourage the children to make a game by writing on pieces of card a) the instructions for planting seeds, and b) the materials needed for the job, so that each card represents one particular item or step in the planting process. They can then offer the cards in a mixed-up order for their friends to sort into two sets. Once the two sets have been sorted, can they sort each set into a logical order?

The children can cut out advertisements for gardeners or garden centres from an old copy of the *Yellow Pages* and delete, say, every tenth word. They can then write out or word-process the text allowing a line for each gap. Other groups of children can read these, then discuss and supply the missing words.

Suggestion(s) for support

Some children will need the support of an able reader throughout to assist with locating and retrieving, and with reading chunks of text. Older children in the school (or more experienced peers) could be very useful here, or adult helpers could be used. Helpers would need to encourage discussion to reinforce learning.

In small groups, with adult support if necessary, children can cut out, match and order the instructions and illustrations for planting seeds on photocopiable pages 153 and 154.

Assessment opportunities

Look for children's confidence and ability in formulating good questions, in using guides for selecting and retrieving information from texts, in finding the important points and representing them in an alternative form, and in matching, resequencing and completing modified texts.

Opportunities for IT

Children could write their instructions for planting seeds using a word processor. The instructions could be printed out and mounted on card for the children to create their own sequencing game. Alternatively, the instructions could be presented to other groups in a mixed-up order on the computer itself and the children could be asked to re-order them into the right sequence. This would involve the use of 'cut' and 'paste' commands to move the sentences around the screen. A similar activity could be undertaken using framework software like *My World* (available from SEMERC), where the children can drag the instructions on to the working screen in the correct order.

Display ideas

The children could 'publish' a gardeners' magazine featuring articles, adverts, descriptions, funny stories, gardening tips, weather reports and recommendations for gardening tools.

Other aspects of the English PoS covered

Speaking and listening – 1a, b, c; 2a, b.
Writing – 1b, c; 2a, b, c, d, e; 3a.

Reference to photocopiable sheet(s)

Photocopiable sheet 152 requires children to identify the most important words in a passage. Photocopiable sheets 153 and 154 require children to match instructions to pictures.

SEASONAL WEATHER

For the children to:

▲ *formulate questions to interrogate a text;*

▲ *use a range of reading strategies to retrieve information from non-fiction books and brochures;*

▲ *read information presented in the form of a map or a globe;*

▲ *read and carry out a set of instructions.*

†† *Session One: whole class, then pairs or individuals; Session Two: whole class, then pairs; Session Three: working in pairs; Session Four: whole class, then small groups; Session Five: whole class, then small groups.*

🕐 *Session One: 30 minutes; Session Two: a) 15 minutes, b) 20 minutes; Session Three: 25 minutes; Session Four: 30 minutes; Session Five: 35 minutes.*

Previous skills/knowledge needed

It is expected that the children will already have had experience of writing poems.

Key background information

This activity provides the context for children to develop effective strategies for reading information texts. It encourages them to use prior knowledge from first-hand experience, linked with information gleaned from other sources, to describe seasonal changes and their effects on our everyday lives, and to note the similarities and differences between their own locality and another.

Preparation

Collect clothes that are worn in the snow and rain to form part of an initial stimulus display in the classroom. If possible, include some specialist items such as ice-skates, skis and umbrellas.

Collect books, photographs and posters about the weather in autumn and winter here in Britain and elsewhere. Below are some suggestions to ensure that you offer a range of books for children to evaluate (some of the following, for instance, do not offer the support of structural guides but operate in a different way from the accepted conventions of an information book, and it is important to discuss this with young readers): Wayland's *Seasonal Weather* series by John Mason for more experienced readers, Wayland's *The Weather in...* series by Miriam Moss for less experienced readers; *See for Yourself* by Kay Davies and Wendy Oldfield (A & C Black, 1994); *Sunny Weather, Snowy Weather, Rainy Weather, Windy Weather* by Jillian Powell (Wayland, 1992); *What Happens When...* series by Daphne Butler (Simon & Schuster, 1993); *Starting Points* series by Ruth Thomson (Franklin Watts, 1989); *The Rainbow* series on the weather (Evans, 1993); *Get Set Go!* series by Ruth Thomson (Franklin Watts, 1993); *Weather and Climate* by Judy Langthorne and Gaye Conroy (Wayland, 1992); *Weather and Climate* by Barbara Taylor (Franklin Watts, 1993); *Early Birds* series (Franklin Watts, 1993); *Facts at your Fingertips: Weather* by David Marshall (Simon & Schuster, 1993); *Walkabout* series (Franklin Watts, 1993); *Snow: Causes and Effects* by Philip Steele (Franklin Watts, 1991); *Clothes in Hot and Cold Places* and *Homes in Hot and Cold Places* by Simon Crisp (Wayland, 1994).

Resources needed

A tape recorder, materials for writing and drawing, materials for making rain gauges (plastic bottles, scissors, rulers, waterproof felt-tipped pens, tape, bricks), a computer, one copy of photocopiable sheets 155 and 156 for each small group of children.

What to do
Session One: Introduction to the topic
Ask the children what changes they notice in the world around them as the autumn term moves towards winter. Encourage them to comment on the weather and mention falling temperatures, the wind, rain and fog. Point out how it gets dark earlier as the days get shorter and that the weather may grow very cold, with some frost, hail, sleet and even snow. Draw their attention to changes in the landscape such as leaves changing colour, the appearance of conkers, rosehips, haws, acorns and the trees losing their leaves. Ask the children if they know about any crops that are harvested in autumn, such as apples, pears, blackberries, damsons, plums, elderberries, and so on.

Talk about the effects that all this has on their lives, for instance how it affects their play: gathering conkers, conker games, crunching through leaves, blackberry picking. Is it getting too cold and too dark to play outside? What do they do instead? What problems does it cause being indoors all day? What are the dangers of going home from school in the dark? What would they be looking forward to if it snowed: sledging, making snowballs and snowmen, sliding?

Then look at how all this affects what they wear — for instance, changing from shorts or dresses to long trousers,

from socks to tights, from T-shirts to jumpers, from cotton to woollen clothes, from a single layer of clothes to several. What do they wear to keep their heads, hands and feet warm and dry?

How does the time of year affect what they eat — for instance, changing from salads to hot meals, from ice-cream to apple crumble and blackberry pie, from cornflakes to porridge, from squash to hot chocolate?

Ask the children how their houses are kept warm and cosy. What sort of heating do they have? How do they keep draughts out? How do they keep warm at night? Discuss the safety aspects of some types of heaters and the possible dangers of burst pipes in freezing weather.

Point out how vulnerable the old and the disabled are in severe weather conditions when roads are icy or blocked, and discuss ways of helping those in the local community. You may be able to set up a rota to check on the old, infirm people who live in the roads near to the school if the weather turns bad. Ask for the children's advice about how to do this – whether by phone from school, by calling at the door or by dropping a note through the letterbox.

It is important to scribe all the children's comments on to a flip chart or a large sheet of paper so that they can reread them during the week. They could follow up this discussion by writing a poem individually, in pairs or in small groups, focusing on 'What I like about Autumn or Winter' in the first verse, then 'What I hate about Autumn or Winter' in the next. Alternatively, different children could contribute different verses. The children can then read the finished poems in class before displaying them or 'publishing' them in an anthology.

Session Two: Development
Focusing on winter conditions to link with the previous session, find out if the children think the whole world has the same climate as we do. Ask if anyone has ever lived anywhere else, has relatives living elsewhere, has been on holiday to another country or seen television programmes about other countries that they could tell the class about. Perhaps you, or some of the children, have been on a winter sports holiday and could tell the class about the weather conditions there and what you enjoyed doing most.

Discuss aspects of weather around the world and list, on a flip chart or board, the questions that the children would like answered about cold winter regions, for example: Which countries have such conditions? What do people wear in those countries in winter? How do people travel around?

Distribute winter holiday travel brochures to pairs of children and remind them how to use structural guides to find information quickly. Ask them all to start by listing all the countries they can find, and then gather again as a class to share the findings and locate all these countries on a large world map or a globe — for example, Norway, Switzerland, France, Germany, Italy, Scotland, Austria, Spain, Andorra,

Romania, America, Canada, New Zealand. Point out the characteristics that these areas have in common (such as mountains).

Session Three: Gathering information
Start off by running through the effective, time-saving ways to find information from a text with the children. Then divide the class into pairs again to find out the answer to the next question from their list, for example: 'What clothes do people wear in cold countries?' Allow them to look through the brochures, then discuss what they have found out and the reasons why people would wear such clothes – such as protection against the cold, protection from the sun, protection from falling, to help with movement, and so on.

Introduce non-fiction books from the class collection to add to the brochures and investigate all the different ways of travelling on snow and ice, such as skiing, sledging, skating, snowshoes, snowmobiles, horse-drawn sleighs, dog sleighs.

Continue researching until all the questions from the children's list have been answered.

You could then broaden the canvas to discuss issues such as the dangers that snow can bring (for instance, avalanches), the damage to the environment caused by tourism in winter resorts and the effect this has on the local population.

Session Four: Writing a brochure
Working in small groups, children can begin the process of writing a brochure advertising their own area as, say, the ideal spot for a weekend break. Discuss with the children what things they will need to find out and write down their first thoughts on a large piece of paper.

▲ *What does the area have to offer?* For example: walks in the wood, romps by the sea, jogging along the canal, fishing, a special local festival, excellent shops for early Christmas shopping, good museums, old buildings, places of worship, special features such as historical events that happened there.

▲ *What accommodation is there?* Think about places to eat, places to stay, and the prices involved (hotels, guest houses, bed and breakfast, farm houses, camping sites). List all the different types of restaurant available in the area, such as Indian, Chinese, Greek, Turkish, fast food, cafés, bars, fish and chip shops, doner kebab shops, take-aways.

▲ *How can people get there?* Look at routes by car, coach, bus, train,

boat and/or aeroplane that can be used to reach the area.

▲ *What would people need to bring?* Obviously, the likely weather conditions will have a bearing here.

The children will then need to decide who will be involved in the writing, who will write which section, who will be the editor, the illustrator, the designer, the publisher, and so forth. Remind them to provide structural guides for their readers – page numbers, contents page, index, headings and illustrations with captions.

This project will take several sessions to complete.

Finally, the groups can show and read their finished brochures to the class, who can evaluate them in terms of aesthetic appeal, information included and accessibility to the reader. The groups can then give an account of their work and display the results in a school assembly.

Session Five: Following instructions
Explain to the children that they are going to keep daily weather reports describing the cloud conditions, the wind and the rain.

Find out what they already know about monitoring and keeping records of the weather. Have they seen weather forecasts on the television or in newspapers? Suggest that the children add to their knowledge by consulting a selection of books such as *Be Your Own Weather Expert* by Janet Kelly (Simon & Schuster, 1991); *What Makes the Wind Blow?* by Alison Niblo (Franklin Watts, 1993) and *Storms* (Franklin Watts, 1990).

Explain that you will need special equipment to keep accurate reports of rainfall. Unfortunately, a hurricane blew all the papers around and the instructions for making a rain

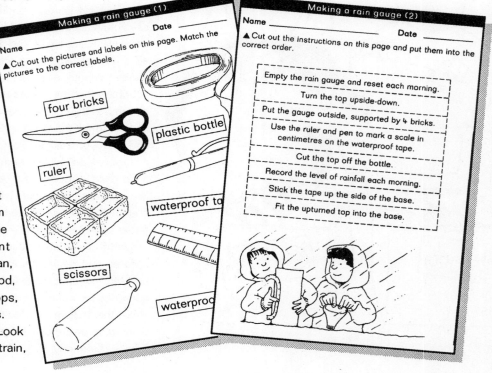

Making a rain gauge (1)

Name

Date

▲ Cut out the pictures and labels on this page. Match the pictures to the correct labels.

four bricks

plastic bottle

ruler

waterproof ta

scissors

waterproo

Making a rain gauge (2)

Name

Date

▲ Cut out the instructions on this page and put them into the correct order.

Empty the rain gauge and reset each morning.

Turn the top upside-down.

Put the gauge outside, supported by 4 bricks.

Use the ruler and pen to mark a scale in centimetres on the waterproof tape.

Cut the top off the bottle.

Record the level of rainfall each morning.

Stick the tape up the side of the base.

Fit the upturned top into the base.

gauge were muddled up. Divide the class into small groups and give each group a copy of photocopiable sheets 155 and 156. Tell them that their task is first to label the articles correctly, then to cut out and sort the instructions for making a rain gauge into the correct sequence, then to carry out the instructions. When this is done, the children will have to decide where best to place the rain gauges in the school playground.

They will also need to decide on methods of recording daily measurements of wind, rain and clouds, prepare charts or diaries to do this, decide on the time and frequency of monitoring these, and then make a rota for carrying out the tasks. The children might like to take turns to read a daily report to the class in the style of a radio or television weather forecaster.

Suggestion(s) for extension
Try to set up a school link by letter or e-mail to one of the European, American or Antipodean countries found in the winter sports brochures. Personal contacts with you or the school would be ideal; otherwise, write to the Director of Education or the mayor of one of the places featured in the brochures and ask to be put in touch with a primary school for the purpose of setting up a regular writing link to exchange diaries, photographs and tapes on various aspects of lifestyle and interests.

NB You may feel more confident with an English-speaking community to start with, but do not be put off by concerns about language mismatch – you will be amazed at how well you can manage, and how much the children learn about language from links with speakers of other languages.

Experienced readers could investigate autumn and winter festivals both in Britain and in other parts of the world, such as Harvest Festival, Guy Fawkes' Night, Diwali, Thanksgiving and Succoth. They could first conduct a survey in the school to find out what different people celebrate during the autumn and winter months, and encourage other children to ask relatives at home. The *Seasonal Festivals* series by Mike

Rosen (Wayland, 1990) will be of help here; *Let's Celebrate World Festivals* by Rhoda Nottridge (Wayland, 1994) has a similar content but an easier text.

For more experienced readers and writers, you could extend the investigation to temperate zones in the southern hemisphere where the seasons occur at the opposite time of the year to our own; or to cold conditions in a different kind of zone such as the polar regions, where the weather patterns are quite different from those in temperate zones.

Suggestion(s) for support
Some children will need a more experienced partner or adult helper when searching for information in brochures and non-fiction texts.

Assessment opportunities
Observe children's ability to compare and contrast weather conditions here and elsewhere and to draw inferences from the information gathered. Note the ability to ask appropriate questions before reading a text; and watch for awareness and use of structural guides, and the capacity to read headings and match names on a map. Note the children's use of structural guides and accuracy in reporting when they are creating their own non-fiction texts.

Children's confidence and accuracy when reading their brochures, their letters to twin schools and their poems about winter are good indicators of their reading and writing development.

Opportunities for IT
In Session One, the children could write their autumn or winter poems using a word processor and print them for display in the class.

The children could write their brochure for Session Four using either a word processing or a desktop publishing package. They could either create the whole brochure on the computer or use the word processor to print out text, which they could cut out and stick on to their own 'brochure'.

The method used may depend on the age and competence of the children and the number of computers available.

In Session Five, the children could use a database to record their weather measurements or use a simple graphing package to display weather data such as rainfall, temperature, and so on. Children could be introduced to software like *Weathermapper* (available from TAG Development Ltd), which enables all aspects of weather to be recorded and the results then used as a database.

Display ideas

The initial stimulus display of clothes for cold weather can be added to as the project progresses.

The children could put together a multimedia display about the hazards of winter conditions, including paintings, drawings, children's writing, photographs and official posters.

Make a collection of photographs and pictures of a mountain resort in the winter and encourage the children to write about their experiences, real or imagined, in prose or poetry for inclusion in the display.

Other aspects of the English PoS covered

Speaking and listening – 1a, c; 2a, b.
Writing – 1a, b, c; 2a, b, c, d, e; 3a, b.

Reference to photocopiable sheet(s)

Photocopiable sheets 155 and 156 relate to the same physical activity: sheet 155 involves matching pictures to labels, sheet 156 rearranging a set of jumbled instructions.

MAKING BOOKS

For the children to:
▲ *develop their knowledge of upper- and lower-case letters;*
▲ *develop their knowledge of alphabetical order;*
▲ *consider the needs of their audience when making an alphabet book for the nursery;*
▲ *reinforce their knowledge of linguistic terminology – noun, verb and adjective;*
▲ *carry out instructions successfully;*
▲ *use clear, precise language in a logical sequence when giving instructions.*
†† *Session One: whole class; Session Two: whole class, then small groups; Session Three: working in pairs.*
🕐 *Session One: 25 minutes; Session Two: 45 minutes; Session Three: 25 minutes.*

Previous skills/knowledge needed

It is expected that the children will have some knowledge of the alphabet, and that they will be familiar with the term 'landscape position'.

Key background information

This activity provides a meaningful context, book-making, in which children can develop their phonic skills and which will sharpen their awareness of the need to cater for the requirements of a specific audience.

Preparation

Assemble a collection of alphabet books in a range of formats (dual language, pop-up, lift the flap, rhyme), such as: *The Calypso Alphabet* by John Agard (Collins, 1989), *Alphabet Puzzle* by Jill Downie (Picture Mac, 1988); *Caribbean Alphabet* by Frané Lessac (Macmillan, 1991); *Animal Characters* by J.C. Knaff (Faber & Faber, 1987); *The Guinea Pig Alphabet* by Kate Duke (Methuen, 1987); *The Minister's Cat ABC* by Lynley Dodd (Picture Puffin, 1994); *A Four-tongued Alphabet* by Ruth Brown (Andersen Press, 1991); *A is for Africa* by Ifeoma Onyefulu (Frances Lincoln, 1993); *Alpha Bugs Pop-up Book* by David Carter (Orchard Books, 1994).

Also provide a selection of books about making books, such as: *Children Making Books* by Paul Johnson, *Writing in Multilingual Classrooms* by Viv Edwards (both published by the Reading and Language Information Centre at Reading University); *Building Blocks: Resources for a Multilingual Classroom* (Multilingual Matters, 1994); *Bright Ideas: Writing and Making Books* by Moira Andrew (Scholastic, 1995).

Resources needed

Materials for making books, such as card, paper, adhesive tape, pencils, rulers, wool, needles; writing and drawing materials, a computer, one copy of photocopiable sheet 157 for each pair of children.

What to do
Session One: Introduction to alphabet books
Explain to the children that they are going to be literary critics, deciding on the annual world-famous prize for the best non-fiction book for young children. This year, the prize is for the best alphabet book.

Brainstorm with the children what qualities they think are required to make a good alphabet book, and note their responses on a board or flip chart – size, durability, appeal of the cover, style of lettering, colour choices, illustrations or photographs, how easy it is to follow/pop-up/lift the flap.

Consider the choices that would have to be made about how each letter should be represented – with a noun, an adjective, a verb? Should there be more than one word for each letter – an alliterative sentence, perhaps? Should the alphabet be written in lower- or upper-case letters? Should it be in more than one language?

Ask the children to work in pairs to assess the qualities of one of the alphabet books in the light of the points they have just raised. After they have done this, three pairs could join together to share their findings. (Try to achieve a range of types of book within each small group.) Each group then has to consider the candidates and decide on *one* book to take through to the final round. Each group then presents its candidate for the prize to the whole class, giving reasons for the choice.

Take a class vote to decide on the winner, and together look at the features that make this book the best.

Session Two: Book-making
Explain to the children that they are going to work in groups to make alphabet books for the Nursery children.

Recap the features that proved most popular in the alphabet book competition, then ask the children to run through the general features of non-fiction books that will need to be considered – page numbers, authors' names, blurb, date of publication, publisher, and so on. Discuss whether a contents page and index are appropriate for an alphabet book.

Working in small groups, the children should then talk together and decide:
▲ what type of book the group wants to make – for example, lift the flap, pop-up, dual-language;
▲ the size and the shape of the pages;
▲ the words used to illustrate each letter;
▲ who will be involved in the illustration or the writing, whether the text will be handwritten or word-processed, and who will be responsible for each letter.

Decisions about which drawing tools will create the best effect for the reader will have to be taken. The children will also have to write the wording for the blurb, design the page borders, make the covers and decide on how the book will be bound.

The project will require several sessions. When it is completed, the children can then read their books to a class from the Nursery.

Finally, encourage the children to evaluate the project. What did they learn about publishing? Were they pleased with the end result? What response did the Nursery children make to the books?

READING

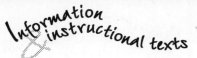

Session Three: Following instructions

Divide the class into pairs and give each pair a copy of photocopiable sheet 157. Explain to the children that they should read through the instructions and speculate on the article they think can be made by following the instructions. Then they can then carry out the instructions to see if they were right.

Now they have a ready-made zigzag book, they can write a story to fill it.

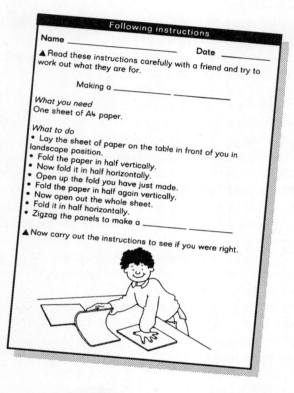

Note also the children's strategies when they are reading the instructions.

Opportunities for IT

In Session Two, children could use a word processor which enables them to mix text and graphics on the page. The illustrations for the alphabet book could be produced using a simple art package, or taken from commercial clipart collections – these could be in colour. Alternatively, children could draw their own illustrations and scan them into computer format. They will need to be taught how to position their pictures on the page, how to re-size them and how to select appropriate font styles and sizes for the page, remembering that the book is for younger children.

If the computer is to be used for the full publishing process, it might be better for the class to make one book between them to ensure that there is sufficient time for the artwork and word processing to be finished. Each group could then be responsible for one or two letters, plus the corresponding text and illustrations.

Suggestion(s) for extension

Ask the children to write the instructions for making, say, a paper bag puppet and then to ask a friend to follow these instructions. The puppets can then be used to perform puppet plays for other classes. The children will need to write scripts for the plays and 'publish' these in book form, then make programmes, tickets and advertising posters for their performances.

Suggestion(s) for support

Inexperienced readers will need adult support to make the alphabet book. An adult will also need to read aloud the instructions from the photocopiable sheet.

Assessment opportunities

The children's comments when making the alphabet book for the nursery can reveal much about their overall awareness of the relationship between reader and writer. Note their ability to match letter and sound, to match upper- and lower-case letters, to name words beginning with the right letter and to distinguish between nouns, verbs and adjectives.

Display ideas

The children's own alphabet books can be added to the initial stimulus display for class reference.

Other aspects of the English PoS covered

Speaking and listening – 1a, c, d; 2a, b; 3a.
Writing – 1a, b, c; 2a. b, c, d, e; 3a.

Reference to photocopiable sheet(s)

Photocopiable sheet 157 requires children to predict the outcome of following a series of instructions, and then to follow them and identify the object made (a zigzag book).

TOYS AND GAMES

For the children to:

▲ *recall factual information presented in an oral form;*

▲ *formulate questions to interrogate a text;*

▲ *use structural guides to find specific information from a text;*

▲ *represent newly-acquired information in a different form from the original text;*

▲ *use an appropriate format for writing instructions.*

†† *Sessions One, Two and Three: whole class; Session Four: working in pairs or individually; Session Five: whole class; Session Six: whole class and group work; Session Seven: whole class and individual work; Session Eight: whole class and group work.*

🕐 *Session One: 15 minutes; Session Two: 20 minutes; Session Three: 30 minutes; Session Four: 25 minutes; Session Five: 30 minutes; Session Six: 30 minutes; Session Seven: 40 minutes; Session Eight: 35 minutes.*

Previous skills/knowledge needed

It would be helpful if children were familiar with evaluating books and were aware of structural guides in books (see 'Evaluating information books' on page 102).

Key background information

By focusing on a subject that is close to children's hearts and therefore highly motivating, you can continue to build their reflective reading skills through modelling approaches used by fluent readers.

Preparation

Provide a collection of books, toys, teddy bears and board games, together with photographs, posters and videos about toys and games from the present day and from the past.

Arrange for a grandparent to visit the class to talk about the toys and games of his or her childhood.

Arrange for the class to visit the nearest toy museum, if possible. There are several scattered across the country, such as the Bethnal Green Museum of Childhood, London; Arundel Toy Museum, West Sussex; Brewhouse Yard Museum, Nottingham; the Museum of Childhood, Edinburgh. *Museums and Galleries in Great Britain and Ireland* (Reed Information Services) is a comprehensive guide that is updated each year.

Resources needed

Materials for making peg dolls (wooden pegs, scraps of different materials, wool, adhesive, felt-tipped pens), a tape recorder, writing and drawing materials, a copy of *Victorian Toys and Games* by Katrina Siliprandi (Wayland, 1994) or a similar book on the history of toys.

What to do

Session One: Introduction

Talk to the children about the toys they have at home. Which are their favourites and why? Who gave the toys to them? How long have they had them? What do they do with them? When and where do they play with them? Note how many different types of toys and games are suggested, and encourage the children to identify broad categories such as those you play with indoors or outdoors, those you play with in summer or winter, those you play with alone or with friends, those you play with at home or at school, and so on.

Ask the children to bring in a range of different types of toys to add to the initial stimulus display in the classroom. Encourage them to write comments and stories about their own toys to enrich the display.

Session Two: The history of toys

Find out what the children already know about toys from the past. Ask them if their parents or grandparents still have any

of their old toys. Have their relatives ever talked about the days when they were young and the toys they used to have? Have they seen photographs of their relatives when they were young playing with any toys? Have they seen programmes on the television, perhaps, showing old toys? Write down all their comments on a flip chart or a board, and consider how much they know already. This will also give an indication of gaps in their knowledge. Bear in mind that thinking of relevant questions is a crucial part of the process of retrieving information from books, so it is important that children have plenty of experience in doing this. Help them to pose questions about what things they would like to find out about toys in the past. Remind them of all the useful question words they can use – What? Why? Who? Where? When? How? – to stimulate their questions. These might include:

▲ When were toys first made?
▲ Have children always had toys?
▲ Where were toys first made?
▲ Who made the toys?
▲ What were toys made of?
▲ What different sorts of toys were there?
▲ Who played with them – boys, girls, babies?
▲ Where did children play with them?
▲ When did children play with them?
▲ How expensive were toys?

The next task is to try to find the answers to these questions. Display your list of questions in a prominent place, so that the children can read it at leisure and record any answers they find.

Session Three: Finding answers

As a starting-point, show the children an information book you have discovered, such as *Victorian Toys and Games* by Katrina Siliprandi (Wayland, 1994). Have any of the children heard of the Victorians, and if so, what do they know about them? Look at the front and back cover of the book together and discuss the information that can be picked up from the photographs of the toys on the front, the border pattern, and the lettering style of the title.

Read the title, blurb and 'about the author' notes to the children and, indicating the question list from the previous session, discuss whether this book will be likely to provide answers to any of the children's questions.

Talk with the children about what else *inside* the book might give them a valuable indication of whether it will be worthwhile consulting this book in search of answers; then consult the contents page. They will quickly realise that there is useful information inside, and will want to read more.

Tell the children that instead of reading a story this week, you will be reading this book to them chapter by chapter, and together you will be trying to find the answers to the questions they have asked about toys from the past. After a quick recap of their list to see what they are looking for, encourage everyone to listen very carefully in order to pick up the information needed.

As you read the first chapter, you may need to adapt or simplify the text to suit your particular class. Point out the subheadings, the photographs, the illustrations and the captions to the children and, at each subheading, briefly ask the children which of the questions from their list this section

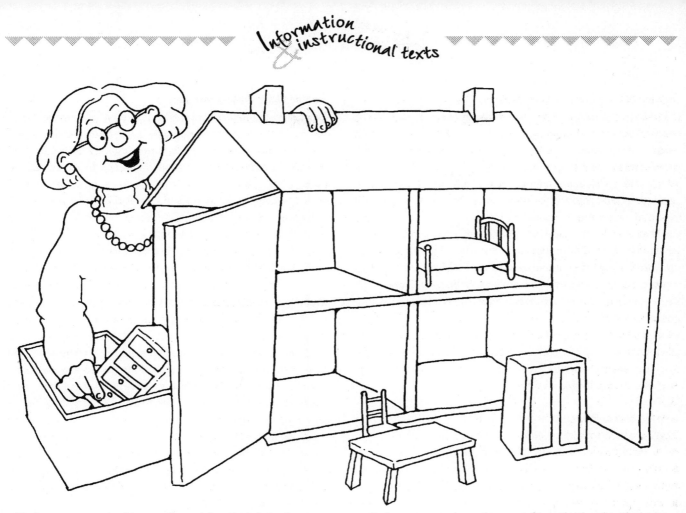

is likely to answer. In this way, by guiding their listening, you model for them what an active, purposeful reader does habitually.

At the end of the chapter, close the book and scribe on the flip chart any answers the children think they have found. If they miss any (which they rarely do!), prompt them by recalling something yourself and checking in the appropriate section if necessary.

Encourage the children to offer general responses to what has been read. Can they tell you what they would have liked about living during that time, and what they would have missed from today? Ask if anyone has been on a rocking horse. What do they feel about children working instead of going to school? What would they feel about having to wear clothes like the ones shown?

In subsequent storytimes, continue through the book in the same way, encouraging the children to note the structural guides in the chapters and to approach the text with their questions at the ready.

Finally, check to see if all the children's original questions have been answered. If not, discuss what they might do about this.

Session Four: Extending the search

In response to the fact that some questions still remain unanswered, move on to look for information in other books about toys from the past.

To develop the children's survey techniques and use of structural guides, tell them that they will have two minutes

to find out as much as they can from the books about toys and games, and then they will all share their findings. Run briefly through the features that help readers to find things out quickly in a non-fiction book – blurb, contents, chapter headings, photographs, illustrations, captions, and so on – before starting. Give out a selection of books such as *Toys* by Gill Tanner and Tim Wood (A & C Black, 1993), *Toys and Games* by Ruth Thomson (Franklin Watts, 1992) and *The Doll Book* by Caroline Goodfellow (Dorling Kindersley, 1993), then tell the children to begin and set the stopwatch.

Share their findings and add any new information to the list of questions and answers.

Session Five: Using other sources

The arranged visit of a local elderly couple or grandparent/ great-grandparent of one of the children, to talk about the toys they played with when they were young, can now take place. Emphasise that this is a different source of information about the past that is equally valid.

Children could decide beforehand who will ask which questions to get the interview going, such as: Which toys were available? What games were played? How much time was available for playing? How safe were the streets for playing? How safe were the toys? What things did they love best of all, and what did they look forward to most? Was there anything they longed for but couldn't have?

The interview could be taped to facilitate follow-up work in which children could check for any additional information that has come to light to add to their list.

Session Six: Comparing information

Working in groups and using the information they have learned so far from the various sources, children can list on large poster-sized sheets of paper the different toys and games available today under appropriate headings, such as electronic toys, board games, street games, construction toys, dolls, and so on. Then they can do the same for different kinds of toys from the past.

They then need to look carefully at each category, compare similarities and differences between the old and new toys and games, and then make a list of their findings. They might note such things as what the toys were made of, how much they cost, who played with them, how they worked and where the children played.

Bring the class together again for the groups to report on their findings and discuss any interesting issues that arise – for instance, safety rules and regulations for toy manufacturers today.

Session Seven: Putting information to use

Suggest to the children that they make a peg doll, dressed as a child from a well-off Victorian family (or family from another period, if appropriate). Recap what they have learned about Victorian children so far, and show photographs and books to reinforce points raised. Discuss construction techniques, the sort of materials they will use and the style of the clothes that will be needed; then each child can make a peg doll in a 'workshop' session.

Evaluate the finished products before displaying them in the school library or entrance hall. Point out that other children in the school will certainly want to know how to make these dolls, so it might be a good idea to write down the instructions for doing this and include them in the display.

Session Eight: Writing instructions

Discuss with the whole class what needs to be provided in a set of instructions – for example, a list of all the things you need plus step-by-step guidance for making the item.

Talk through exactly what was needed to make the peg dolls: pegs; scraps of different types of material such as velvet, silk, lace, cotton; balls of wool for different hair colours; adhesive; felt-tipped pens; scissors; needle and thread... Talk through the first step in the construction process, the second step, and so on through to the final stage.

Show the children a range of examples of different ways to set out instructions, and talk about how easy or difficult these are to follow. Remind them of the needs of other children in the school who will be reading the instructions they provide.

Arrange the children into pairs and tell them that they now have to write a set of instructions for making peg dolls. They have to decide whether to use only words, only drawings, or a mixture of the two; whether to write the instructions as a list, as a flow diagram, or in any other way they can think of, bearing in mind that the aim is to make these instructions easy for readers to follow and carry out.

Finally, the children can read their instructions to the class and compare their results, explaining the reasons for the choices they have made.

Suggestion(s) for extension

Children could make their own non-fiction book about 'Our toys' and 'The games we like to play'. Perhaps they could write a diary entry for a day in the life of a poor Victorian child and/or a rich Victorian child.

This activity offers many opportunities for developing language across the curriculum, through mathematics

(calculating and recording data related to toy surveys) and through science (investigating the materials and properties of toys).

Suggestion(s) for support

Children can work with an adult helper and, through discussion, create a timeline of toys from 1900 through to 1990. They can then draw carefully-observed pictures to represent the various toys and games.

To support those with little writing stamina, organise oral work with an adult focused on creating a time capsule for future archaeologists to find which will tell them about toys in the 1990s. Children will need to decide which actual toys, if any, to include; which photographs or drawings of toys to include; whether to include a set of instructions (scribed by an adult) explaining how to play certain games; whether to include a diary entry or a letter to inform the people of the future about who played with the toys, and when and where they did so.

Assessment opportunities

Listen to, and observe, children when they are brainstorming ideas about toys now and in the past, formulating questions, responding to non-fiction texts, discussing structural guides in books and reading their findings to the class. Record the individual children's confidence and skills.

The children's written instructions for making a peg doll, their comparisons between toys of different generations and their 'published' books will demonstrate what they have learned from reading non-fiction texts, as well as providing evidence of their writing skills.

Opportunities for IT

In Session One, the children could write stories or labels for their toy display using a word processor. They could experiment with different font styles or sizes to make their labels easy to read.

In Session Eight, the children could use a word processor to write their instructions for making a peg doll. They could include pictures by either scanning in their own hand-drawn pictures or by drawing them on to the final printed pages. In both cases, they will need to allow space on the page for their pictures. The children should be given opportunities to originate their work using the word processor, so that they have to think about the correct sequence (possibly moving sections around) and how it can be presented in the best form.

Display ideas

Classroom displays could include children's toys with labels, captions and stories relating treasured moments involving the toys; a selection of teddy bears (old and new) with information about how teddy bears have changed over the years, safety features and durability; clockwork toys with reports of experiments carried out in class; and the peg dolls made by the children with instructions for making them.

Accounts of the visit by a senior citizen, with drawings and paintings showing children of that day and age at play, could also be included.

Other aspects of the English PoS covered

Speaking and listening – 1a, b, c; 2b.
Writing – 1b, c; 2c, d, e.

MAKING AN INFORMATION BOOK

For the children to:
▲ **draw on previous knowledge about structural guides and supports for readers in retrieving relevant information from print;**
▲ **put this information to use in writing a non-fiction book for the class collection.**
†† *Introductory session: whole class. Subsequent sessions: individual or pair work.*
🕓 *Class session: 30 minutes. Subsequent sessions of 20–30 minutes depending on children's stamina.*

Key background information

Children will need a wide range of experience in using non-fiction books. From this activity, you will be able to measure the progress children have made in using information retrieval skills.

Preparation

Spend time with the children, helping them to decide on a toy or a pet that they would like to write about.

Resources needed

A range of non-fiction books for children to browse through as appropriate, book-making materials, a computer.

What to do

Explain to the children that during the next few weeks, they are going to make an information book about a favourite toy or pet; and that before they start, they are going to recall together all that they now know about the ingredients that make a good non-fiction book. Collect their ideas on to a chart or a large sheet of paper, so that they can refer to this throughout the project as an *aide-mémoire*; these might include an attractive cover, the title of the book, careful illustrations, contents page, logical sequence, chapter headings, captions, index.

Children can choose to work on their own or with a partner. In this session, they will need to make a list of questions about the topics they have chosen that they think a reader might want to have answered. This list will form the basis for their research and planning.

In subsequent sessions, they will have to retrieve information from books, make choices regarding the final selection of material to include, re-present that material and organise it, draw accompanying illustrations, make the cover and design the contents page.

The finished books can then be shared with the whole class before you add them to the school library collection.

Throughout the project, you can observe and listen to the children as they plan, read, talk and write, to assess how effectively they handle information (that is, their information processing skills). The quality of the finished product will provide further evidence to support your summative assessment. Annotated photocopies of pieces of work can be included in children's portfolios.

Suggestion(s) for extension

Older children might like to make a 'big book' version of their book for the Nursery and an accompanying tape of the text.

Suggestion(s) for support

Inexperienced readers and writers may prefer to work as a small group and undertake part of the work each. Some children may need the support of an adult helper, who will need to keep notes on the children's awareness of structural guides, their setting of questions and their recognition of relevant information.

Display ideas

A 'Work in progress' display could act as a useful model for other young writers to learn from. A 'local authors' display in the school library of all the books the children have made would encourage other aspiring authors.

Other aspects of the English PoS covered

Speaking and listening – 1a, b, c; 2a, b; 3b.
Writing – 1a, b, c; 2a, b, c, d; 3a, b.

Photocopiables

The pages in this section can be photocopied for use in the classroom or school which has purchased this book, and do not need to be declared in any return in respect of any photocopying licence.

They comprise a varied selection of both pupil and teacher resources, including pupil worksheets, resource material and record sheets to be completed by the teacher or children. Most of the photocopiable pages are related to individual activities in the book; the name of the activity is indicated at the top of the sheet, together with a page reference indicating where the lesson plan for that activity can be found.

Individual pages are discussed in detail within each lesson plan, accompanied by ideas for adaptation where appropriate – of course, each sheet can be adapted to suit your own needs and those of your class. Sheets can also be coloured, laminated, mounted on to card, enlarged and so on, where appropriate.

Pupil worksheets and record sheets have spaces provided for children's names and for noting the date on which each sheet was used. This means that, if so required, they can be included easily within any pupil assessment portfolio.

Beneath the surface, see page 18

Labels

▲ Which of these labels is easiest to read? Why?
▲ Does each label give all the information you would need?
How could the labels be improved?

Food fair, see page 22

Preparation guidelines (1)

The words from these instructions on how to cook soup have been muddled up.

▲ Cut out these words and put them in the correct order.

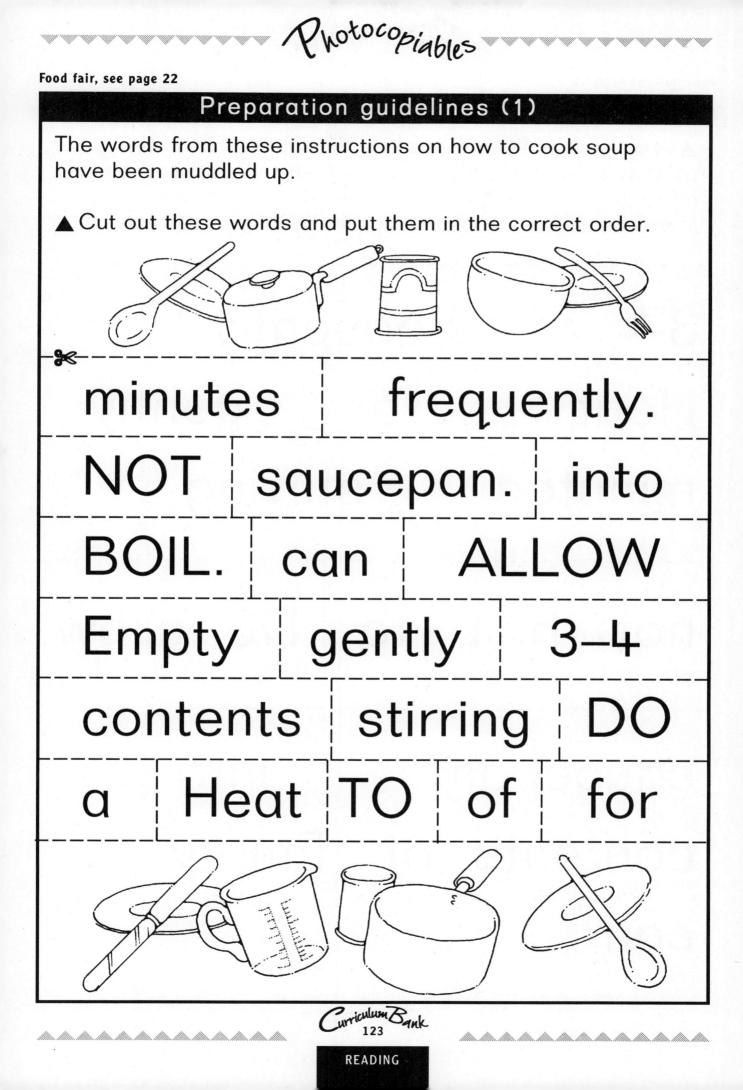

minutes	frequently.
NOT	saucepan.	into
BOIL.	can	ALLOW
Empty	gently	3–4
contents	stirring	DO
a	Heat	TO	of	for

READING

Food fair, see page 22

Preparation guidelines (2)

▲ Each sentence below has been muddled up. Cut up the word strip for each one, and arrange them into the correct order to make complete sentences. Then put the sentences in order to make the instructions for heating a can of soup.

3-4   frequently.

Heat   for   gently

minutes   stirring

---

not   boil.   to   Do   allow

---

saucepan.   into

contents   of   Empty   a

can

Food fair, see page 22

In the soup

Name _____   Date _____

▲ Fill in the missing letters to complete the names of these soups.

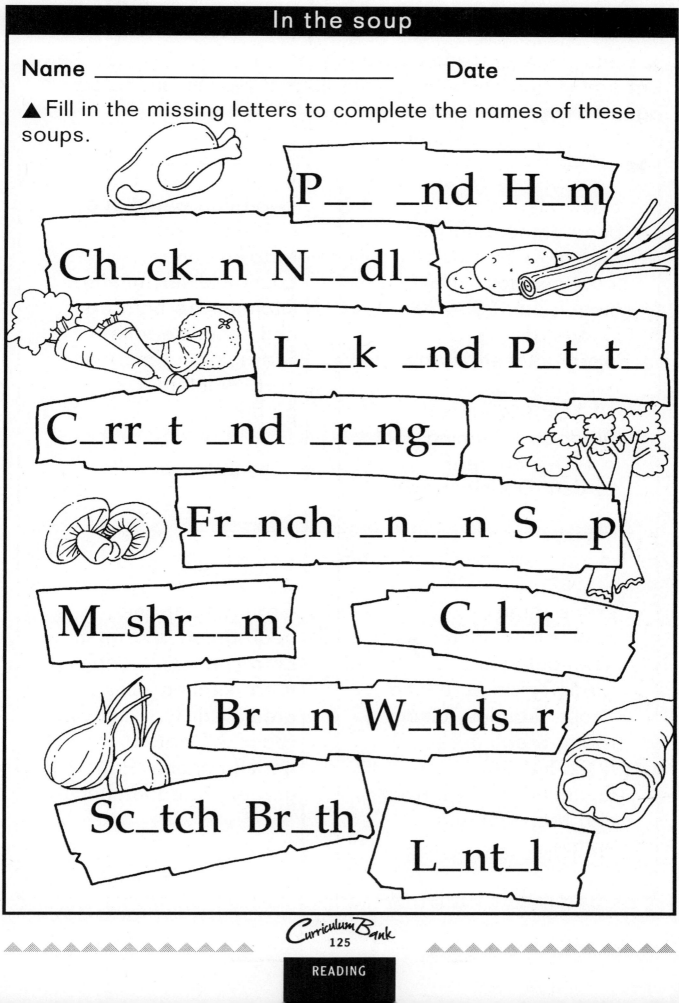

P__ _nd H_m

Ch_ck_n N__dl_

L__k _nd P_t_t_

C_rr_t _nd _r_ng_

Fr_nch _n__n S__p

M_shr__m

C_l_r_

Br__n W_nds_r

Sc_tch Br_th

L_nt_l

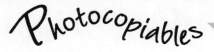

Estate agents' advertisements (1)

▲ Read through these house advertisements, then cut them out and match each one to the correct picture on 'Estate agents' advertisements (2)'.

✂

Spacious four-bedroomed detached bungalow in village location. Hall, d/s cloakroom, 25' x 30' lounge, dining room, luxury kitchen, study, two bathrooms. Gas c/h. Double-glazed. Outdoor swimming pool in 100' x 50' rear garden. Double garage.

Two-bedroomed end terrace property near to town centre. Lounge/diner, modern kitchen, d/s bathroom and separate toilet. Storage heaters. Car port. Small rear garden.

Large three-bedroomed Victorian semi-detached property close to local shops. Lounge, dining room, breakfast room, fitted kitchen. Enclosed garden, front and rear. Parking space.

Ground floor one-bedroomed apartment. Entrance hall, lounge area, kitchen/dining area, bedroom, shower room. Allocated parking space. Patio garden, fitted kitchen.

READING

Estate agents' advertisements (2)

▲ Use this sheet with 'Estate agents' advertisements (1)'.

Underlining exaggerations

Name _____   **Date** _____

▲ Read through this estate agent's advertisement for a cottage. Underline any words you think may be exaggerations.

Located in a picturesque village setting overlooking open woodland, this charming 400-year-old character thatched cottage with internal beams and original fireplaces is a real bargain. In good condition throughout and recently redecorated, it comprises a quaint hallway, 2 reception halls, 2 bedrooms, a fully-fitted kitchen, modernised bathroom and separate toilet. Electric radiators throughout. Lawned garden and off-street parking.

Television advertisements, see page 32

Filling the gaps

Name ______________________________ Date ______________

▲ Fill in the gaps to make an advertisement for your favourite chocolate bar.

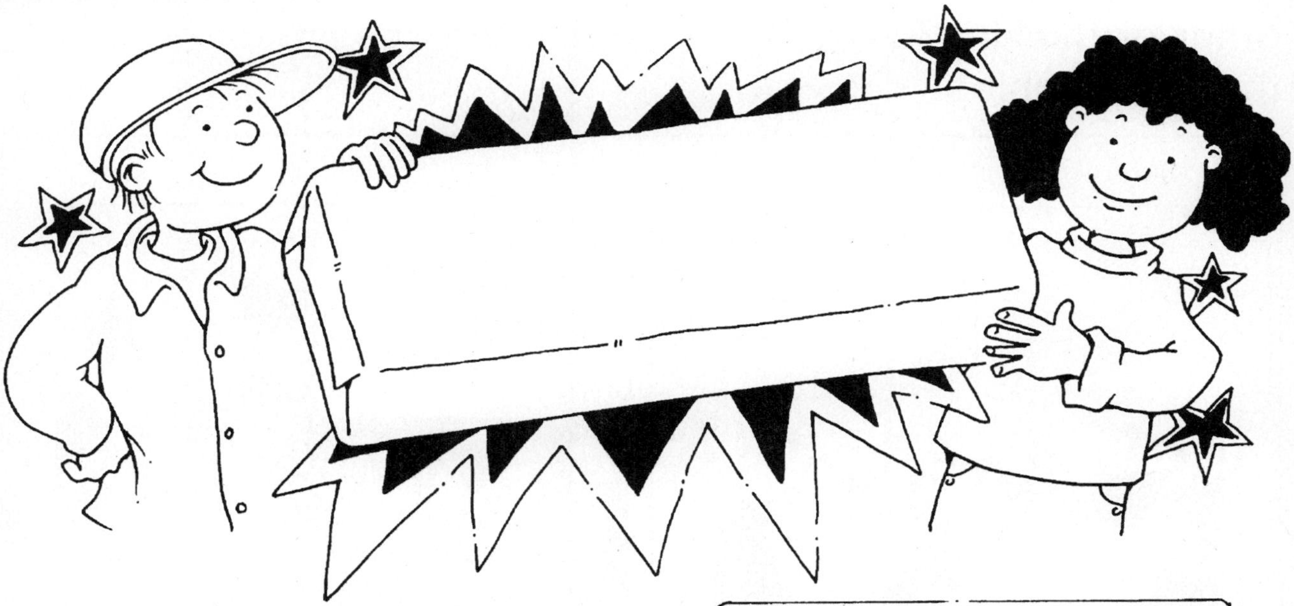

When you're feeling hungry, [ ]

will ________________ your hunger, because it's filled

with ________________. It's more satisfying than

________________ and more ________________

than ________________. So, stop at a ________________

and buy a [ ] ____________.

Television advertisements, see page 32

Speech bubbles

Name _____   **Date** _____

▲ These pictures are from an advertisement for chocolate. What do you think the characters might be saying to each other or thinking? Write the words in the speech and thought bubbles.

Inventing names

Name _____   **Date** _____

▲ Make up a brand name for each of the following:

1 sweets or chocolate

2 a toy or game

3 fast food, cake or biscuits

4 toothpaste or soap

5 washing powder or shampoo

▲ Now create a catchy slogan to advertise each one:

1 _____

2 _____

3 _____

4 _____

5 _____

Television advertisements, see page 32

What's on offer?

Name _____   Date _____

▲ What do you think these catchphrases might be advertising?

Everyone's a fruit and nut case

_____

Keeps hunger locked up till lunch

_____

Only the best chick, chick, chicken

_____

Aunt Bessie's always rise to the occasion

_____

A step in the right direction

_____

Tackles stains first time

_____

▲ Choose a new product you would like to advertise. Invent a name and catchphrase for your product.

Name _____

Catchphrase _____

_____

_____

Children's comics, see page 36

Crafty Cat

Name _____ **Date** _____

▲ What do you think these characters are saying?
Write the words in the speech bubbles.

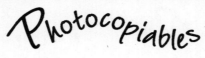

Introducing a children's author, see page 42

Introducing a children's author

Name _____   Date _____

▲ Answer these questions and fill in the missing words.

Who had dinner early?   _____ had dinner early,

Who played with Kate?   _____ played with Kate,

Who needed burping?   _____ needed burping,

So who had to wait?   So _____ had to wait.

Refrain: Quiet! said her father, Hush! said her mum.

　　　　　Nora! said her sister, Why are you so dumb?

Who was very filthy?   _____ was very filthy,

Who cooked with Kate?   _____ cooked with Kate,

Who needed drying off?   _____ needed drying off,

So who had to wait?   So _____ had to wait.

Refrain: Quiet! said her father, Hush! said her mum.

　　　　　Nora! said her sister, Why are you so dumb?

Who was getting sleepy?   _____ was getting sleepy,

Who read with Kate?   _____ read with Kate,

Who needed seeing to?   _____ needed seeing to,

So who had to wait?   So _____ had to wait.

Introducing a children's illustrator, see page 46

Sequencing illustrations

▲ Cut out these pictures and put them in order to make a story.

▲ Write what you think the people are saying in the speech bubbles.

Babysitters, see page 50

Babysitters (1)

Name _____ **Date** _____

▲ Fill in the gaps in this passage.

The night the babysitter came, Mum and Dad left in a hurry. 'Goodbye,' they said, 'and be good.' The babysitter smiled at us and sat down to watch the television in peace and quiet. But we had other ideas!

My big brother Dan said, 'I'm going to _____

_____ ,'

My big sister Pauline said, 'I'm going to _____

_____ ,'

My little sister Susie said, '_____

_____ ,'

And my little brother Gary _____ .

So the babysitter had to _____ .

No wonder she was exhausted when mum and dad came home!

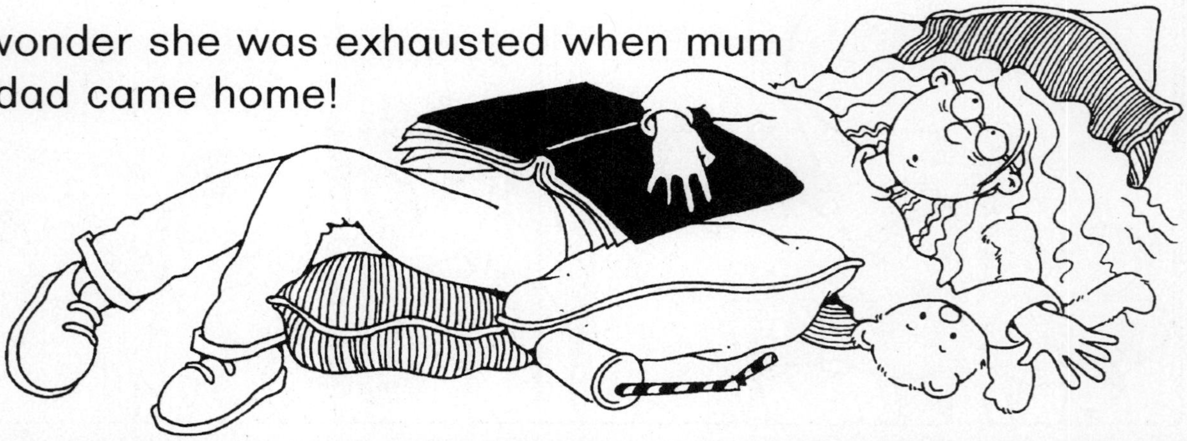

Babysitters, see page 50

Babysitters (2)

Name _____   Date _____

▲ Match the words to the pictures and write the correct letter in each box.

A	crawl
B	cry
C	bump
D	bang
E	juggle
F	jump
G	slide
H	sleep
I	hug
J	hide

READING

Pets, see page 54

Pet phrases

Name _____   Date _____

▲ Fill in the gaps in this passage.

Who _____ out through the back door?

Who _____ [_____] down the garden?

Who _____ [_____] along the wall?

Who _____ down into the alley?

Who _____ [_____] against the fence?

Who _____ [_____] between the bottles?

Who should watch out? Cat!

Who _____ [_____] round the corner?

Who _____ [_____] between the bottles?

Who _____ [_____] down the alley?

Who comes back safely through the back door? Cat!

Making Tiddalik laugh

Name _____ **Date** _____

▲ Complete these jokes, then write some of your own on the back of this sheet.

Why do birds fly south in the winter?

Why do bees hum?

When is water like a kangaroo?

What did the mouse say when he broke his tooth?

Traditional tales, see page 64

Nabunum's special dance

Name _____ **Date** _____

▲ Fill in the gaps in this passage.

At first, his dance was slow and

graceful, like _____

_____

_____.

He _____

his long, thin body.

He _____ twirled.

He sh_____.

He fl_____.

He did _____

_____

and arabesques to make Tiddalik laugh.

African folk tales

Name _____ **Date** _____

▲ Fill in the blanks from this passage.

Many years ago, the rain did not fall at the end of
the _ _ y season. The _ _ ops died and the rivers
turned to dust. Aio called to the ancestors to send
rain. 'The leopard is so _ _ irsty, he has no
_ _ rength to _ _ ase the antelope. All he can do is
sit in the _ _ ade of the baobab _ _ ee. The
antelope has lost his streng _ _ . He is so thir _ _ y,
he ju _ _ sits all day under the baobab _ _ee.

'The _ _ ameleon has no strength to _ _ ange his
colour. The parrot cannot _ _ y. The monkeys sit in
silence in the bran _ _ es. The _ _ ogs sing no more
in the evenings. Even the py _ _ on has no strength
to _ _ ed her _ _ in. The _ _ orpion cannot carry
her _ _ ildren.'

'Aio, we hear your song. If you remember us, we
will _____

_____

_____
                                                          ,
_____

Traditional rhymes

▲ Cut out the word strips and arrange them in order to make nursery rhymes.

We all fall down.

A pocketful of posies.

Ring-a-ring o' roses.

Atishoo! Atishoo!

So are you!

Hark don't you,

I'm wet through.

I hear thunder,

Pitter patter raindrops,

Hark don't you?

Pitter patter raindrops,

I hear thunder.

Out came the sunshine

Down came the rain

Incey Wincey Spider climbed up the water spout,

and washed poor Incey out.

and dried up all the rain.

So Incey Wincey Spider climbed up the spout again.

READING

Games, rhymes and songs, see page 74

Bits and pieces

▲ Someone's broken the teapot! Can you put the pieces back together to make a well-known rhyme?

short

I'm

stout

Tip

little

I

up

teapot

my

the

me

and

a

out

my

spout

and

me

me

When

shout

see

hear

handle

Here's

here's

pour

teacups

Nursery rhymes, see page 76

Name the rhyme

Name _____   **Date** _____

▲ Label these items, then list the names of the nursery rhymes they could have come from on the back of this sheet.

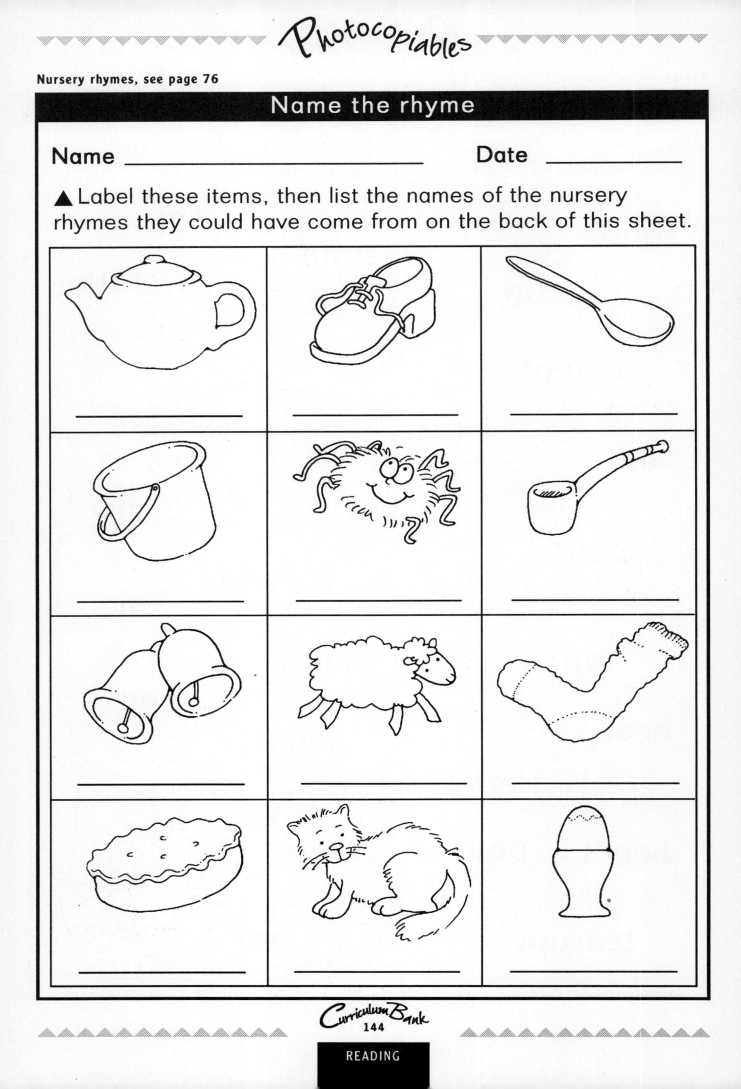

Rhyming stories, see page 80

Question and answer

Name _____ **Date** _____

Can you remember who caused the rumpus?

_____

Who had a troublesome beak and gave Hairy Maclary a tweak?

_____

Who had a bottlebrush tail and jumped over the rail?

_____

Who came from Parkinson Place and joined in the chase?

_____

Who forgot he was sore and clattered all over the floor?

_____

Who, in a thundering rage, crashed into a cage?

_____

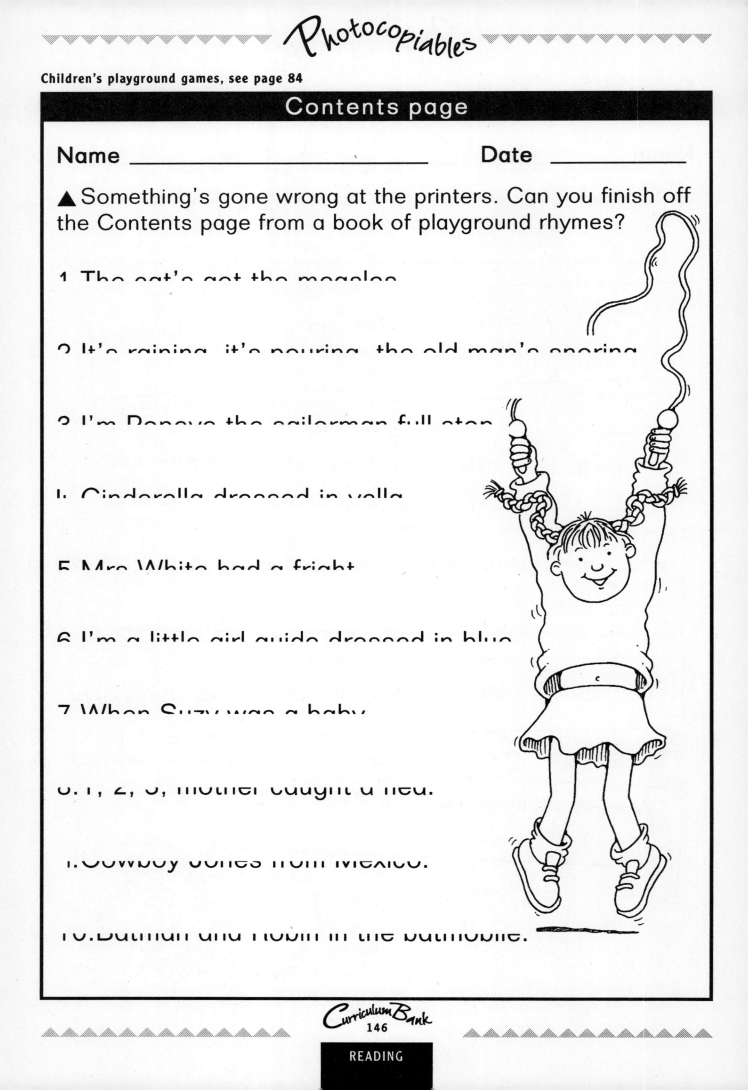

Photocopiables

Children's playground games, see page 84

Contents page

Name _____ Date _____

▲ Something's gone wrong at the printers. Can you finish off the Contents page from a book of playground rhymes?

1 The cat's got the measles.

2 It's raining, it's pouring, the old man's snoring.

3 I'm Popeye the sailorman full stop.

4 Cinderella dressed in yella.

5 Mrs White had a fright.

6 I'm a little girl guide dressed in blue.

7 When Suzy was a baby.

8 1, 2, 3, mother caught a flea.

9 Cowboy Jones from Mexico.

10 Batman and Robin in the batmobile.

READING

Photocopiables

In the playground

Name _____   Date _____

▲ Write a second verse for this poem.

I felt ...
As lost as an abandoned puppy
As lonely as the last man on Earth
As miserable as a king without a kingdom
As awkward as a fish without a tail.

Six months later ...
I felt ...

As

As

As

As

READING

Cloze procedure, see page 99

The Dark

Name _____   Date _____

▲ Fill in the gaps to make your own version of this poem.

I don't like the dark coming down on my head

It feels like _____

I don't like the dark coming down on my head.

I don't like the dark coming down over me

It feels like _____

I don't like the dark _____

I don't like the dark coming _____

It feels like _____

I _____

Original poem by Adrian Henri

Cloze procedure, see page 99

Clankety clank

Name _____   **Date** _____

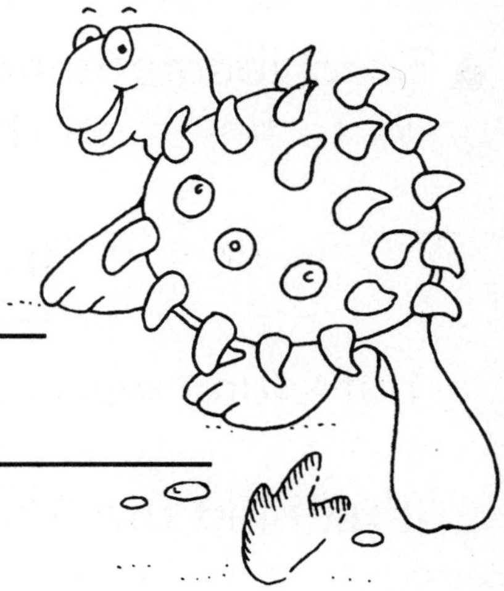

▲ Fill in the gaps to complete the poem.

Clankety, clankety, clankety clank

Ankylosaurus was built like a _____

its hide was a fortress as sturdy as _____

it tended to be an inedible meal.

It was armoured in front, it was armoured _____

there wasn't a thing on its minuscule _____

it waddled about on its four stubby _____

nibbling on plants with a mouthful of pegs.

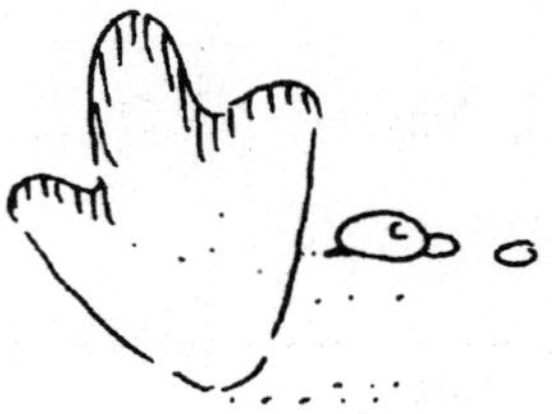

Ankylosaurus was best left _____

its tail was a cudgel of gristle and _____

_____

_____ was built _____

Jack Prelutsky

Cloze procedure, see page 99

Filling the gap

Name _____   **Date** _____

▲ Brachiosaurus has been nibbling again! Please fill in the gaps to finish off the poem.

Brachiosaurus had little to do

but stand with its _____ in the treetops and chew,

it nibbled the leaves _____ were tender and green,

it was a perpetual eating _____.

Brachiosaurus was truly immense,

its vacuous mind was uncluttered by _____,

it hadn't the need to be clever and wise

_____ beast dared to bother a being its size.

Brachiosaurus was _____ and slow,

but then, there was nowhere it needed _____ go,

if Brachiosaurus were living today,

no doubt it _____ frequently be in the way.

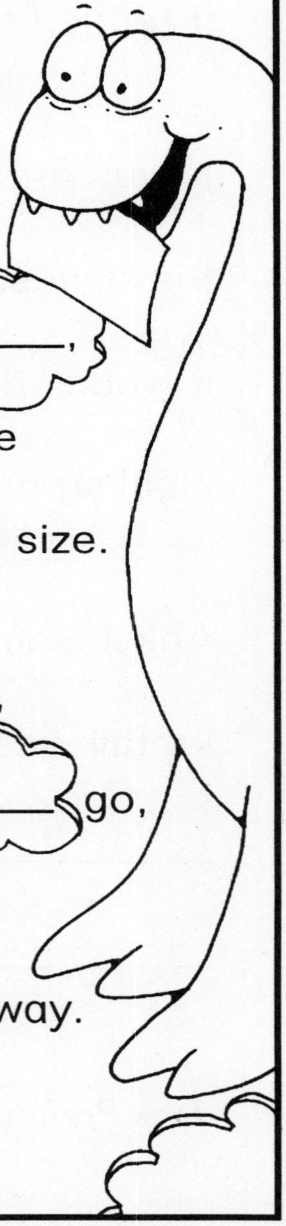

Jack Prelutsky

READING

Evaluating information books, see page 102

A book record sheet

book title			
contents			
chapters			
page numbers			
headings			
pictures			
photographs			
diagrams			
captions			
index			
glossary			
bibliography			

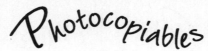

Underlining important words

Name _____ **Date** _____

▲ Decide with a friend which are the most important words in this passage. *You can choose no more than ten!* Underline the ones you have chosen.

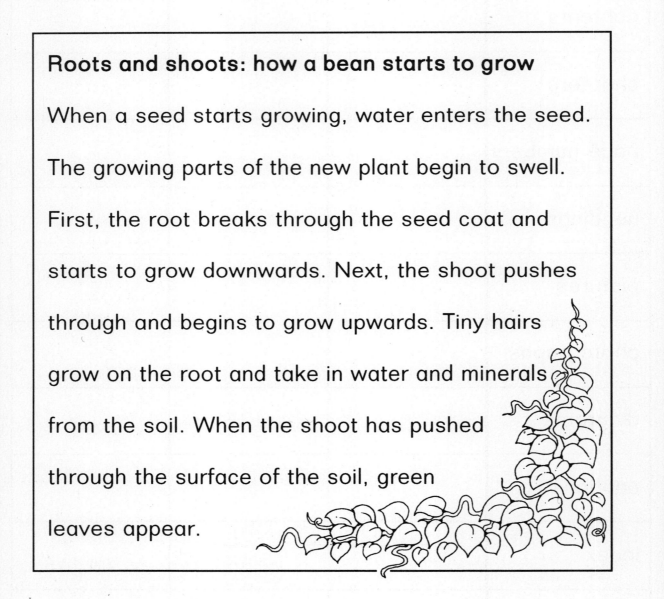

Roots and shoots: how a bean starts to grow

When a seed starts growing, water enters the seed.

The growing parts of the new plant begin to swell.

First, the root breaks through the seed coat and

starts to grow downwards. Next, the shoot pushes

through and begins to grow upwards. Tiny hairs

grow on the root and take in water and minerals

from the soil. When the shoot has pushed

through the surface of the soil, green

leaves appear.

▲ Now draw pictures on the back of this sheet to show what you have learned about how a bean starts to grow.

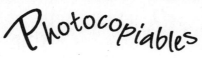
Planting seeds (1)

Name _____ **Date** _____

▲ Read the captions below carefully with a friend, then match the captions to the pictures on 'Planting seeds (2)'.

1. Fill the seed trays and flowerpots with compost, and water so that it is moist but not soaking wet.

2. Plant the big seeds in the flowerpots about 1cm below the surface of the compost. Label the pots with the names of the seeds.

3. Sprinkle the small seeds over the compost in the seed trays, then cover them with a thin layer of compost. Label the trays.

4. Spray the trays and flowerpots with water. Cover both with plastic bags and put them in a warm, dark place.

5. When shoots appear, remove the plastic bags and move the seeds into the light.

6. When the seedlings become too big for the pots or trays, remove them very carefully and plant them in separate flowerpots.

Planting seeds (2)

Name _____ Date _____

▲ Use this sheet with 'Planting seeds (1)'.

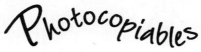

Seasonal weather, see page 108

Making a rain gauge (1)

Name _____   **Date** _____

▲ Cut out the pictures and labels on this page. Match the pictures to the correct labels.

four bricks

plastic bottle

ruler

waterproof tape

scissors

waterproof pen

READING

Seasonal weather, see page 108

Making a rain gauge (2)

Name _____   Date _____

▲ Cut out the instructions on this page and put them into the correct order.

Empty the rain gauge and reset each morning.

Turn the top upside-down.

Put the gauge outside, supported by 4 bricks.

Use the ruler and pen to mark a scale in centimetres on the waterproof tape.

Cut the top off the bottle.

Record the level of rainfall each morning.

Stick the tape up the side of the base.

Fit the upturned top into the base.

READING

Making books, see page 112

Following instructions

Name _____   Date _____

▲ Read these instructions carefully with a friend and try to work out what they are for.

Making a _____ _____

What you need
One sheet of A4 paper.

What to do
• Lay the sheet of paper on the table in front of you in landscape position.
• Fold the paper in half vertically.
• Now fold it in half horizontally.
• Open up the fold you have just made.
• Fold the paper in half again vertically.
• Now open out the whole sheet.
• Fold it in half horizontally.
• Zigzag the panels to make a _____ _____

▲ Now carry out the instructions to see if you were right.

INFORMATION TECHNOLOGY WITHIN READING

Word processors

During Key Stage 1, pupils will be developing their confidence and competence in the use of the standard computer keyboard. They should be taught a range of basic keyboard and word-processing skills. These should include:

▲ an understanding of the layout of the keyboard and where the letter and number keys are found;

▲ how to get capital letters and characters found above the number keys, using the *shift* key;

▲ how to use the *delete* key to erase words and letters;

▲ how to use the *cursor/arrow* keys or the mouse to place the cursor in the desired position;

▲ the use of more than a single finger or hand when typing, particularly once they know where the letters are located;

▲ how to use the space bar (pressing it with their thumbs);

▲ how the word processor will 'wrap' the text around the end of the line, so there is no need to press *return* at the end of each line;

▲ how to join text using the *delete* key;

▲ how to break up text or create lines using the *return* key;

▲ how to move the cursor to a mistake and correct it, rather than deleting all the text back to the mistake, making the correction and then retyping the deleted text;

▲ how to print out their completed work, initially with support from the teacher, then eventually on their own.

Children will also need to save their work if they are unable to finish it in one session. They should be taught how to save it on to a hard or floppy disk, so that eventually they can do this without teacher assistance. They will then need to be shown how to locate and retrieve their work later.

Young children will take a long time to input text at the keyboard, so it is important to ensure that the writing tasks are kept short and that, where possible, there is support available. If parents or other adults are available, they can often be used in this way, provided they have the relevant skills. Alternatively, they can be used for scribing during longer tasks: typing in the children's work and then going through it with them to edit and amend it.

For many writing tasks, children can use the standard page format available to them when they start using the software. However, for more complex tasks the teacher may wish to set up the page layout beforehand and save it as a master page. Children can then start with this basic layout and alter it if they need to.

Concept keyboards

Many schools have access to concept keyboards which can be linked to the word processor. These can be used with great effect for children at the start of Key Stage 1, when keyboard and writing skills are at an early stage of development. The small squares of the concept keyboard can be programmed so that when a child presses the word *nail* or a picture of a nail, *nail* will appear on the screen of the word processor.

Teachers can make their own overlays by using drawings or pictures taken from magazines or other sources. Words can also be included. It is also possible for children to use the computer keyboard itself to enter words which are not on the overlay. Although the overlays take a little time to set up initially, they can help to give children access to the computer. In many of the activities, they can be used as a simple form of assessment.

Art packages

A number of simple art or graphics packages are available for children. They tend to fall into two categories:

▲ *Graphics packages* enable children to draw lines and shapes, and add text. The lines and shapes can be manipulated: resized, moved, stretched and rotated. Colours can be changed and shapes filled. On more sophisticated packages, the shapes can be combined to form a single object – so that, for example, all the components of a house can be drawn separately, combined and then kept as a house. Text can be typed on the page, and in some packages different fonts, sizes and colours can be added. In such packages, it is easy to move shapes around the screen and position components of a picture wherever you wish. These packages are sometimes called *vector graphics*.

▲ *Art or painting packages* use a different approach, but can often achieve similar results. The drawing process is more akin to using a pencil or brush. Lines and shapes are drawn by colouring in the individual pixels of the screen. Very detailed work can be done to create pictures which mimic the effects of paint on paper. Such packages usually have a range of tools such as brushes, sprays and rollers for creating different effects. Text can be added, coloured and resized. The scanned images that children create using a hand scanner can be combined in such packages and edited, changing colours or masking out parts of the picture. Such packages are often referred to as pixel painting packages, and can produce very large datafiles.

The skills that children need to be taught using such software are similar to word processing skills and include:

▲ selecting appropriate drawing tools;

▲ changing features such as line thickness;

▲ drawing different lines and shapes;

▲ editing and erasing shapes and lines;

▲ resizing and rotating shapes and lines;

▲ moving shapes and lines around the screen;

▲ selecting and adding colours;

▲ adding, resizing and colouring text;

▲ saving and then retrieving their work;

▲ setting up the printer and printing out their work.

IT links

The grids on this page relate the activities in this book to specific areas of IT and to relevant software resources. Activities are referenced by page number rather than by name. (Bold page numbers indicate activities which have expanded IT content.) The software listed is a selection of programs generally available to primary schools, and is not intended as a recommended list. The software featured should be available from most good educational software retailers.

AREA OF IT	TYPE OF SOFTWARE	ACTIVITIES (page nos.)			
		CHAPTER 1	CHAPTER 2	CHAPTER 3	CHAPTER 4
Communicating Information	Word Processor	14, 16, 18, 22, **28**, 32, 36	42, 46, **54**, 58, 62, 64, 68	74, 77, 80, 87, **92**	104, **108**, 112, 115
Communicating Information	Concept keyboard	22		74	
Communicating Information	Art/graphics	16, 18, 22, 32	42, 46, 58		112
Communicating Information	DTP	40	42, 58, 64	84, 87, **92**	**108**
Communicating Information	Developing Tray	22	**54**		
Communicating Information	Authoring	14	**54**	87	
Communicating Information	Scanner	40			
Communicating Information	E-mail			84	
Information Handling	Database	**28**			**108**
Information Handling	Graphing Software	18, 36	**54**		**108**
Information Handing	CD-ROM	14			
Information Handling	Thesaurus		**54**, 68		
Control	Tape recorders	16	46		

SOFTWARE TYPE	BBC/MASTER	RISCOS	NIMBUS/186	WINDOWS	MACINTOSH
Word processor	*Stylus* *Folio* *Prompt/Writer*	*Phases* *Pendown* *Desk Top Folio*	*All Write* *Write On*	*My Word* *Kid Works 2* *Creative Writer*	*Kid Works 2* *Easy Works* *Creative Writer*
Authoring		*Rainbow* *Hyperstudio*		*MMBox2*	*Hyperstudio*
DTP	*Front Page Extra*	*Desk Top Folio* *1st Page* *Front Page Extra*	*Front Page Extra* *NewSPAper*	*Creative Writer* *NewSPAper*	*Creative Writer*
Framework	*Developing Tray*	*My World*	*Developing Tray*	*My World*	
Art Package	*Picture Builder*	*1st Paint* *Kid Pix* *Splash*	*Picture Builder*	*Colour Magic* *Kid Pix 2*	*Kid Pix 2*
Database	*Our Facts* *Grass* *Pigeonhole* *Datashow*	*DataSweet* *Find IT* *SeeLinks*	*Our Facts* *Datashow*	*Sparks* *Claris Works* *Information Workshop*	*Claris Works* *Easy Works*
Graphing Software	*Datashow*	*Pictogram* *Picture Point* *DataSweet*	*Datagraph*	*Datagraph* *Easy Works*	*Easy Works*

READING

	MATHS	SCIENCE	HISTORY	GEOGRAPHY	D&T	ART	MUSIC	RE/PSE
ENVIRONMENTAL PRINT	Shapes and patterns in the locality. Sorting and matching: signs seen on the walk. Estimating and measuring: time taken for the walk, materials for making models. Recognising numbers: houses, buses, prices, dates; odd and even. 3-D shapes: volume and capacity of tins. Coin recognition, adding and subtracting money.	Washing and drying clothes. Wear and tear experiments on fabrics. Sources of heat for cooking soups. Tasting experiments. Properties of materials used for building.	Using a range of sources – books, photos, oral accounts. Changes in local area over time. Changes in clothing styles. Language changes. Advertising: past and present. Changes in houses, kitchen utensils.	Amenities in the local area. A plan of the route taken on the walk. Places where T-shirts are manufactured. Homes and eating habits of people from different parts of the world, effects of climate.	Making choices about appropriate materials and tools when designing and making. T-shirt logos. Posters, programmes, invitations for a fashion parade. Labels for soup tins.	Rubbings made on the walk, sketches. Printing T-shirt logos and patterns on fabrics. Collages of labels.	Describing sounds heard on the walk. Composition for the fashion show. Choral composition with water noises. Rhythmical patterns of words in adverts, with musical accompaniment.	Safety on the road, at home. Caring for the environment. Appreciating the problems of the homeless. Respecting alternative ways of life: travellers. Valuing bilingualism. The morality of advertising. Violence in comics.
NARRATIVE	Counting/number songs. Sequencing events. Surveys of pets – graphs. Measuring and comparing sizes, shapes, ages of pets. Symmetry, pattern. Counting money: other currencies.	Human needs: healthy eating and exercise, growth. Using the senses. Environmental concerns: seaside, countryside. Animals' camouflage and habitats, threat of extinction. Shiny things, reflection and light.	Human growth. Life cycle of pets. Ancient civilisations. Changing traditions in developing countries.	Exploration of space: map of the Bunny Planet. Habitat of birds. Features of holiday resorts. Seasons: effects of the weather. Daily life in other countries; climate.	Making books, bookmarks. Designing a book cover, 'Wanted' poster, postcard. Designing and making a home for a pet.	Comparing book illustrations. Representing personal experiences. Drawings and clay models of pets and story characters. Appreciating artists and craftspeople of other countries. Tie-dyeing: making jewellery, masks.	Rhythmical patterns. Listening to music from other cultures. Learning songs about animals. Creating sounds to accompany a poem. Composing music to accompany choral reading. Comparing musical instruments across cultures.	Expressing feelings and emotions. Sharing tasks, eg., tidying up. Similarities and differences between people; respecting other people. Celebrations in different cultures. Beliefs about Creation: Dreamtime.
POETRY	Learning action and counting songs, dipping rhymes. Classifying rhymes. Skipping or saying tongue-twisters for a timed minute. Language of shape, texture and size. Fractions: half, quarter.	Senses. Naming body parts. Change of state when cooking bread. Light and dark. Dinosaurs.	Traditional rhymes. Rhymes and word games in grandparents' childhood. Change over time: gender issues.	Children's rhymes and games from other countries. Climate, the effect on crops: Kapiti Plain.	Making books of riddles, poems, jokes. Poster for Dog Show.	A frieze of a dog show. Book illustrations. African animals – colour mixing, camouflage.	Recognising and keeping the beat with body parts, percussion. Learning songs with rhythmical patterns. Counting and clapping syllables in dogs' names.	Similarities and differences in children's rhymes across cultures. Discussing the behaviour of nursery rhyme characters. Celebrating language diversity. Expressing feelings.
INFORMATION AND INSTRUCTIONAL TEXTS	Estimating, measuring and comparing the growth rate of plants. Surveys of gardens and toys. Money: role play in Garden Centre. Sorting/matching toys.	Growth cycle of plants. Materials toys are made of. Clothes to keep us warm. Heating systems in homes.	Changes in local environment. A 'Victorian toys' timeline. Change through the seasons. Alphabet books from the past.	The effect of weather on plants and on how we live. The effect of seasons on climate. Weather reports. The effects of tourism.	DTP, book-making. Design and make a mechanical toy. Design and make a tourist brochure or class book. Making peg dolls. Making a rain gauge.	Observational drawings of plants. Clay miniatures of toy characters. Painting winter landscapes. Illustrating a tourist brochure.	Investigating musical toys. Songs about plants and toys. Creating music to match emotions. Listening to mood music.	Caring for and sharing toys. Caring for old people in winter; hazards. Festivals in autumn and winter.